Acclaim for Paul Goldstein's

ERRORS and OMISSIONS

Paul Goldstein
ERRORS and OMISSIONS

Paul Goldstein is the Lillick Professor of Law at Stanford Law School and is widely recognized as one of the country's leading authorities on intellectual property law. A graduate of Brandeis University and Columbia Law School, he is Of Counsel to the law firm of Morrison & Foerster LLP, where he has represented motion picture studios, among other clients. He has regularly been included in *Best Lawyers in America*. A native of New York, he now lives outside San Francisco with his family.

ERRORS and
OMISSIONS

ERRORS and OMISSIONS

A NOVEL

Paul Goldstein

Anchor Books
A Division of Random House, Inc.
New York

FIRST ANCHOR BOOKS EDITION, JULY 2007

The Library of Congress has cataloged the Doubleday edition as follows:
Goldstein, Paul.
Errors and omissions / Paul Goldstein.
p. cm.
1. Intellectual property lawyers—Fiction. 2. Hollywood (Los Angeles, Calif.)—
Fiction. 3. Motion picture authorship—Fiction. 4. Blacklisting of authors—
Fiction. 5. Motion picture industry—Fiction. 6. Americans—Germans—Fiction.
7. Polish Americans—Fiction. 8. Munich (Germany)—Fiction. I. Title.
PS3607.O4853E77 2006
813'.6—dc22
2005051872

Anchor ISBN: 978-0-307-27489-2

Book design by Caroline Cunningham

www.anchorbooks.com

Printed in the United States of America
10 9 8 7 6 5 4 3 2 1

For Jan and Lizzy

ERRORS and OMISSIONS

ONE

The worst part of being drunk before breakfast is the hangover that returns before noon.

Michael Seeley's head throbbed. He was tall and ruddy, with an athlete's vigor, but he felt compressed by the narrow room. Like the courtroom next door, the anteroom to Judge Randall Rappaport's chambers was designed for intimidation, not comfort: high ceiling, dark wood, brass fittings, wood chairs with no padding. There were no magazines or newspapers for distraction, not even a legal newspaper or law journal. A leather-bound volume the size of a Bible was carefully centered on a mahogany side table: *The Collected Opinions (1985–2005) of the Honorable Randall Rappaport, Justice of the Supreme Court of New York*.

The other person in the room, Noel Emmert, hadn't acknowledged Seeley when he came in, and it wasn't until after Seeley inspected the book and returned it to the table that Emmert spoke.

"How's the intellectual property business, counselor?" There was an edge to Emmett's voice, as if he were delivering the punch line to a story.

Emmett's law practice was in county and state courts like this one, in a gray warren of pillared buildings off Foley Square at the bottom of Manhattan. Seeley practiced mainly in the federal courts on Pearl Street, around the corner.

Seeley said, "How's the real property business?"

Emmett gestured, so-so. "Is this going to be a long waltz, counselor, or are we ready to settle?"

Seeley said, "Precisely."

Emmett's eyebrows arched and he shot Seeley a look. "You know," he said, "the law is truly humbling, if you think about it. Your guy sells a piece of crap sculpture to my guy, my guy decides to fix it up with a coat of paint, and before you know it, we have a lawsuit. Two professionals, me and you, spending our time and our clients' money fighting over an issue that's worth—what?—peanuts."

Seeley said, "It's funny, the way you do that."

"What's that?"

"The way you don't say, 'law.' You say '*the* law.' There's a nobility to it."

"I never thought about it. Maybe I picked it up in law school."

"That's what I was thinking."

Given a choice, Seeley preferred the public theater of the courtroom where the playing field is level and a lawyer who does his homework has a better than average chance of winning. In judge's chambers, where decisions are private and unreviewable, the averages were out of his control.

The previous night, fueled by gin, Seeley had plotted his strategy for the morning meeting until he passed out on the bed in his room at the University Club. He came to five hours later, murderously hungover. He fumbled a small handful of ice cubes from the insulated bucket on the nightstand, pressed them against his forehead, then dropped them into an empty tumbler. As he staggered to the dingy bathroom, Seeley's single thought was to dissolve the thick layers of gauze that encased his brain. He uncapped the fresh bottle of Bombay gin he had hidden beneath the sink and filled the tumbler to within a quarter-inch of the rim. He sipped tentatively at the bright, metallic liquid, took his time to study the University Club crest etched neatly into the glass, then, shuddering, gagging once, took the rest of the contents down in a succession of short, greedy gulps. He reached through the plastic curtain behind him and turned on the shower full force. Filling the tumbler a second time, he nursed the drink while he waited for the steam to rise. When he climbed through the curtain into the punishing needles, his mind was already clearing.

Now, in Rappaport's anteroom, the two tumblers of gin were dying inside him, and a burrowing thirst had taken over. He needed a drink. His hands clenched his knees. When he looked down he saw that the suit pants and jacket didn't match—both were dark gray, but one was glen plaid, the other herringbone. Although the light in the room at the University Club was poor, this hadn't happened before. Rappaport's secretary came in and announced that the judge was ready to see them.

Busy signing papers, Rappaport took a full minute before indicating the two empty chairs that faced him, still not looking up from his desk. It was September and the weather was warm, but the judge had on a three-piece suit with a gold chain looped through the vest and black judicial robes open over that. A few strands of gray hair had been carefully combed and plastered across a white scalp. He could have been a child in the tall chair. Seeley would bet that when Rappaport told people he was a supreme court justice he didn't bother to add that there were almost four hundred other supreme court justices in the state. Because of a historical quirk in the way courts were designated in New York State's judicial hierarchy, the supreme court was in fact among the lowest courts in the judicial system, not the highest.

Rappaport read from the paper in front of him. "*Minietello v. Weber Properties*." When he finally looked up, his expression was a scowl. "Where are your clients, counselors? Where's Mr. Minietello? Where's Mr. Weber?" The voice was nasal, aggrieved. "Surely, when he scheduled this meeting, my clerk reminded you of the standing order. Your clients must be present any time there is a settlement conference before a justice of the supreme court. Mr. Emmert, you have practiced here long enough to know that."

"It's a new requirement, Your Honor—"

"But a mandatory one."

"I have consulted with my client on the point, Your Honor, and he has agreed to waive a personal appearance."

"This is not a requirement that can be waived, counselor." The two could have been volleying at tennis. "*I* want your clients here. I see too many lawyers rejecting settlements that, if the client knew the details, the client would gladly accept. And you, Mr. . . ." Rappaport's tiny fingers, a busy rodent's, sorted through a pile of papers, searching for an appearance sheet or an appointment diary. This was playacting, Seeley knew, the way a small man bullies a newcomer to his domain. The judge knew his name; it was on the same sheet as the names of the parties. Finally, Rappaport found the paper he pretended to be looking for. "Mr. Seeley. What about your client? Is he waiving, too?"

"He was detained, Your Honor, but he's on his way."

Seeley had made a detour from his room at the University Club to his office on Sixth Avenue in midtown to collect a briefcase, and there had fallen into a long conversation with one of the mailboys about the Mets losing a double-header the day before. Leaving the building in a hired car, he forgot his promise to pick up Gary Minietello at the sculptor's loft so they could review strategy for the settlement conference. Only when he was walking up the granite courthouse steps, already late for the meeting with Rappaport, did Seeley remember the promise. He made a rushed call for Minietello to meet him in chambers.

"So, we shall sit here and wait for Mr. Seeley's client."

Seeley had dealt with difficult judges before, but he had the feeling that Rappaport was going to be a special challenge.

The judge swiveled in his chair to Emmert. "You're Fordham, aren't you?"

"Two years behind Your Honor. Your name still echoed in the hallways. All the time I was there, the professors were still talking about when you destroyed the Columbia team in the moot court competition."

Rappaport beamed. "Harvard, too. In the finals. The Jesuits field a fine moot court team. Where did you attend school, Mr. Seeley?"

"Canisius."

"The Jesuit school upstate?"

Seeley nodded.

"I didn't know they had a law school."

"They don't. I went to college there."

"I was asking where you went to law school," Rappaport said.

Seeley knew that's what he had meant. "Harvard."

"I thought so. An Ivy Leaguer." The judge paused to think if he could make something more of that, and instead made a show of studying his wristwatch and adjusting the cuff of his shirt. "I have a heavy schedule today, counselors, and unlike you, I'm not paid by the hour. So why don't we get started. You can fill your client in when he arrives, Mr. Seeley. Mr. Emmert, I want you to brief your client, too." Again he searched through the papers on his desk. "Let me see if I can help you frame the issue here."

Every first-year law student knows that how a legal issue is posed inevitably determines how it is decided. Seeley said, "If Your Honor would allow me to state the issue—"

Rappaport waved him off. He had found the briefing memo. "Correct me if I am in error, counselors, but, as I understand it, what this little tempest is about is that your client, Mr. Seeley, sold one of his sculptures to Mr. Emmert's client, and now he wants to stop him from putting a coat of paint on it."

Minietello's sculpture consisted of a dozen or so rusted structural girders exploding through a brick wall in the lobby of a Park Avenue office building, the girders' extremities twisted and shredded as if from a violent explosion. The building, owned by Emmert's client, had been on the market for more than a year. A buyer had at last made an offer on the property, but insisted that the sculpture be cleaned up and painted. Minietello objected. None of his works had ever been painted; to do so, he told anyone who would listen, would violate the integrity of his vision. Seeley didn't care much for the sculpture, or for Minietello, but nonetheless won a temporary restraining order enjoining any alteration of the work. His next step, unless the Honorable Randall Rappaport forced a settlement on him, would be to go to trial and win a judgment making the injunction permanent.

Seeley had been waiting years for a case like this—the opportunity to establish a foothold in New York law for the principle that artists have moral as well as economic rights; that no one, not even the owner of a work of art, can alter the work without the artist's consent. "If Your Honor will—"

"So we have a straightforward clash of interests here," Rappaport said. His chair squeaked as it rocked in a steady rhythm. "Your client's aesthetic wishes on the one side, Mr. Seeley, and on the other side, the interest of Mr. Emmert's client in selling his property. What's not clear to me, Mr. Seeley, is how your client has been injured."

The judge might be a sanctimonious jerk, Seeley thought, but he was no fool. He had stripped the case to its core, leaving no rough edge on which Seeley could build an argument. Seeley could argue that Minietello's interests were not only aesthetic but that his reputation, and consequently his future income, would suffer as soon as word got out that one of his works had been altered. But that wasn't the principle for which he had filed the case.

Emmert nodded at Rappaport's words but didn't speak. When a judge is making your case for you, you don't interrupt.

"I would be interested in hearing what precedents you think you may have on your side." Rappaport was still looking at Seeley.

If the judge had read his brief, he knew there were no direct precedents to support his position. But neither had there been direct precedent for any of the great decisions that had challenged, and ultimately reversed, the authority of existing law. For Seeley, that was the great beauty of American law: if you were persistent, prepared thoroughly, and had justice on your side, you could change the law. "Your Honor, federal law already—"

"This is not federal court, counselor. This is New York Supreme Court."

Seeley's thick hair felt matted as he tried to massage away the throbbing at the back of his head. He was parched; just speaking felt like fingernails clawing at his throat. The meeting was not going as he had planned it the night before. His thoughts ricocheted from the judge to Noel Emmert—the lawyer had the flushed look of a man who liked a drink—to the bottles he had stashed in the credenza in his office uptown. What if the chrome carafe on Rappaport's side table were filled with iced gin? How else would a judge get through the tedium of the day?

"Every civilized country in the world," Seeley heard himself saying, "England, France, Germany—every one of these countries recognizes an artist's moral right. No court in any of these countries would hesitate to enjoin Mr. Emmert's client from disfiguring a work of art."

"Even assuming that to be the case," Rappaport said, still rocking, "this is not a federal court and this is not a French court, either." He tilted back in the chair and clasped his hands over his vest.

Seeley's thoughts turned to the number of ways he might strangle Rappaport. "It's a fundamental principle of decency that you can't take away an artist's right to the integrity of his work."

Emmert said, "What about my client? Maybe he's an artist, too. Maybe he thinks this piece of junk looks better painted."

"That's a foolish argument, and you know it." Seeley hadn't intended it, but his voice had risen. "Painting someone else's sculpture isn't art."

Rappaport smiled. "You must forgive Mr. Emmert. He lacks the advantage of a Harvard education."

Seeley tried to think of a smart remark that might turn this bond between Rappaport and Emmert in his favor, but realized he was lost. Still, the words flew out. "This case isn't just about sculptors. It will set a precedent for painters. Writers. Musicians." Why was he having such difficulty controlling his voice? This was closing argument, a high schooler's imitation of Clarence Darrow. "It makes no difference if the work is Picasso's *Guernica* or the image some prehistoric man painted on the wall of his cave." His voice rose perilously. "A work of art—any work of art—touches something sacred in us. To violate it—" Words that had seemed so eloquent the previous night now tasted like paper in Seeley's mouth; he gagged on them and hated himself for believing them.

"I don't know what they put up with in federal court, but I will not have voices raised in my chambers. Do you understand that, counselor?" Rappaport's voice was level, his chair still. He waited for Seeley's acknowledgment before continuing. He leaned over the desk, his hands spread before him. "Look, let's be practical about this. If ever there was a case that should settle, it is this one. On your client's side, Mr. Seeley, there are some injured sensitivities. That is understandable. As you have already acknowledged, there is no precedent, but I'll grant that juries can be unpredictable. Also, the appellate process may fail to correct an error by the jury. So I expect"—he turned to include Emmert—"Mr. Emmert might be prepared to offer a reasonable figure for settlement. Reasonable, but not exorbitant. After all, Mr. Emmert's client presumably paid the artist good value when he purchased the sculpture."

"Your Honor, that's correct," Emmert said. "My client paid top dollar."

"I would be very interested to hear what Mr. Emmert's client is proposing as an offer of settlement."

Seeley didn't know what was going on between Rappaport and Emmert, but they had been exchanging looks for the past several minutes. "My client isn't interested in settling. He has never allowed a work of his to be altered. Putting money on the table isn't going to change his position."

"That is why this court would like your client to be present, counselor. So I can determine whether he is as committed to this principle as his lawyer appears to be." He nodded at Emmert to go ahead.

"My client," said Emmert, "is prepared to offer—and this is solely as a gesture of goodwill, with no admission of liability on his part—the sum of fifty thousand dollars. I'll be honest with you—my client needs to sell his building. But this is his top figure. There is no room here for bargaining. As I said, it is a gesture of goodwill, and I trust your client will accept it as such."

The judge pressed his palms together, steepling his fingers under his chin. "This is a generous offer, Mr. Seeley. I would strongly recommend that you advise your client to accept it."

Seeley was certain Rappaport already knew what the settlement figure would be. The two sons of Fordham had talked. Seeley nodded at the chrome carafe on the side table. "Is that water in there?"

"Help yourself," Rappaport said.

Seeley was pouring water into a glass when the door in the back of chambers opened and Gary Minietello came in. For the first time that morning, the judge rose from the too-big chair. He greeted Minietello with a two-handed politician's handshake, introduced Noel Emmert, and took Minietello's hand back again. "It is an honor, sir, to have an artist of your stature in my chambers."

Minietello shot a questioning look at Seeley. He didn't know whether this was real or a put-on. Seeley didn't know either. He had many artist clients, and more than once he had seen people like Rappaport, with no shortage of ego themselves, genuflect extravagantly before a painter, sculptor, or photographer who was barely known outside his own neighborhood. Then he saw what Rappaport was up to. The judge was going to seduce his client into settling. He nodded to Minietello to take the chair next to him.

"So, Mr. Minietello"—Rappaport was back in his chair—"we have been having a little discussion of how best to approach this case. As your lawyer, Mr. Seeley, has pointed out, there is an important principle at stake here—your moral interest in seeing your creation respected. But Mr. Emmert is a realist, and so is his client—and so am I. We believe, and just now we were trying to persuade your lawyer, that the most appropriate resolution—strictly confidential of course, this is all off the record—would be an honorarium of sorts, a proper recognition of your efforts and your reputation that would at the same time preserve the rights of Mr. Emmert's client as a property owner."

"Your Honor—" Seeley began, but Rappaport cut him off with a look and said to Emmert, "Do you have something to add to this, counselor?"

Seeley started out of his chair, but the room suddenly bucked and lurched, throwing him off balance. The glass of water, mixing with the residues of gin still in his blood, had blossomed into a cocktail. He was drunk again. He reached to the judge's desk for support. "With all due respect, Your Honor, I must insist on my client's right to confer with me."

A silent communication passed between the judge and Noel Emmert. "You can use my reception area," Rappaport said. "Of course, you won't object to my sitting here with Mr. Emmert in your absence. No claims of improper ex parte communications?"

None that hadn't already taken place. "Of course not, Your Honor. The thought wouldn't have occurred to me." As soon as he turned to go, Seeley realized his mistake. With the alcohol again working in him, he couldn't move without reeling. He placed an arm on Minietello's shoulder as a wise, avuncular counselor might, and concentrated on placing one unsteady foot ahead of the other. Proceeding this way, he made it to the anteroom without stumbling.

Minietello hadn't noticed or, if he had, there was something more important on his mind. Even before Seeley could close the door, the words were out of Minietello's mouth, "How much?" The sculptor's voice had the ring of a cash register opening.

Seeley's head was spinning and a wave of nausea passed through him. "If you take their money, Gary, they're going to destroy your sculpture."

Minietello was all in black: T-shirt, jeans, chrome-studded belt. He had grown up in the estate country of northern Westchester, gone to prep school in Vermont and from there to Princeton. The New York accent and rough manner were affectations. He was bone-thin, and the muscular hands weren't from handling rough metal—a foundry in New Jersey fabricated his sculptures from papier-mâché maquettes—but from a pocket exerciser he played with when he was anxious or angry. All of this grated on Seeley more than it usually did.

"How much?"

"Fifty thousand dollars," Seeley said.

"I have to supervise the painters. This guy has to pay me for my time."

"What about the integrity of your work? Your reputation?"

Minietello sucked at his lower lip. He took the chrome exerciser from a back pocket and flexed it. "They're going to need me for the . . . ah . . ."

This is going to be truly repellent, Seeley told himself.

". . . the reconceptualization. You wouldn't understand this. You're not an artist. It's a question of presentation. Artistic intention."

Most of Seeley's artist clients—not the paying ones like Minietello but the many he took on pro bono—were serious people who labored steadily and earnestly at their art, taking part-time jobs, driving taxis, waiting tables, struggling at the edge of poverty, spending any cash that came their way on tools and materials. Hard up as they were, none of them would accept the $50,000. Seeley had no illusions: any one of them would kill to get a two-week show at a SoHo gallery. But sell out their art? Not one of them.

"You're not listening, Gary. When I agreed to represent you, it wasn't just to file papers and go to court. I'm advising you to reject the offer."

This confused Minietello. He leaned forward, making his voice confidential so the judge and lawyer on the other side of the wall wouldn't hear. "You really think I can get more? They've got to be desperate to sell that dump. How much do you think I can get?"

"I didn't take this case to settle it. We have a better than fifty-fifty chance of winning with this judge."

If he could get Minietello to reject the settlement offer, Seeley was confident he could win the case. The cozy byplay between Rappaport and Emmert in chambers would evaporate once the trial started and they were in the bright light of the courtroom. Rappaport knew that Seeley would appeal any judgment he rendered against him; as a result, his conduct of the trial would be scrupulously fair.

"Even if we lose," Seeley said, "we have a good chance of getting the decision reversed on appeal."

"If I win, how much do I get?"

They had been over this. Seeley had already explained to Minietello that no money would be awarded. Talking to his client was draining the last dregs of his spirit. His voice rose. "You haven't suffered any damage. That means the court won't award you anything. What's important is that you get to see your piece stay the way it is. Intact."

"I thought we were playing poker," Minietello said. "This was a bluff."

Seeley's jaw ached. He had been grinding his teeth. "I signed my name to the complaint, Gary. It wasn't a bluff." His voice rose, and again he had to work to keep it under control.

"So if I win, I lose." Minietello's face darkened. His eyes became hooded behind the outsized black frames of his glasses. "All I get is a bill from you."

"When we win, the court will order the other side to pay my fee." In deposing Arnold Weber, the building's owner, Seeley had maneuvered him into admitting that he loathed Minietello's sculpture by implying, truthfully, that he didn't care much for it himself. Weber's admission would be the evidence Seeley needed to demonstrate the bad faith that courts require before they will award attorney's fees. "If the court doesn't award fees, the firm will eat anything you owe us. A decision in this case will be a landmark."

"And when the TV cameras show up, who gets to be the hero? You."

"I'll make sure you're the one on the evening news," Seeley said. "I'll be the gray figure behind you. Banquo's ghost."

"Do you have any idea what my overhead is? Do you know what my payroll is like? My bookkeeper, my manager, my publicist, my foundry—"

Judge Rappaport was in the doorway. "As I already informed you, Mr. Seeley, I do not tolerate raised voices in my chambers." He could have been reprimanding a wife beater on his way to prison for twenty years. The client conference was over. Rappaport led them back to the chairs facing his desk, but remained standing.

"My obligation as a justice of the supreme court of New York," he said, speaking directly to Minietello, "is not only to apply the laws of this state but to ensure that justice is done. Law is for the courts. Justice is what we seek to achieve here in chambers. Mr. Emmert's client has made a reasonable offer. A just offer. It is my opinion that you would be wise to accept it. Of course, the decision is up to you." He glared at Seeley. "You, and not your lawyer." He walked around to the front of the desk. "Now, Mr. Minietello, if you and Mr. Emmert will excuse me, I would like a private word with your lawyer." He motioned the two to stay where they were and, grasping Seeley's elbow, led him through the open door and into the anteroom.

Rappaport thrust his face upward, to within inches of Seeley's. "Your presence here is a disgrace, counselor. You're drunk. I smelled the booze as soon as you walked into my chambers."

A tight fist of rage swelled inside Seeley. He wanted to hoist the man and fling him against the wall. "You," he tried to say. "You. You." *You, what?* No words came. Then all at once they flew out: "You toad! You pompous toad!" Just as quickly, the rage turned back on him, filling him with disgust at his own recklessness.

The judge's face was crimson. "From here on," Rappaport said, "I own your license." Unaccountably, the judge had grown tall. How had it happened that this pipsqueak was looking down on him? "You will get a hearing, and I'm sure a big-firm lawyer like you will take every appeal you can. But at the end of the day, counselor, have no doubt: you will be barred from practicing law in New York State—including your federal courts." A drop of spittle attached itself to Rappaport's upper lip, forming a translucent thread, so that when he spoke it was a marionette's mouth moving up and down. "If you don't know the meaning of the term 'moral turpitude,' I would suggest you look it up. That's the charge you're going to have to defend against." Rappaport stepped away. "You may leave my chambers now."

In the empty corridor leading to the courtroom, Seeley waited for Minietello. It was 11:45. In less than an hour, he had managed to let the case he had waited years for slip away. The disbarment meant nothing. It was a small man's threat and Rappaport would drop it once he calmed down. But his case: Seeley pictured the judge writing out for Minietello the name and telephone number of another lawyer, a political crony, who would settle the sculptor's case for him.

He paced the corridor. When he looked at his watch again, it was well past noon. He tried the door to the secretary's office, but it was locked. So was the door to the anteroom. Evidently everyone had gone to lunch, using another exit. And, no, he didn't need a dictionary. He knew the meaning of the term. Moral turpitude: moral depravity, weakness. The words fit like they had been invented for him.

Clare was waiting for him outside the restaurant, on a block of Madison Avenue crowded with diners at sidewalk tables. In their three months apart, she had grown thinner. Her cheekbones, when she turned in Seeley's direction, were planes beneath a summer tan. He would admit this to no one, not even to Clare, but it was her looks he had first fallen in love with. Vaguely spoiled and aristocratic, they implied lazy summer days in Saranac or Southampton, winter holidays in Aspen, private schools, a small exclusive women's college somewhere in New England. (As it turned out, she had graduated from Smith.) There was an aura about her that he coveted. Yet if someone told him he was a snob, in the way that only a boy who grew up hard and poor can be, and that he had married Clare Putnam so she could rescue him, Seeley would have denied it.

"Hi," he said.

Clare studied him, the intelligent blue eyes revealing nothing about what she was thinking.

Seeley said, "Let's go inside."

"You're half an hour late. They didn't hold the reservation."

He started to the door. "I'll talk to them."

"Forget it. They're packed. I really don't feel like eating. Let's walk over to Henry's."

Henry's was what Clare called the Frick Collection, a museum a few blocks away, on Fifth Avenue. It was where they had first met, and Henry Clay Frick's century-old mansion had become a recurring destination, a sanctuary in a way their own home, a three-bedroom apartment in an anonymous gray Park Avenue building selected by Clare, was not.

"Old times' sake?"

"It's close. It will be cool. We can talk."

As much as he loved the paintings at the Frick, it was the quiet and the elegant order of the place that regularly drew Seeley back, with or without Clare. Filled with old masters, the museum was a compact lesson in art history. Standing in what had been Frick's dining room, with Hogarth, Reynolds, and Gainsborough on the walls, was like being inside a jewel box.

"How are you?"

"Okay," Seeley said.

The consuming thirst that had somehow abated during the cab ride uptown suddenly returned, as punishing as before. What would Clare think if he told her what had happened in Randall Rappaport's chambers? The memory of the encounter stabbed at him. He was less certain now that Rappaport's talk of disbarment was just a threat.

"I miss you."

"You said we wouldn't talk about that."

Seeley didn't remember the promise. "Then why did you come?"

"You said it was important. I believed you." Her posture on the upholstered bench was upright, unrelenting.

Seeley didn't have the vocabulary for this kind of conversation. Over the course of the marriage, their usual dinner talk was about what had happened at work that day—for Seeley the case he was trying or the one he was preparing for trial, for Clare the doings in the trust department of a bank downtown—and Seeley suspected that she listened to his tales no more intently than he did to hers.

"It's been three months, Clare. I want to come back."

Clare's jaw was set; her voice turned to a harsh whisper. "Are you drunk?"

"For God's sake, Clare, I was just in a judge's chambers." She smelled the gin on him, as had Randall Rappaport. "Look," he said, "I can cut back on the drinking."

"I don't believe you. Do you know how many times you've told me that? Your whole life is nothing but working and drinking. That's all you do."

"I can change."

"You need to go away somewhere." Clare brushed back her abundant gold hair with a hand. "Get into a rehab program."

He wasn't a drunk. He didn't need rehab. She had other reasons for wanting him to go away. "Are you seeing someone?" Unexpectedly, the question produced a small, cold knot inside him.

"That's not what I'm talking about."

"But are you?"

"It's none of your business." Clare's brave shoulders slumped. "Do you know how hard this is for me? You're my husband. I'm not going to sit around and watch you destroy yourself."

"I'm not a drunk, Clare. Sometimes having a drink is the only way I can keep going. Do you have any idea what it's like to try a string of cases, one after another, without a break?"

"I'd think it would be a lot easier to do sober."

"Then you don't know what it's like."

"Nick told me you're down to your last case."

Nick and Clare, Seeley thought.

"He said the other partners are picking off your clients. All you have left are your pro bono cases. He said you're not carrying your weight at the firm."

Seeley had been in the same law firm with Nick Girard for twenty-one years, first in Buffalo, now in New York. He played squash with him three mornings a week, and when he was still single had dinner with Girard and his wife, Maisie, two or three times a month. But he remained as uncomfortable with them as he was when he first met them; it was as if an invisible but impenetrable barrier surrounded them. Yet soon after Clare came into his life and he introduced her to the Girards, the three threw themselves at each other like long-lost friends, avidly discovering the places, schools, and acquaintances they had in common, sharing confidences as comfortably as if they had grown up together, which in a way, Seeley realized, they had.

"All the important artists in New York used to come to you. At least the young ones did. You'd take me to an opening and you were as much of a celebrity as anyone there. They could still be your clients."

"They all have big galleries behind them now. Their work stopped being interesting. *They* stopped being interesting." Like Gary Minietello, he thought; my last celebrity artist.

"What about the other clients you used to have—the real clients—book publishers, film studios, record companies? Some struggling artist comes along and you drop their work so you can take his case."

"My artists have principles, Clare. They're challenging the establishment."

"That's fine, Mike. Some of them may even turn into paying clients. But they can't support a law practice."

"There's no rule that says everyone has to work in a large firm."

"Go out and practice on your own if you want, but if you keep drinking you're not going to have any clients. You won't even have the ones who don't pay. You won't have a home, either."

Seeley said, "That was your choice, not mine."

Seeley noticed the Frick's ceiling and wondered if it was like this throughout the mansion: deeply coffered mahogany, the same color as the trim in Randall Rappaport's anteroom but, in its depth, welcoming rather than austere.

"If you believe that, you're even more self-absorbed than I thought you were." Clare glanced down at her watch. "Do you realize that in forty minutes you haven't once asked me how I'm doing?"

"How are you, Clare?"

"Pissed off, if you really want to know."

For some reason Seeley found that promising. Unlike anything else she had said, it had the sound of a door opening. "Pissed off, why?"

"You really don't have any idea, do you, how lonely and miserable I've been?"

On a bench in the Fragonard Room they were surrounded by large painted panels recounting love's breathless evolution in stilted, saccharine poses: *The Pursuit*, *The Meeting*, *The Lover Crowned*, *Love Letters*. If you looked not at the lovers but at the grim statuary painted above them—gray somnolent cherubs, anguished goddesses—you knew how matters were going to end. And, after the love letters? *The Lover Being Sued for Divorce*.

If Clare's fantasy in marrying him had been that her husband was going to be the lawyer of choice for the stars of the art world, giving her access to the best parties and the most important museum committees, what had his own expectations been when he married her? Until the last three months, it was not a question he thought about much, and even now he hadn't made a significant dent in it. He never got deeper than the inchoate yearning that ran like a current through his life. "I want to come back, Clare."

"You haven't heard anything I've said. This isn't about what you want."

"I told you, I can cut down on the drinking."

"I don't think you can."

"But what if I do?"

Clare hesitated before answering. "I'm still sorting things out."

He should never have asked her to lunch. Things were worse now than they were before. "Well," Seeley said, "I hope you don't sort me out." He had meant it to be light, but it came out leaden.

"I'm glad you haven't lost your sense of humor." Clare didn't have to finish the thought because Seeley already heard it in her voice: *You're going to need it.*

Seeley removed a crystal tumbler from inside the credenza and had just opened the other door, behind which he stored his liquor, when the harsh fluorescent light flashed on in his office. Daphne Hancock, formal in dark jacket and skirt, filled the doorway.

"Do you have a minute?"

He pressed the door shut. "What can I do for you, Daphne?"

He knew she wouldn't take a chair. Along with her gaudy scarves and floppy hats Daphne used height and bulk to her advantage. At a firm event, years ago, Seeley had met Daphne's husband, a construction executive in Manhattan, and now when he saw her the picture that came to mind was inevitably of a bulldozer.

She said, "You haven't been returning United's calls."

"The firm's chairman doesn't come down three floors to tell a partner to return a phone call."

In her rare lighter moments Daphne might refer to herself as "overhead," but the title had been her choice. She refused to be the chairwoman, or even chair or managing partner. She had fought too hard for the position, she said, to be called any-thing but chairman of Boone, Bancroft and Meserve.

"A lawyer named Jack Elm called me. He said he wanted to talk to you about an errors and omissions opinion."

"I already told him I'm not interested." Elm worked in the legal department at United Pictures and was Seeley's contact there when he handled copyright litigation for the studio. The man was fussy, ambitious, and jittery, and Seeley didn't like working with him.

"Elm said they've got a film waiting to shoot, and they can't close the financing until you give them an opinion that will sat-isfy their insurance company. The bank won't release funds un-til the insurance company issues a policy."

Seeley said, "There are half a dozen lawyers in LA who can write an E&O opinion for United."

"We're not in the lawyer referral business, Mike. He specif-ically said they wanted you. I'm not going to wait for Beau Callaway to call and ask me whether we still want to be his company's law firm. Do it, Mike."

Even the head of a major law firm is only as strong as the firm's most important clients let her be. Beau Callaway had been an Oklahoma oil-and-gas man when Daphne brought him to the firm as a tax client eight years ago. But as Callaway began acquiring media properties—his conglomerate, Interme-dia, now owned radio and television stations, a national bill-board company, a large magazine publisher, a video rental chain, and, most recently, United Pictures—Daphne made cer-tain that all of the conglomerate's legal work came to Boone, Bancroft, and she parceled the work out to the partners as a sovereign might dispense favors. Any work that Intermedia took elsewhere was one less foundation stone in Daphne's power base.

Daphne's tone softened and Seeley immediately distrusted it.

"It'll be easy duty. Fly out there, stay at a nice hotel. After you're done, take two or three weeks for yourself. Make it a vacation."

There was a knock at the open door, and Nick Girard came in. His shirt was wrinkled and the crease had long since gone from his suit pants, but the dishevelment was a deception. The only thing casual or disorganized about Nick Girard was the surface. He practiced law—mostly negotiating large corporate transactions—the way he played squash: hanging back, loping about, making the fewest possible moves, all with a fierce economy that inevitably wore down his opponent. He was also the only broad-chested former college athlete Seeley knew who could wear a bow tie and not look like a rube.

"Am I interrupting something?"

The timing was transparent, but Seeley didn't trust his voice to ask why Daphne and Girard were double-teaming him. His attempt at banter had failed with Clare, and it would fail him now.

Daphne said, "Maybe you can explain to your friend where his duty lies. A client needs him in Los Angeles."

Girard was a lousy actor, and the look he exchanged with Daphne confirmed that they had planned this.

"I can't go to Los Angeles. I have clients who need me here."

Daphne colored. She nodded to Girard, who pushed the door closed, shutting out the background noise of computers and telephones.

"I review all the billings," Daphne said. "Apart from your retainers and the Minietello matter, you haven't billed any real time in months."

"That's why they call it pro bono, Daphne. Even if there aren't any bills, it's still real time."

Daphne and the other partners took great pride in the

firm's pro bono program. It was the lure they used to recruit the brightest young graduates from the country's best law schools. Only the program's reality disappointed them: Seeley's sometimes ragged artists, musicians, and writers waiting in the firm's mahogany-and-leather reception area. All those lawyer hours spent but not paid for.

"You've written dozens of opinions for the studios. Your calendar's open. I can't understand why you won't do this one."

There was a tremor in Daphne's voice, and for a moment Seeley experienced an uneasy closeness to her. A mallet hammered inside his head. He pictured the bottle behind the credenza door.

"Doesn't it tell you something that, after I turn him down, Jack Elm keeps coming after me instead of going to another lawyer? Why does it have to be me?"

"Because insurance companies care about a lawyer's reputation, and no other lawyer comes close to yours."

"I think the studio has a problem with their rights and they want an opinion that will cover it up. They think that because we're their regular lawyers, I'll be more . . . flexible than a lawyer at some other firm."

Daphne said, "If there's a problem, you don't have to sign the opinion."

Nick Girard looked from Daphne to Seeley. "Maybe you're afraid United has a problem with its rights and you'll be tempted to sign anyway."

"Why would I do that?"

"Stranger things have happened," Girard said. "Even to a guy with principles, like you."

This was one of Girard's negotiating tactics, shaming his adversary into doing what he wanted him to do. But why, Seeley wondered, would he use the tactic on me?

"If there's a problem with the rights, there's no chance I'd sign."

"Of course not," Daphne said. "And no one would ask you to."

In the long silence that followed, the air in the room grew heavy. Girard flexed his knees and took a practice swing with an invisible squash racket. Daphne's hand moved to the back of her neck and kneaded it, a reflex Seeley had seen when she was about to deliver news to the partners in Boone, Bancroft and Meserve of a drop in billings or the loss of an important client.

"I never told you this," Daphne said. "Nick doesn't know either, but when Ed Meserve was getting ready to retire, and he told us you were the best intellectual property litigator on the East Coast and we better hire you if we wanted to start winning cases, I was the one who sold you to the younger partners. They didn't want to break our rule about not hiring partners from other firms. I wasn't even in management then, but I fought for you because I knew that if our litigation practice was ever going to make it to the first tier you had to be part of it. You have no idea how proud I was to be in the same firm as you. You were a real leader around here—" The sight of a thick volume precariously overhanging the bookshelf stopped her, and she went to straighten it. "Every chance I got, I told people you were the firm's future."

"You want the office back, don't you?"

Ed Meserve had been the firm's senior litigator and this had been his office. Seeley was still practicing in Buffalo when he met Meserve. Boone, Bancroft, with Meserve in the lead, was representing Overhead Door, Inc., the largest manufacturer of garage-door openers in America, in patent-infringement lawsuits against a dozen or so much smaller manufacturers across the country. Meserve's approach was to bully his opponents into settling—persuading them to buy a license from Overhead Door, rather than go through a risky and expensive trial challenging the validity of the company's patents. All the manufacturers settled but one, B and G Doormasters, two brothers with a single factory in Cheektowaga, New York, just outside Buffalo. The brothers had wanted to settle, but Seeley convinced them that Overhead Door's patents were vulnerable.

In a short jury trial, Seeley succeeded in overturning every one of Overhead Door's patents, a victory so decisive that Meserve advised his client against taking an appeal. Meserve was sufficiently impressed with Seeley's work on the case that he lobbied his partners to offer Seeley a partnership in the firm, and Seeley was sufficiently attracted to the challenges offered by a high-stakes New York practice that he accepted their offer.

"You were still a rainmaker when the firm gave you this office." Daphne glanced at Girard. The quick, knowing looks, like Rappaport's and Emmert's that morning, were becoming tedious. "Things have changed. You've changed. We're concerned about you," she said. "We want to help. This is a big firm, but we're still family. We pride ourselves on that." She continued massaging her neck. "I was sorry to hear about you and Clare."

Win a dozen hard trials back to back and no one says a word. But let your wife kick you out and they can't talk about anything else. Trial practice had taught Seeley never to trust an eyewitness for an accurate account of events. Daphne was wrong. Things had started falling away from him long before Clare asked him to leave. Longtime clients didn't renew their retainers. New clients just disappeared after a first or second meeting. Even the stream of pro bono clients seemed to be thinning.

Girard said, "You need to get out of the office, Mike. Bring in some new clients. Catch your wind. In all the time I've known you, you've never taken a break."

"Look," Daphne said, "I'm not good at this kind of thing. Write the opinion for United. When you finish, go out to the desert. Take a break. When you come back, we'll see if there's still a place for you."

Seeley's eyes traveled painfully around the office. When they reached Girard, his friend averted his look.

Daphne said, "You really don't like being in a big firm, do you? Remember that lunch when we interviewed you? Even then, I figured you for a loner, but I hoped you'd get used to being part of a team. For a while I thought you had. When you come back from LA, if you decide you want to leave the firm and start a solo practice, I'm sure the partners will be glad to guarantee a loan, refer clients to you. You still have a lot of friends here." She looked at Girard, who nodded.

Thirst had cauterized Seeley's insides. "How did you know I was thinking about that?"

"Going solo? You told me at the last firm outing. It's not the kind of thing I'd forget."

This had happened to him before, entire conversations sucked from his memory, if they had even briefly lodged there. Whole evenings and afternoons filled with meetings and people that the next day were a blank.

"I must have forgotten." He hadn't forgotten telling Daphne. He never knew that he had told her.

"Go to Los Angeles."

Seeley said nothing.

"No sane man, if you throw him a life jacket, will throw it back because he doesn't like the color." To Seeley's surprise, there was emotion in Daphne's voice. "This is the last life jacket."

"I got the allusion," he said. "Is there anything else?"

Daphne studied him for a long moment before turning away. "You talk to him, Nick." She went to the bookshelf, pushed in a second offending volume, then opened the door and left.

Girard took another practice swing with the invisible racket. Seeley had never seen him this fidgety.

He and Girard had started out together at the same law firm

in Buffalo before moving to Boone, Bancroft—Seeley first, Girard six months later. Lawyers at Boone, Bancroft called them the Buffalo Twins even though their backgrounds couldn't have been more different. Girard came from the Buffalo establishment, where the family name showed up on the boards of the symphony, the art museum, and half a dozen other local philanthropies. While Girard was gliding through prep school, Princeton, and Yale Law, Seeley was working twenty or thirty hours a week to put himself through college and law school, using loans and a college athletic scholarship to make up the difference. Girard and Maisie had lived in a sprawling house in Buffalo's still-grand Delaware district. Until Seeley went to dinner there the first time, he didn't know that people outside of the movies actually dined at home by the light of silver candlesticks.

"How'd you make out downtown?"

"Minietello wants to settle. The other side wants to settle and the judge wants them to settle. I told Minietello he was making a mistake if he went along with them." Seeley weighed how much he could tell Girard about what had happened in Rappaport's chambers. "The judge thought I was out of line. He's sending my name to the disciplinary committee."

"They don't hand out reprimands for disagreeing with a judge."

"He isn't filing for a reprimand. He wants me disbarred."

Like an alarm, a vein in Girard's temple pulsed. "That's crazy. You get disbarred for stealing client funds, missing court dates. Not for crossing a trial judge."

"Maybe he wants to set a precedent."

"If he's really serious about this—I'm sure he's not—we can take care of it. Stan Trupin used to be on the committee. He can ask around, head off anything that looks like it might develop into a problem."

That was how people in Nick Girard's world handled things. A phone call, cocktails, a favor returned, and the law as Seeley knew it just slipped away.

"This thing about not going to Los Angeles. What do you really want, Mike?"

What did he want? How long had he been shadowboxing with that question? Whatever it was he wanted, it had a density to it, a weight and feel, sometimes even a taste, coppery and dry, at the back of his throat. He could no more put a name to it than he could fly to the sun.

"That's the big one, isn't it? The question the philosophers get all lathered up about."

"I give up." Girard took a last swing at the imaginary ball. "Some of us have a law practice. Game tomorrow? Usual time?" He tossed the ball at Seeley.

Seeley wondered if Girard knew what it was like to chase a small, hard ball around an echoing court while painfully hungover. It had been like that three mornings a week for years now. Yet the more dreadful it got, the more important it became to keep up the locker-room camaraderie, the appearance of normalcy. Which is why, at an hour most people in Manhattan were turning off their alarm clocks for another half hour's sleep, Seeley was careering about the ferociously white walls of the University Club's squash court, his stomach sour and his head throbbing.

"Sure," he said to Girard's back. "What Daphne said about my going to Los Angeles—did she mean it? If I don't go, I'm out?"

Girard turned. "That's a bit more direct than I'd put it, but sure—in on the opinion for United or out of the firm. And you know, if you're not a partner here, there's nothing the firm can do for you on this disbarment thing."

"Friends aren't supposed to threaten friends."

"It's not a threat, Mike. It's reality. I'll be there for you, but there are other partners who, if Daphne tells them to, will vote to cut you loose."

"So much for partnership being like a marriage."

Girard said, "I suppose you're the one to know."

When Girard had gone, Seeley locked the door and went to the credenza where he scooped ice cubes into a crystal tumbler—the ice maker had been Ed Meserve's legacy to him, along with the rest of the furnishings—and filled the tall glass to within a finger of the top. The office furniture had not been designed for a six-footer, and when Seeley crossed his legs on the desktop, they extended several inches over the other side. With the filled glass cooling in his hand, as reassuring as a handshake, the urgency that had accumulated through the day slackened.

Had he really told Daphne about his ambition for a solo practice? Seeley spread the plans out in his mind and examined them as he would a map. Clear up this mess with Rappaport; he would call the judge in the morning. Make a fresh start, but not with partners or being tied to any one place. Travel the way the old circuit lawyers did, from city to city, taking only the hardest cases. Picking his clients. Los Angeles could be the first stop. Why not? See what the studio was up to with its E&O opinion, stretch out the billing. He thought about Nick Girard's bullying remark that if there was a problem with United's rights he might be tempted to sign anyway. What if doing that was all it took to regain everything he had lost over the past year: Clare, the paying clients, and, if Rappaport persisted, his license to practice law. Short of the real thing, disbarment is as close as a lawyer gets to death.

Seeley held the glass up to the light, toasted his departed partners, and took a long, cool sip, a perfect circle closing on a day that had begun in his bathroom at the University Club. No, he'd throw the job back in the studio's face if it didn't look right. Clare was wrong. He didn't need rehab, just a change of scene. Spend some time by the water, maybe go down to Baja for a little sport fishing off the coast. Eat well. Cut back to a martini or two before dinner. *This* was a plan. Los Angeles glowed in his mind like a promise.

TWO

At midday, the lighting in the United Pictures commissary was subdued. Bow-tied waiters in gold jackets moved with the self-possession of movie stars past brown walls lit by golden sconces. The only details to distinguish the low-ceilinged room from any of a hundred other darkened eating places around Los Angeles were the colorful framed posters of the studio's current releases and the gold Oscar statuettes next to the maître d's station. Stacked in tiers and sealed off in a glass case, they were illuminated from below like religious icons. The maître d' could have been hired for his resemblance to the statuettes: bald, erect, feet pressed together as if preparing for a backflip from the high board.

"Your meter's been running for more than a week." Jack Elm was across the table from Seeley in the commissary, fussily tearing at a dinner roll and letting the pieces drop onto his plate. "You can't sit there and tell me you won't write an opinion for us."

"It's not that simple, Jack."

In late 1963, when the second of the James Bond films was making a fortune for its producers at the box office, Mayer Bermann, the chairman of United Pictures, ordered one of his producers to search United's library for a film with a flavor of international intrigue, something like *The Third Man*, on which the studio could base a spy series of its own. The producer picked *Spykiller*, a noir film from the early 1950s, and the film and its hero became the source for the *Spykiller* franchise, with ten sequels released to date. Unlike the solemn, black-and-white original, the action-filled *Spykiller* sequels gushed money. As currently practiced, the formula for each picture prescribed that no more than $80 million be spent on producing the film and another $40 million on releasing and promoting it. The formula predicted with unerring accuracy that no film in the series would earn less than $250 million worldwide. Most did considerably better, even before adding in the revenues from DVDs and product tie-ins. It was *Spykiller*, as much as the amusement parks and the studio tour, that kept United Pictures in business after a long string of box-office failures.

Spykiller presented only one problem for the studio, a problem that dated to the studio's lax, even negligent, contracting practices many years earlier. Contracts in the film industry have always been casual—a dinner menu with two or three deal points scrawled in the margins, a corner torn from *The Hollywood Reporter* with the producer's initials at the bottom, a blot of lipstick on a cocktail napkin filled with numbers. Fifty years ago, instead of getting a formal transfer of rights from a screenwriter, studios simply printed on the back of his royalty check that, by endorsing and cashing the check, the writer assigned all his rights to the studio in perpetuity. Forced to choose between haggling with the studio and paying for his groceries, the writer would cash the check. Sometimes United Pictures didn't bother to do even that. Although the writer was usually a freelancer,

United simply declared him to be a studio employee and claimed the rights in the script as a work made for hire.

Then, after decades of this casual industry practice, the U.S. Supreme Court dropped a bombshell, ruling that to call a free-lancer an employee was not enough to make him one. In a single stroke, the Court transferred ownership of thousands of copyrighted works worth hundreds of millions of dollars from the studios that commissioned them to the freelance writers who created them; it threw into doubt United Pictures' rights to almost half its film library. The decision set off a panicked search by studio lawyers like Jack Elm for some scrap of paper, a check endorsement, anything that might serve to evidence a true transfer of ownership. The decision was particularly fearsome for United's future: if the studio no longer owned the rights to the script on which the original *Spykiller* was based, it also had no rights in the film's characters, and without these rights it could not produce another sequel.

After the Supreme Court decision came down, the studio offered Bert Cobb, the author of *Spykiller*, increasingly larger sums to sign over his rights to the script, but he refused. Now United was paying Michael Seeley his hourly rate to search through the dozens of file boxes stored in its Panorama City warehouse and, from what he could piece together there, to write an opinion for the studio, its insurance company, and its bankers that Cobb had in fact been a studio employee and, if he hadn't, that he had at least said or done something in the past that a court might reasonably construe as a transfer of his rights to the studio.

If, fifty years ago, Bert Cobb had occupied an office on the studio lot or let the studio pay his medical bills, that fact and a liberal reading of the California Labor Code might have made it possible for Seeley to write an opinion that he was a studio employee. If Cobb had told someone, even in passing, that he intended to sell United his rights to the screenplay, or left a telephone message or scrawled something on his calendar, that might have given Seeley enough to conjure a transfer of rights sufficient to support a legal opinion. Even then, Seeley would have to state that it was a long shot.

"You already knew I wouldn't find anything. There's nothing in the files to prove Bert Cobb was your employee or that he transferred his rights to you."

Elm pushed the remains of a green salad around a chipped dinner plate. "We thought you could find a legal theory. We were expecting some creativity."

"I'm a lawyer, Jack, not a magician. I don't create facts. You're asking a bank to lend you, what, seventy, eighty million dollars to make a picture—"

"They're covered by insurance."

"That's exactly my point." Elm was being willfully obtuse. "You're asking me to write an opinion that will deceive your insurance company into thinking the studio owns the rights."

"You're at the top of their approved list. You're the go-to guy."

Seeley let the exaggeration pass. "I didn't get there by writing inflated opinions."

Elm said, "What about Cobb's signature on the canceled check?"

Even in the brutally air-conditioned room, Elm's forehead glistened with perspiration. He had insisted that they drive the two blocks to the commissary from the studio's office tower, and now at the table his nerves hummed like the engine of his idling Corvette.

"The check doesn't say anywhere he was assigning his rights."

When Seeley arrived in Los Angeles, Elm had met him at the airport, and Seeley had done his best to avoid him since.

Most days Seeley spent at United's warehouse in Panorama City or its offices in Burbank reviewing the production and business files for the first *Spykiller* film. He spent a pleasant day at the UCLA Law Library looking for judicial decisions to support the studio's claim to Cobb's script, even though he knew that, with the few facts he had found, no precedent would even come close to making the case that Bert Cobb had transferred his rights to United. It was years since he had researched cases himself—that's what eager young associates were for—and he had forgotten how much pleasure could be had in tracking down citations, moving systematically from one case to the next. It was like tracing a pathway in a maze. Finally, though, he could put Elm off no longer, and had agreed to lunch.

Elm said, "There's got to be some room for interpretation here. Lawyers in Los Angeles shade E&O opinions all the time."

"Have you thought about getting one of them to write your opinion?"

The insurance companies maintained a short list of lawyers whose experience and integrity qualified them to write E&O opinions. Seeley knew that no lawyer on the approved list would give the studio the opinion it wanted.

Seeley let the waiter remove his plate. The rare steak sandwich and grilled onions had been first-rate. Even the choice of bottled water that Elm had agonized over had been fine. Curiously, Elm's jitters had a calming effect on him, just as the depressing decor of the room boosted his spirits.

Elm said, "I'd think that a client that gave you and your partners as much business as we do would be entitled to some consideration in return. Not just United's business. Intermedia's, too."

"Then give your business to another firm. Let them write an opinion for you."

Elm bunched the tablecloth between his fingers and released it. The heavy white linen Seeley remembered from his last lunch at the commissary had been replaced with a slippery synthetic, the same gold color as the waiters' jackets.

"This has to stay under the radar. We've got a crew that's been sitting in Spain for more than a month waiting to shoot. If word got out that we're shopping for an opinion"—Elm rapidly surveyed the room, then drew a finger across his throat—"we can kiss *Spykiller* goodbye."

There was a commotion in the front of the dining room by the Oscars. A girl in a brown uniform with gold trim, a small megaphone at her lips, was directing a line of Asian tourists to a place by the display cabinet. The adults, erect and trim, could have been visiting dignitaries, and the children at their sides were so still they were almost invisible. The guide spoke rapidly, pointing to one Oscar after another. Then she turned and began gesturing, randomly it seemed, at the tables in the dining area.

"It's a premium we added to the studio tour," Elm said. "It was one of Beau's ideas."

The one time Seeley had seen Beau Callaway up close was in New York, coming out of a Boone, Bancroft conference room trailed by three lawyers, all talking at him at once. Slight and fair, with a bland, distracted smile under startling gray eyes, Callaway made no effort to listen to the lawyers; he moved with the lightness of a dancer or an escape artist. Seeley imagined a cold breeze as he passed. The man could have been a streak of quicksilver.

"You'd be amazed how much money celebrity sightings can bring in."

"It looks like you're giving them real value." There were no film stars in the room, but Seeley vaguely recognized a few character actors from television. Two of the tourists made their way toward an ancient comedian who had been in a television sitcom in the seventies. He was sitting alone at a table, his face as brown and creased as a walnut. Seeley thought he had died years ago.

"Mayer thought he had three years to meet Beau's profitability targets. Last month the order came from New York to meet the targets by the end of next year. The television stations and theaters are doing okay. So is merchandise. With gas prices going through the roof, the park's financials stink. Our first animated feature's coming out, but it's not going to release until Christmas. You didn't hear it from me, but it took Mayer sixty years to figure out what kind of genius Walt was. *Snow White. Pinocchio. Sleeping Beauty.* Animated characters don't hold out for twenty-million-dollar salaries or a percentage of gross. They don't have a union, either."

"What about the artists who create the characters?"

"They're kids. You can hire them off the street corner. The Artists Rights Alliance tried to organize them, but gave up." Elm finished shredding the last roll from the basket. "If the animated release craps out, *Spykiller's* all we have."

"Your boss doesn't look worried."

At a table across the room, Phil Mendelson, the studio's general counsel, was making his way through a massive slice of chocolate cake while a man and woman on either side of him, young corporate types in gray suits, sipped at their coffee. Elm was the point man, but it was Mendelson who hired counsel—a fact he never let Seeley forget.

"Those are Beau's people. Strategic planning. They flew in from New York to talk about selling off what's left of the film library."

"Callaway won't sell the library," Seeley said. The U.S. Supreme Court may have left Beau Callaway with only half the films he paid for, but the library was why he bought the studio. Without it, all the wheeler-dealer from Oklahoma oil country really owned was a movie lot, the parks and billboards, some television stations, and a studio whose production schedule should have been printed in red ink. "Callaway didn't get out of oil and gas to become a real estate operator."

"You're wrong," Elm said. "If we don't wrap up the rights to *Spykiller*, Beau's going to unload the studio."

A man on the commissary tour, a camera hanging from his shoulder, haltingly approached their table. Several feet behind him and to the side, a well-dressed woman waited. The man put on a tight grin, bowed modestly, and, with both hands, presented Seeley with a sheet of stationery from the studio hotel next door. A gold pen rested along the edge, under his thumb. The eyes were expectant. "Please sign?"

Seeley looked around the room. The other tourists had scattered through the commissary, and this routine was being repeated at several tables. Some of the diners seemed amused. Others turned their backs and continued their conversations. The television comic amiably wagged his walnut head. Seeley scribbled rapidly and handed back the paper. The man studied it for a moment, beamed broadly, and bowed again.

"What did you write?"

"When he gets home, he can tell his buddies he had lunch with Richard Gere."

Elm studied him intently. "Richard has a lot more gray hair but, you know, there's a resemblance."

Behind Seeley, there was a movement of air.

"You see how easy it is to sign a piece of paper?" Mendelson had come up from behind; he moved quietly for a big man. "There's nothing to it."

Mendelson turned to the man and woman from strategic planning. "Mr. Seeley here is the leading copyright lawyer in the United States. Isn't that right, Mike?" He rested a plump hand on Seeley's shoulder.

"Like most of our outside counsel, Mr. Seeley is stretching

out the hours, pumping up his bill. But at the end of the day he's going to sign a letter to the insurance company that we own clear title to *Spykiller*." Mendelson squeezed Seeley's shoulder, hard. "A letter from him is like money in the vault. He's right at the top of their list."

Seeley wondered who had made up the lie—Mendelson or Elm. Mendelson, he decided.

The man in the gray suit wasn't listening, but the woman absorbed every word. "If you're as good as Phil says you are, you wouldn't need to pad your hours. Clients would be waiting in line for you."

She was attractive in a smart, hard-edged way, and Seeley liked how she wore her suit jacket with no blouse underneath, only unblemished fair skin and a string of pearls.

"Then why don't you tell me why I haven't signed the opinion."

"If I had to guess, I'd say there's a problem with the studio's rights that Phil's not telling us about."

"There's nothing wrong with our rights." Mendelson looked at Seeley as he spoke. "If there was a problem, I promise you, Mr. Seeley would tell you about it. He's a man who speaks his mind. You won't believe this, but just last week, he told a New York Supreme Court judge exactly what he thought of him. Can you imagine that—right in the judge's chambers, with his client sitting there."

The woman looked at Seeley again, interested.

"One of his law partners told me about it." Mendelson leaned into Seeley, his hand clasping his shoulder again. "One thing I don't miss, working for the studio, is having law partners." He straightened. "We're expecting the opinion by tomorrow at five. If you get writer's block, you might try calling your partners in New York and see if they can't give you some encouragement."

Mendelson left, trailed by the two executives. Elm silently picked at the crumbs on the table.

Seeley said, "Did Cobb tell you why he won't sign over the rights?"

"He wouldn't give a reason. Hersh went out to see him twice."

Hersh Landau, the president of the studio and Mayer Bermann's son-in-law, wasn't someone Seeley would describe as a deft negotiator.

"Hersh was ready to pay him more money than the old guy's seen in a lifetime. You'd think he'd jump at it. This is the only script of his that ever got made. He's a wedding photographer out in Pacoima. He used to do publicity stills for the studios. How much can he be making? But he told Hersh no matter how much we offered, he wouldn't sign."

"Maybe," Seeley said, "you should get Mayer Bermann to talk to him."

"Mayer said if Hersh couldn't get him to sign, no one could."

Across the room, Seeley's tourist was showing off the autographed sheet of stationery and gesturing in Seeley's direction. It was time to go.

A busboy came to the table with coffee and Elm waited for him to leave before continuing. "Look, forget anything I said about our relationship with your firm. What Phil said, too. Water under the bridge." With the edge of his hand, Elm brushed a scattering of bread crumbs to the side. In the chilly room he was still perspiring. "You might want to consider whether it would be in your interest for us to switch from your hourly rate to a flat fee. This is strictly between the studio and you. It doesn't have to go through your partners."

"Forget it. I'm not interested."

Elm put up a hand. "Don't say anything until you see what

we're talking about." He removed a long black wallet from inside his jacket, laid it open on the table and extracted a business card. When he closed the wallet the glossy surface showed his moist fingerprints. Behind a cupped hand, he quickly wrote on the blank side of the card, then pushed it across the table.

The figure on the cream-colored card was $125,000. If that was Elm's opening offer, it meant the top number Hersh or Bermann had authorized him to pay for a cooked opinion was between $200,000 and $250,000.

"You get half when you sign the letter. The other half is yours when the insurance company issues its policy and the bank funds the loan. You can have a check for $62,500 in your pocket this afternoon."

"Do you come up with these ideas on your own, Jack, or do you get help?"

"What do you mean?"

"Extortion. Bribes. You already told them, didn't you? You told your insurance carrier and the bank I'm going to sign the opinion."

Elm drummed the table with his fingertips and looked away. A knot of Asian men was coming toward them pens and paper in hand.

"Let me tell you what the deal's going to be," Seeley said. "It's the only offer you're going to get, and you can take it or leave it. Tomorrow I'm going to drive out to Pacoima and get Bert Cobb to sign over his rights. That will get you your insurance policy and your financing. When I hand you Cobb's signature, the studio pays me a flat fee, one lump sum, no installments."

As soon as he made it, Seeley realized how reckless and grandiose the promise to get Cobb's signature was. Money in hand, the studio's president had struck out with Cobb, and the studio's chairman had written off further effort as futile. This was how Seeley made trouble for himself: reaching for people, cases, ideals—his next drink—impulsively and without regard for the consequences. He hadn't had a drink for more than a week, but he was still the same person.

Elm said, "How much do you want?"

"A quarter of a million dollars." The sum wouldn't be enough to support his first year of solo practice, but it would be a start. He caught himself: if he still had his license to practice law.

Elm put a hand under his chin, as if he were thinking. "If you're going to try to get Bert to sign over the rights, you've got to be careful. Diplomatic. Tell him we want his signature just to confirm our earlier relationship with him. Don't let him know how important this is to us. Make it sound like a formality."

"You're absolutely right. The president of the studio goes out to see him twice, throws a blank check at him, and Cobb understands from this that you're just trying to fix a small book-keeping error."

"One condition. You don't tell anyone you didn't sign the opinion."

"My condition is, you don't tell anyone I did."

"That's acceptable," Elm said.

Seeley had no idea what he could do or say to get Bert Cobb, a man he had never met, to sign over his rights to *Spykiller*. He didn't even know if the old photographer would be willing to see him. Why, then, did he think there was a chance he could pull it off? Perhaps it was the odd kinship he felt with this stubborn man. Bert Cobb, whatever his reasons, would not sign a deed turning over his rights to the studio, and Michael Seeley would not sign an opinion that would turn over to the studio whatever was left of his reputation. Not under any circumstances.

THREE

Used-car lots and auto junkyards lined the main road into Pacoima, where Bert Cobb lived. Closer to the small downtown were liquor stores, fast-food outlets with names unfamiliar to an easterner, and a few dusty motels. The surroundings drained whatever hopes Seeley had set off with. Before leaving the studio's offices, he had picked up United's standard form for transferring rights in a motion-picture script, but even then he knew it would be useless. If the studio's president had failed, and its chairman hadn't thought it worth his while to try, what could Michael Seeley, who didn't even have the authority to make an offer, hope to accomplish?

The previous night, to prepare for the visit with Cobb, Seeley had watched the original *Spykiller* for the seventh or eighth time. The film was set in Kraków. Unlike the cartoonish sequels that followed, the movie was all nuance and layered tones of black and gray, an artful embodiment of weary European attitudes after the Second World War. Its hero was Jack Wilbern, an American intelligence operative whose service during the war had left him distrustful of everyone, but particularly of his controllers in Washington. Wilbern had no desire to remain in Poland, but none, either, to be anywhere else. The screenplay had given him a single, redeeming edge of wit: his gift as an amateur magician. At any moment, Wilbern might extricate himself from a fix by producing, seemingly from out of nowhere, a knife, a length of rope, and even once a bouquet of roses.

Although the trailer billed the film as an espionage thriller, and the female part was small, the story was at its heart about a love affair, the romance between Wilbern—brooding, cynical, endlessly inventive—and the Russian double agent, Natalia, who on the seesaw of their relationship perfectly balanced the American with her somber gravity. Plain, even homely, in the film's early parts, Natalia was invested by some trick of light or camera angle with a stunning, dark-eyed radiance in the later scenes. In her final speech, made directly to the camera, all language and pretense fall away, revealing in her fine eyes a limpid, childish love for the American agent. A moment after she finishes her lines, a revolver suddenly appears in Wilbern's hand, he shoots her point-blank between the eyes, and the film ends.

It struck Seeley as unusual that a minor character should occupy such a central place in the film, or at least in his memory of it, and he found himself thinking about Natalia at odd times during the day. He inquired at the studio about the actress—Carlotta Reyes—who had played her but she had appeared in no movies before or since. Nor was Natalia the only aspect of *Spykiller* that seemed off balance. From the first viewing, Seeley had the sense that the film had at some point in its creation been brutally truncated or twisted off the course of its original intentions. If the movie were a painting, he would say the composition was wrong in a way the artist hadn't planned, as if in framing the canvas, someone had cropped or altered it.

Cobb's shingled bungalow was on a side street, mostly hidden by spiky shrubs and a single desiccated cactus towering over the low roof, its gray-green flesh consumed by rot. The front yard was hard-packed clay with a few patches of dead grass. It was only a few minutes past ten and already the ground was baking.

Seeley knocked on the door to the bungalow and, soon after, it opened a crack and a pair of faded blue eyes studied him warily before it opened wider. There was no depth to the eyes; it was as if they looked only out, not in. More bony than thin, Bert Cobb reached no higher than Seeley's chest. He had a full head of greased-down gray hair and his hands, hanging gracelessly at his sides, were like a farmer's, swollen and sinewy. He took his time examining Seeley and, when he finished, a rude glint went on in his eyes.

"You're the big-time lawyer from New York, right? The one the studio said was coming out. You're wasting your time and their money. I'm not signing anything. But you're here, so come in."

Seeley followed the man's rocking, bandy-legged walk into a low-ceilinged hallway. The place smelled of damp and of something older than that, mildew maybe, or the sediment of a frugal old age. There was a small kitchen, its curtains drawn. A flowered apron hung from the doorknob. Beyond that was a closed door with white printing engraved on a black plastic strip. PHOTO LABORATORY. Along the hallway hung museum-size black-and-white photographs in yellowing mats and old-fashioned frames of blond wood. Even in the dark passageway, the portraits glowed, as if from an inner light. They appeared to be of film actresses, or girls who wanted to be, dressed and lit extravagantly in the style of the 1930s and 1940s, with lots of opalescent flesh, shadowed cleavage, long legs, and dark painted nails. If these were Cobb's, the photographer liked bearskin rugs and flimsy tops riding down pearly shoulders.

Their destination, a den off the hallway, had more framed photographs. Cobb jerked open a folding chair and handed it to Seeley, taking the black vinyl recliner for himself. The furnishings were the same vintage as the photographs. The desktop next to Cobb's chair was covered with cheap paste-on shelf paper, the grains and knots simulating oak. On it were a dusty glass ashtray with the worn logo of a Tahoe motel and a pipe rack holding a single meerschaum, its yellow stem chewed down to an angry stub. A calendar in a tin frame advertised a local mortuary. Shelves holding wide flat boxes filled an entire wall. Close to Cobb's hand was a small camera, an antique with brassed chrome and peeling vulcanite. Directly across from where Seeley sat, an electric wall clock was framed by a flaking plaster sunburst.

"Let's shoot you, first," Cobb said. The voice was reedy, thin. He reached for the small camera with one hand and with the other switched on a reading lamp, aiming it at Seeley so that for a moment it blinded him. "I don't get many visitors, but I shoot them all. Like a guest book."

Cobb adjusted the light so it fell across a side of Seeley's face and directed him to turn slightly and tilt his head a few degrees upward. The swollen fingers manipulated the camera's knobs and dials with youthful dexterity and the shutter made a precise, silky whisper. Studying Seeley closely, indicating with his own head how he wanted him to pose, Cobb clicked off three more exposures before returning the camera to the desk and turning off the lamp.

As Seeley's eyes readjusted to the dim room, he studied the photographs on the wall. "You didn't take these with that camera, did you?"

Cobb grinned. "Heck no. This is just for me. The real portraits, I use a five-by-seven. Old Bertha."

Bert and Bertha, Seeley thought. A pair. "They're good," he said.

"*Good?* Hell, they're tops. It's my profession. Not as fine as Hurrell, maybe—the man was a genius—but still the best. Good enough for Goldwyn. For DeMille, too, the whole lousy crowd of them. Even your employer, Mr. Mayer Bermann. They came to me on their knees to do stills for them. You won't see anything like this from the digital boys." He shifted in the recliner. "I bet you can't guess which one's not mine. The one George Hurrell did."

Seeley started to rise, but Cobb gestured him to stay in his chair.

"You can see it from where you're sitting. It's the one right over my shoulder." Without turning, he hooked his thumb in the direction of a double portrait on the wall behind him. The two pictures, one above the other, were of the same head and shoulders in an identical pose. When Cobb twisted the reading lamp so that it shone on the wall, Seeley saw that the face on top was unblemished, eggshell smooth, while the one beneath it was uneven and freckly. The eyes and mouth looked familiar.

"It's Joan Crawford. George printed it as a joke. He said she was one of the three most beautiful women in the world. The others were his wife and some model whose name I forget. The bottom one's before he retouched the negative. Crawford went crazy when she saw it, told him he had to destroy the print. He kept one and made one for me. It wasn't just Crawford, you know. They all had that cruddy skin. Dietrich, Garbo. Now that George is a big thing with the fine-art boys, they're saying he was a master of light and shadow. He was that, sure. But if you want to know, he was a master of the retoucher's brush. Did you know George was a painter before he took up photography? A pretty good one, too."

From when they sat down, Seeley had tried not to stare at Cobb's fingernails, lustrous black from bottom to top, like chips of hard coal. "You're still working?"

"I keep my hand in. I pick up a Mexican wedding here and there. The Mexican girls are real beauties. I bid the senior pictures at the high schools around here that know my work. Everyone's using digital now—a trained monkey can do that work, the retouching, too. They try to beat me on price. All the parents want digital. A day before the senior portrait, Sonny shaves his head like a cue ball and sticks a gold ring through his nose. The parents go nuts. There's nothing I can do in the darkroom, but the digital boys, for a few bucks, they'll pull that ring out and put hair back on his head like nothing happened."

Seeley figured the man was lonely and without much work. He decided to let him talk.

"I know what you're thinking. Give the old guy a paper to sign and hand him a few bucks so he can buy some new equipment. But I'll tell you right now, I won't go near that digital crap!" Cobb leaned forward, half rising from his seat. "You're a big-shot lawyer? You don't know anything! If a kid shaves his head and sticks a ring in his nose, you've got to show him like that. Anything else is fake."

"Isn't that what your buddy, Hurrell, did with his retouching?"

Cobb's expression darkened. "That shows how much you know. George worked with silver, just like me, with light and shadow. When he retouched, he had a vision of what he was doing. To hell with the digital boys! They don't know the first thing about art."

"Silver?"

"Silver's what they call real photography, after what they coat the film and paper with. You need a darkroom for it."

Seeley pictured the old guy traipsing from high school to

high school with those blackened fingers, trying to sell his old-fashioned portraits.

"Your fingers got like that in the darkroom?"

Cobb shot him a puzzled look before drawing the backs of his hands in front of him, as if noticing the jet-black nails for the first time. "Amidol," he said. "An old developing formula. A classic. You don't use tongs. Only the amateurs do. Let your fingers stay in the soup long enough, and the nails go black on you."

Like most artists Seeley knew, not only the prima donnas like Gary Minietello but the serious ones, too, Bert Cobb had encased himself in a shell of self-regard that would make it impossible to reach him on any terms other than his own. Hersh Landau had no doubt blundered in and out without making an impression.

"George Hurrell worked that way, too?"

Cobb shook his head and laughed. "No, not George. You want to know a secret? George never did his own lab work. He stayed out front where the girls were. He didn't like the stink of the darkroom. Or the stains. You know what he said? 'I'll never disfigure myself for art, Bert, it's not worth it.' Those were his exact words." Cobb sucked in his bottom lip, making the thin cheeks pucker.

"Did Hurrell write?"

"What do you mean write?"

"Did he write movie scripts, like you?"

"Oh, you mean why you're here. Well, you could say George got me into it." Cobb's effort at a smile came out as a grimace. The even, yellowish teeth weren't his. "Back in the forties he got me mixed up with a bunch of writers and painters that came here from Europe. George got in with them through one of the artists—did I tell you George started out as a painter? There were some big-name writers in that crowd. I took some of their pictures. Thomas Mann, but he didn't socialize much. Fritz Lang. There were some movie writers, too. Dalton Trumbo, but he wasn't a refugee, Max Kanarek, Billy Wilder. Everything was wide open then, not like now. Even Johnny Weissmuller came to their parties. Starlets. They loved George, thought he was the real Hollywood. Back then the refugees were all trying to get into movie work, even the composers."

"Where did the writing come in?"

Cobb rocked in the recliner. "I had a little money put away by then, and I owned this house. So I stood collateral for a couple of the newer fellows. Before Uncle Sam would let a refugee come into the country, he had to have a sponsor, someone that would stand collateral for him if he ran out of money. So I did that and they invited me around. The ones that got here earlier, like Mann, they had loads of money, but we were in the war by then, and they were Germans, so they couldn't stand collateral.

"They pretty much lived over on the west side. They were always at each other's houses. If you can believe it, after what they'd been through where they came from, they were a real happy-go-lucky crowd. If they had any sorrows, maybe they put them in their books. I don't know. I'm not much of a reader. They liked having natives like George and me at their parties. We were sort of like cover for them. If you didn't look too close, you know, the whole gang of us was just a bunch of American patriots having a good time. One of the wives, a friend of Greta Garbo, wrote screenplays. She's the one that talked me into writing the script. She gave me some tips, but, you know, seeing how she did it, I caught on to how easy it was."

"But you wrote only that one script."

Cobb's eyes collapsed into watery slits. "That shows how much you know about making art. Writing's too easy to be art. There's no struggle to it. So I went back to photography. Besides, the script wasn't that big a deal, just another potboiler. The actors and the director did all the work."

Spykiller may have barely paid back its production costs, but it was no potboiler. And, whatever changes had been made during production, the film had a resonant, indestructible story at its core.

"Let me show you some of my pictures."

When Cobb went to the shelf, Seeley checked the clock on the opposite wall. The drive out had taken less time than he'd expected, but in two hours he had to be downtown. He had promised to meet Elm at a fund-raiser lunch to fill him in on what happened with Cobb.

Cobb pulled down a flat yellow box with a Kodak label on it. He laid the box on the desk, opened it, and, with Seeley looking over his shoulder, lifted a sheet of tissue paper off the print on the top, an eleven-by-fourteen, the head and shoulders of a craggy-featured man.

"A character actor. I don't remember his name." Holding the print by its edges, he handed it to Seeley who took care to hold it as Cobb had.

Seeley had never cared for photographic portraits; stiff, posed, lifeless, they made him think of death masks. But this picture had so much vitality, the subject could have been standing in the room with them. The light in the actor's eyes was not from a posing lamp, but from inside the man himself. Cobb's shaping of light and shadow gave the man a presence—nobility was the only word Seeley could think of—that transcended life. Cobb continued silently through the box—Seeley recognized a few of the actors from movies on late-night television—and though the prints all had the same lambent quality, each was as distinct as its subject.

Cobb stopped abruptly, slipping the tissue paper back over the print he had been about to remove.

Seeley said, "What's that one?"

"Nothing. The rest are all writers." He placed the cover back on the box. "No one important."

None of the others had been important either. "Thomas Mann?"

"No. Not Thomas Mann." Cobb put the box back on the shelf and returned to the black recliner.

Seeley wondered what he was hiding.

"Do you still see any of these people?" George Hurrell was fine if Seeley only wanted to keep the conversation going, but he needed someone living, an old friend, who might persuade Cobb to sign over his rights.

"You can't be serious. I was a kid then. Most of these people are dead. During the Red business in the fifties, a lot of them left the country. Some of their kids may be around, but I don't have any reason to get chummy with them."

"What about Carlotta?"

Cobb looked confused, then embarrassed. "Carlotta?"

"Carlotta Reyes. She played Natalia, the Russian girl."

"Oh, her." The shadow of a thought moved across Cobb's eyes. "An old man forgets. No, she was just a one-time tramp. A real pistol."

"Did the studio tell you to change the script? Or was it the director?" Seeley was thinking about the unexplained twist the film's story had taken. "Who made the changes?"

"These guys always fiddle with scripts. You know that. Nothing's good enough for them."

"No, I mean a big change. Something that moved the plot in a different direction."

"Look, the movie got made. Like I said, it wasn't a great movie, but it got made and that's the end of it. It won't do anybody any good to start picking apart how it got made." Cobb lifted his arms from the chair and folded them across his chest as if to protect himself.

How many times had Seeley seen a witness do that on

cross-examination when he'd caught him in a lie? More than failed memory was making the old man uncomfortable.

"What was Natalia's last line in the movie? Before she's killed?"

Cobb's arms tightened around his chest. "I told you. This was fifty years ago. What do I care what she said? The movie's nothing."

"Have you ever been to Kraków?"

Cobb stared at him.

Seeley suddenly grinned and shook his head. "I'm sorry," he said. "You invite me into your home, you let me look at your photographs, and what do I do—I start cross-examining you. Really. I'm sorry."

Cobb didn't return the smile. "I'm getting the picture you have more than a lawyer's interest in this."

"If you sign the papers, the studio will pay you more than you ever saw from your photographs. Ten times more. You could quit working."

Cobb gave Seeley a wicked look and put a hand against his cheek. "What does an old man need with money? I see the old geezers at the MaxiMart buying lottery tickets."

"Why won't you sign?"

Cobb shrugged. "I can't tell you."

"That's not good enough."

Cobb pressed his hands into the arms of the recliner and in a single movement propelled himself to just inches away so that Seeley could taste the man's stale breath. "You want to know why I can't sign your piece of paper? Ask the man who hired you. He knows."

"Phil Mendelson?"

"Your employer. The great Mayer Bermann."

"Bermann is going to tell me why you won't sign over the rights?"

"I didn't say he'd tell you." The voice had dropped to a whisper. "He won't tell you. But he knows."

This made no sense. Seeley didn't doubt that Bermann knew Cobb. The studio was smaller fifty years ago, and the chairman himself probably hired writers and fired them. But if Bermann knew why Cobb wouldn't sign, why hadn't someone passed the information on to him? If the studio had spent half the effort on Cobb that they had invested in trying to get Michael Seeley to sign an opinion letter, they might have the rights by now.

Seeley thought of the studio moguls on their knees begging Cobb to do their publicity stills. "If I got Mayer Bermann to come out to see you, would you change your mind?"

"There's nothing I have to say to him. Anyway, he won't come. There's nothing you can do to make him come."

"You don't know that."

"He buys and sells people like they were slabs of bacon, but he doesn't have the grit to look me in the eye." Cobb drew his bottom lip under the perfect yellowed denture and crossed his arms on his chest again.

"What about Mrs. Cobb?" The frilly apron in the kitchen suggested the presence of a woman. "Shouldn't she have a chance to say something before you turn down this kind of money?"

It was a crude question, but the response was mild. "Verna hasn't had a say for seven or eight years now."

Cobb caught Seeley's stricken look and gave a choked laugh. "No, she's alive. She just moved away. She used to take care of the business end of things. She'd tell me the business was going to hell because I wouldn't market myself. Like I was a new brand of soda crackers."

"Maybe she was thinking of Hurrell."

"She'd tell me I was as good as Hurrell. Better. But I

wouldn't market myself. She moved out to the desert. We never made a big thing about it. You could say we're separated. We like it better this way."

Cobb caught Seeley glancing at the sunburst clock.

"I've got to be downtown for lunch in an hour."

Disappointment crossed Cobb's face. "I was thinking you might stay for a bit and let me show you some of the other boxes. I've got landscapes from out in the desert."

"I'd like to come back some other time."

"You having lunch with the big shots at the studio? Mayer Bermann?"

Seeley shook his head. "It's the annual alliance lunch, their big fund-raiser."

"The Artists Rights Alliance?"

"Do you belong?"

"I used to. George, too. It wasn't just writers and directors back then. If you were a working artist, they welcomed you with open arms."

"Do you want to come? I can give you a ride and bring you back." Elm had said Bermann would be at the lunch. If the chairman wouldn't come to Cobb, he could bring Cobb to the chairman.

"I'm not going anywhere near the alliance. I quit in the fifties, when they kicked the Reds out. I wasn't pink myself, but the guys that took over were a bunch of chowderheads— they still are. All they care about is money and who's kissing what big shot's behind. If you ask me, they're in cahoots with the studios, the same crooks they're supposed to be fighting." He ducked his head in what looked like embarrassment, and when he raised it he was grinning. "You got me going there." He saw that Seeley was smiling, too. "What's that smile for?"

"I'm thinking I'm not that great a lawyer."

"Why? Because you couldn't sell me your bill of goods? I'm

sure you're a top-notch lawyer. I like the way you look at pictures, too. Most people just want to flip through them. See the celebrities. You were really seeing them. There aren't many people that do that. I like the way you listen. An old geezer like me gets to talking and . . ." He hesitated and dropped the smile. "Don't take it personally. I'm just a tough old bird."

Seeley gave Cobb his number at the studio and at his hotel in case he wanted to talk, then let Cobb show him out. As he turned the ignition in his car, the thought occurred to him: What would it be like if Bert Cobb and Gary Minietello met? What would these two artists have to say to each other?

FOUR

The drive back to Los Angeles took Seeley through a sun-burned landscape of scarred desert flats and brown hills. When he arrived in the city just over a week ago, the pulsing bright-ness of the landscape had stunned him as it always did, the California sun turning everything beneath it to a blinding gold. As usual, after a day or two the dazzle revealed itself as just another slick deceit—not the clear, transforming light that Hollywood puts onscreen in films and on television, the transparent brilliance that turns beaches white and surf blue, but a splotchy, polluted irritant, a sullen presence that scorches the colors from paint and turns foliage a dusty brown. Day or night, the sun-struck palm trees and the pale green lawns had the same dusty pallor. At first exotic, the fragrance of jasmine had become cloying and oppressive. Seeley's time in Los Angeles had been an unbroken succession of such sun-addled days and scented nights.

The studio had booked a suite for him at the Vista del Mar in Santa Monica. The hotel was old and the worn carpets and chenille coverings gave the rooms a tired look. Leaving open the single window in the kitchen did nothing to dispel the ancient, sour smell there. The sitting room looked out on the Ocean Avenue traffic three floors below and, beyond that, a sliver of beach and ocean. Every two minutes, the traffic signal at the intersection gave out a shrill chirp like a trapped bird. Clare hadn't called and, though he came close several times, he didn't call her.

The day had started for him before 5:00 a.m. with a telephone call that, as he groped for the receiver, he was certain would be Clare. It was Daphne Hancock.

"I just got bawled out by my client," Daphne said. "I don't like when that happens. You gave someone in strategic planning the impression that you're not going to sign the opinion."

The woman from lunch, Seeley remembered. The gray suit and pearls.

"They don't own the rights to the script," Seeley said. "They want an opinion that says they do. Do you want me to write a fraudulent opinion?"

"Why do you have to make everything black or white?"

"You're telling me you think I should sign the opinion."

"I'm telling you to consider how important this is to Intermedia, and how important Intermedia's business is to this firm. If United has to shut down *Spykiller*, Intermedia's going to have to write off a good part of its investment. Remember what we talked about. Your office can be waiting for you. Or, if you want, we can arrange a loan for you to start your own practice."

There was a long silence before she spoke again. "It's your call, Mike."

"I don't think there's a decision to be made here, Daphne. If there is, I already made it."

When she didn't respond, he hung up.

Half an hour later Nick Girard called. For some reason, the sound of his friend's voice made him lonely for Clare.

Seeley had been surprised when, ten years ago, Girard followed him from Buffalo to New York and accepted a partnership in Boone, Bancroft's corporate department. Having broken their rule against hiring partners from other firms in order to recruit Seeley, the Boone, Bancroft partners had little difficulty taking Girard, with his extensive business contacts around the state, into the firm. But why would Girard leave Buffalo? His friend had laughed when Seeley asked. "Four generations of Buffalo lawyers named Girard is enough. And if you haven't looked, Mike, the city is dying. The corporate guys aren't practicing law. They're taking in each other's wash." For Girard and Maisie, the move was less of a disruption than Seeley's own, for the couple instantly re-created in Manhattan the social circle they had left behind in Buffalo—a crowd made up of hearty men and their agreeable wives, all as Seeley saw them with an inborn talent for living graceful yet productive lives.

"Why didn't you tell me you were drunk in the judge's chambers?"

Seeley had never heard Girard so furious; the words ripped through the morning like a chain saw.

"Your partners are trying to help you, Mike. I got Stan Trupin to talk to his contact at the disciplinary committee. He told Stan you were completely hammered. You called the judge a toad."

A *pompous* toad, Seeley remembered. "Where do things stand?"

"The guy at the disciplinary committee talked to the judge's clerk. He says Rappaport isn't going to let up on this. We've got a lot of work to do if we're going to straighten it out."

"What about Daphne?"

"She hasn't said anything, and I'm not going to ask. Right now, I think only Stan and I know what happened. But it's just a matter of time before this hits the fan."

If only Stan Trupin and Nick Girard knew what had gone on in Rappaport's chambers, who had told Phil Mendelson?

"You're going to need all the support Daphne can give you. For God's sake, Mike, try to keep your nose clean."

The line went silent as it had with Daphne, and Seeley knew what was coming.

"Have you cut back on the drinking?"

"Sure," Seeley said.

In fact, he hadn't been near alcohol since coming to Los Angeles. Evenings, after a sandwich or takeout Chinese eaten in the small kitchen of his suite in the Vista del Mar, he walked to the Santa Monica Pier, half a mile from the hotel, staying on the tree-shaded, beach side of Ocean Avenue, away from the restaurants and bars. On the pier, he strolled the edges of a boardwalk crowded with aimless tourists. There were always a few locals absorbed in the fishing lines they cast over the rail, but he never saw one pull in a catch. When the light faded, he returned to his rooms and anesthetized himself into unconsciousness, not with gin but with late-night television or DVDs of the mindless *Spykiller* sequels Jack Elm had given him.

Seeley hadn't planned to spend any time with the sequels, but after watching one he found their cartoonish simplicity relaxing. Natalia was missing, of course, and the gray shadows and tense personal connections of the original were replaced in the sequels by bright colors, explosive action, and technological wizardry. As the series progressed, the gadgetry, villainy, rescues, and even hero Jack Wilbern's throwaway girlfriends grew increasingly improbable. Wilbern's magic tricks became more grandiose—a sheet of fire enveloping his adversary, highways suddenly iced over to prevent escape, and, in the last film, the sudden disappearance of an ocean-going yacht as its owner looked on. But, to Seeley's surprise, Wilbern himself remained as *Spykiller's* author had written him: cynical, thoughtful, and with an edge of sorrow and guilt—or had Seeley just imagined this—from his long past execution of Natalia.

Staying off alcohol was turning out to be more complicated than Seeley had anticipated. It was as if he had come to an intersection, and instead of turning left he had turned right, moving into a parallel existence where every detail was at once familiar and completely alien. And, like staying on the other side of the street from the bars and restaurants, Seeley told himself that if he could stay on this side of alcohol, everything would be fine; Clare would have him back, and if that could happen, the rest of his life could change, too.

For the present, though, the difference was not what he had thought it would be. Before this, when he daydreamed about life without alcohol, he had imagined it would restore the clarity of mind with which he walked through his early career, measuring conduct in the most precise fractions of cause and consequence. Instead he found himself in a persisting haze. The sensation was of a camera focusing back and forth on a point in the middle distance, his thoughts a blur until they reached the critical point, then blurring again the instant they passed it. One night, crossing an alley off Ocean Avenue on his way back to the hotel, an SUV hurtled past, just inches from hitting him. The driver jammed on the brakes, took the cell phone away from her ear, and turned to him with a frantic, apologetic look. He waved her on, mildly surprised that no adrenaline pumped inside him.

His plan had been to let the drinking wind down to the same relaxed pace as his chores at the studio. A cocktail before dinner, no more than two; the way other people drank. But, against his intentions, he had stopped completely. The urge to drink was still there, its grip as powerful and unremitting as it had ever been. Yet some entirely different force, at times as palpable as a hand pulling at his shoulder, held him back. Sometimes it was a shuddering physical revulsion that restrained him. Other times, it was a perverse will not to do what he most wanted. Whatever it was, it was not easy. Seeley had the uncomfortable sensation that he had overshot the mark and that there was no safe way back. The reprieve from drinking felt borrowed, not his own; it was tentative and could be revoked at any moment. The moderation he'd planned on no longer seemed possible. Now, if he took one drink, he thought he might never stop.

FIVE

The banquet room of the Biltmore was a kaleidoscope of color and noise—white tablecloths, ruby-filled goblets, glittering silver, centerpieces of tropical flowers, and a din that filled every corner. At the tables closest to the dais, brightly painted logos on plastic daggers burst out from floral arrangements like an animator's fantastic blossoms—the MGM lion, Fox's spotlit billboard, Universal's block letters girdling the globe. At the table where Seeley found Jack Elm, a golden centaur rampant rose through a wreath of brown laurel.

Elm halted his finicky lecture on vineyards and vintages to introduce Seeley to two men from the studio's legal department and a woman from business affairs. The men could have been twins. Younger than Elm, they had surfer tans and longish hair. The woman was heavily made up but her features had collapsed into boredom. On the dais, high on a carpeted platform, Seeley recognized the alliance's executive director. His aviator glasses, dark suit, and fashionably slicked-back hair marked him as one of the chowderheads who, according to Bert Cobb, had taken over the organization.

Only when Elm drew his chair away from the others and close to Seeley did Seeley see that he was as jittery as he had been at lunch the day before. "Did you get him to sign?"

Seeley said, "I didn't know so many people in Hollywood were committed to artists' rights."

"The industry's always supported the alliance. The studios and the big talent agencies pay twenty-five thousand for a table. The lawyers and accountants pay ten thousand. The writers are at the free tables in the back." He was breathless. "Did you get it?"

"Why would you subsidize a group you fight in court?"

"It gives us a say in how the alliance picks its lawsuits and who they're going to sue."

A red-jacketed arm reached over Seeley's shoulder and poured dark wine into the goblet in front of him. The sudden intrusion flustered him. He pushed the glass away, and then the congealing plate of food. The plates at the two places across from him were also untouched.

"Mayer and Hersh," Elm said. "They'll show up right before the speech. They always do." His voice strained to be heard over the noise. "You're in Phil's place. He's on a plane to New York to talk to the Intermedia people. What happened with Bert?"

"He won't sign unless Bermann goes out there and begs him to." Seeley checked himself. "Even if Bermann goes, there's no guarantee he'll sign."

"Bermann won't see him."

"Then he won't sign."

"Then you have to sign the E&O opinion."

"You're real strong at logic, aren't you?"

On the dais, a massive, pale profile, familiar from book jackets and late-night public television, leaned forward to whisper to the alliance executive. The man had a strong nose and chin, a high sloping forehead, and a thick silvery mane flowing almost to his shoulders. James Crowe Hardesty, American novelist and man of letters, had been on the short list for the Nobel Prize for as far back as Seeley could remember. Everything about his posture, even the way he leaned toward his companion's ear, was a model of implied seriousness and statesmanlike discretion. On looks alone, Hardesty should have received the prize years ago. Seeley understood literary politics well enough to know that Hardesty had been running too long to still have a chance. He'd never get the prize on the quality of his writing and his politics weren't far enough to the left to make up the difference.

"Bert was your only chance." Elm's voice was that of a belligerent child accustomed to having his way. "Now you have to sign the opinion."

Seeley surveyed the room. Diners were going from table to table, pausing to clasp a shoulder, pat a back, share a joke, all as intent as bees gathering nectar. Even in conversation, eyes traveled around the room, searching for someone more important to talk to. The studios might be owned by conglomerates, but nothing had changed the gossipy, self-absorbed culture of this tight-knit little community. Break one of its rules, fail to give these people what they want, and you might as well go home.

Seeley was not going to sign the E&O opinion, and if that caused problems for United, it was none of his concern. Mayer Bermann could go out to Pacoima and plead his case if this was so important to him. It made no difference to Seeley whether Cobb signed over the rights or not, or if the studio got to make another sequel in its inane series. He was going back to New York. If his partners wouldn't support him, he'd deal with the disbarment proceedings on his own.

Seeley glanced at the goblet, aware that it had not been out of his thoughts from the moment the waiter filled it. It was more than an arm's length away, but it filled his field of vision. He imagined the cool, consequent heft of the globe in his hand, as fat and full as a summer grape, could taste the rich, slippery liquid on his tongue. Forget what the wine snobs told you—fruity this and oaky that—the goblet in front of him stank of dark and musty oblivion, which is why he longed for it so: its promised release from the futility that even in this loud and gaudy room afflicted him. The irony was, he didn't even like the taste of wine.

"You really aren't going to sign, are you?"

Seeley thought Elm was going to cry. "Don't beat yourself up, Jack." Then, to distract him, "Is that Harry Devlin over there?"

Elm turned to where Seeley was looking at an older man talking to a young woman.

"If you can believe it, after all this time, he's still the alliance's lawyer." The unhappiness in Elm's voice told Seeley he hadn't given up on getting the opinion.

Seeley knew who Harry Devlin was, but had never met him. The first time he'd seen him was in a documentary on the McCarthy era, lean and fierce in a neat fedora, bantering with the press, crafty eyes moving under wiry black eyebrows and a shock of prematurely white hair. When the newsreel camera drew back, Devlin's right hand would be touching an elbow or shoulder of his client, some director or actor accused of being a Communist sympathizer. Later, Devlin appeared in cameo roles in two or three feature films, mostly playing himself. Seeley wouldn't argue if someone told him that he had himself become a trial lawyer because of those clips of Devlin, cigarette dangling from his mouth like a gangster, fighting for justice. There was more than shrewdness in the man's posture; there was defiance, menace.

"Don't let that sweet look of his deceive you. He hasn't mellowed with age."

"I thought you said the studios get along with the alliance."

"The only problem we have with the alliance is its lawyer. Everything's a crusade for him."

Devlin was dictating now, gesturing rapidly as he spoke, all the while chain-smoking what looked like unfiltered cigarettes, using a saucer as an ashtray. The woman wrote furiously, her head just inches from the legal pad as she took down his words. Devlin could have been a king in his castle courtyard, so comfortably was he in command. At something he said, the woman put the pen down, lifted her head, and ran her fingers quickly through short, boy-cut hair. It was a boy's face, too, but fair and fine-boned, the almost translucent skin setting off jet-black eyes. In a room where the few female faces were uniformly hard, varnished, and ambitious, she could have alighted from some distant, wonderful place.

"Who's the scribbler?"

"Never saw her before," Elm said. "Probably a secretary from his office."

Devlin leaned toward the woman and rested a hand on her shoulder. The smile she gave him was at once innocent and intelligent, radiant, even though Seeley thought he saw an edge of sadness at the corners. It was over in an instant but, for some reason, Seeley felt moved by the exchange.

As if in reply, the chime of a knife against crystal rang through the noise in the room. The alliance executive rose to the lectern, rapped on the glass a second time, coughed into the microphone, and hurriedly introduced the president of the alliance, Mark DeSousa, a television writer and producer. With a hawkish face and skier's tan, in his expensively cut suit he looked more like central casting's idea of an international financier than a working writer. Seeley couldn't imagine him hunched over a notepad or word processor, struggling with a plot line or piece of dialogue.

DeSousa welcomed the group in a liquid baritone, cracked a joke at the expense of the lawyers, aimed another at the agents, then introduced James Crowe Hardesty—Crowe, he called him—with a few desultory words, mostly lies about his Nobel Prize prospects. For the briefest moment, at the mention of the prize, a bright leer darted through Hardesty's eyes.

"Over there," Elm said.

Across the vast room, two figures paused at the entrance, Mayer Bermann and Hersh Landau. The chairman and the president. Hersh towered over Bermann, and was at least twenty years younger, but at this distance the older man, erect and formal, created an illusion of greater stature. The light coming from the corridor behind him made an aura of his thick white hair. The two stopped at a table just inside the door where Bermann greeted a man who looked to be the same age, holding on to his hand as they talked, the way a lover would.

"Those two have been at each other's throats for half a century," Elm said. "But every Saturday morning they're playing pinochle in the locker room at the Hillcrest."

Hersh and Bermann moved on to the next table, where the routine was the same, Bermann chatting with another old-timer and repeating the hand-holding business, while Hersh talked with the others, giving an occasional laugh or tap on the shoulder.

Hardesty had started his speech, oblivious to the thicket of noise below him. Straining, Seeley could just barely make out the words. "James Fenimore Cooper, Nathaniel Hawthorne, the intellectual forebears of a distinctly American sensibility . . ." Somewhere between the small Midwestern farm town where Hardesty had been raised and the Ivy League university where he now taught, his accent had acquired the plummy resonances of upper-crust New England. "Theirs was the beginning of a sturdy American tradition of individualism, of *authorship . . .*"

Elm and the two lawyers and the woman from business affairs left the table to join the others circulating through the room. Bermann and Landau disappeared into the crowd. Seeley again found himself staring at the dark ruby globe of the wineglass.

"Michael Seeley!" The voice was a low growl, and a hand hard as hickory gripped Seeley's arm. "I'm Harry Devlin," he said, coming around the table. "I've wanted to meet you."

Devlin's face was strong and complicated, with patchworked lines and guarded blue eyes. He had left his suit jacket draped carelessly over the chair at his table, and was in shirtsleeves and suspenders.

"We've been watching that artist's rights case you filed in New York."

Seeley wondered what he had heard.

"We're hoping you might make some law."

"The client got cold feet. He's going to settle." Seeley guessed that he already had.

"That's too bad." Devlin's regret seemed genuine. "We're working up a case of our own out here. It would be federal, though, not state." Then, as flat as if he were asking about the weather: "Would you be interested in taking it on?"

Seeley tried to keep his voice level. "Who's the plaintiff?"

"It's a class action against the studios. The class is going to be all members of the alliance and any other writers and directors who want to join in. We're going to stop the studios from hacking up their movies to make room for television advertising."

"I already represent a studio. There'd be a conflict."

"You could drop them right now. You're not going to write the opinion for United."

Harry Devlin was the studio's adversary. There was no honest way he could know about the opinion letter or the fact that Seeley hadn't signed it.

"I don't talk about my client's business."

"Have they tried to bribe you yet? What's an E&O opinion worth these days? A quarter of a million? Half?"

"Why aren't you trying the class action yourself?"

Devlin smiled. "I write briefs. That and some counseling and strategy. I haven't tried a case for seven years. It's almost that long since I've argued a motion."

As Seeley remembered, Devlin had started out representing midlevel labor racketeers in New York, then graduated to working for their bosses. When he moved west in the 1940s, he added left-wing writers and directors to his client list, helped them found the alliance, and in the sixties started taking on real celebrities as clients. All this time, he practiced solo, with no more than two or three young associates who did research and investigative work for him before he kicked them out of the nest to make it on their own. Harry Devlin had the law practice that Michael Seeley coveted.

Seeley let himself imagine what Devlin's class action could do for him: with discovery, trial, and appeals, a case like this could easily go on for five or six years, giving him a foundation on which he could build his solo practice. And this was the case—the principle—that Randall Rappaport snatched from him when he talked Minietello into settling. Seeley knew how unforgiving the motion picture industry was: sue a film studio and forget about ever getting that studio, or any other studio, ever to hire you again. But, for him, to leave this crowd would be a blessing.

Devlin said, "I understand United can be a difficult client. I hear that Beau Callaway's been putting the blocks to them on profits."

Why was Devlin pushing this?

"I can't talk to you about your case. Until this engagement's over, I still have a client."

"Law practice would be wonderful, wouldn't it, if it weren't for clients?"

"I'd think you'd get to pick the clients you work for."

"If I started picking and choosing clients, I'd have to figure out which ones are right and which ones are wrong and, other than the alliance, I've never done that. Is that how you do it? You only represent clients who are on the side of right and justice?"

"Whenever I can." Seeley didn't add how easy that had become now that the list of paying clients was down to a handful.

"How do you decide that? Which side justice is on?"

Seeley said, "I'd turn in my bar card if I couldn't tell the difference."

"You're an idealist." Devlin nodded in Hardesty's direction. "Unlike you and our friend up there, I don't have the luxury of knowing that my judgment about right and wrong is better than anyone else's. I let the law sort it out. That's the beauty of the law, you know—it has no ego, only principles."

"That makes you the idealist." Seeley didn't believe that someone who had spent his entire career in the legal system's dark corners could honestly possess a sixth grader's belief in the integrity of law.

"No, it makes me a gambler. I figure it gives me a fifty-fifty chance of working for the right side on any matter. Practice law long enough, and you bat five hundred. That's not bad for an average."

The noise in the room had increased, as had the heat from the milling bodies. Hardesty, virtually screaming now, moved across the Atlantic, to Flaubert, Goethe, Victor Hugo. "These were not just men of letters," Hardesty roared, "these were men of affairs, public citizens who held themselves accountable for the condition of their culture."

"Listen to what's coming," Devlin said.

"You read the speech?"

"Let's say we had a hand in writing it. Julia and I. It's too bad she had to leave."

The boyish scribbler, Seeley thought.

"She had a meeting to go to. Listen to this."

"I challenge you: What eternally fulfilling work of art, what soaring vision, was ever created by a committee? What work of authorship is not, ultimately, the gift to us from a single individual? *Don Quixote*? *Paradise Lost*? *The Sun Also Rises*?"

"Why aren't you up onstage with the other big shots?"

"Too much huffing and puffing. Too much grandiosity." Devlin let the word roll out, syllable by syllable. "That kind of excitement's dangerous for me."

"Heart?"

Devlin smiled. "No, soul. It's why I don't try cases anymore. You try an important case and the press is all over you, other lawyers, all the people you don't want to be spending time with. Before you know it, they're calling you a hero and you're sitting at a table on a platform, your head all puffed up. Of course, it's got nothing to do with you or anything you've done. It's all about the people who need heroes so desperately that they make them up. That's easy to forget. I used to forget it all the time. If I stay down here, I don't give myself the opportunity to forget."

Even in the din, Seeley was aware of the eccentric rhythms of Devlin's speech. Sentences rushed forward, then, unexpectedly, paused for a beat before continuing. It went with how the open, friendly expression turned cold and reserved when it reached his eyes. There was something seductive about the combination, even sensual.

"It's a good thing there's no Nobel Prize in law," Devlin said. "Instead of paying attention to my clients' business, I'd be spending the days polishing my acceptance speech."

"You'd have plenty of company."

"All of it bad." The hard tips of Devlin's fingers touched the back of Seeley's hand. "Wait, here's the good part."

Hardesty was in angry battle with the din below, shoulders rolling and jerking in spasms, eyes flashing, voice at hysteria pitch. "And yet you take this cohering vision, this singular work of art, and hand it over to be hacked and twisted by a crew of thirty-year-olds, their moral sensibility shaped in the crucible of a talent agency mail room. Eviscerated to make room for television advertisements, slaughtered, drawn and quartered to satisfy the common taste! Would William Faulkner have tolerated such indecencies? Ernest Hemingway? Eugene O'Neill?"

All Nobel winners, Seeley thought. Hardesty's putting himself in good company.

"This industry—every one of you—to this day bears the stigma of the blacklist, a cowardly outrage that drove its more fortunate victims into exile and forced the less fortunate, who stayed behind, to see their works—their very children—go out into the world under the names of false parents. How can the industry that once bore this shame now repeat its crime? How can you, who shamelessly denied authors the paternity of their offspring, now deny them the integrity of their works?"

"This is your heads up to the industry, isn't it? The class action against the studios?" The words came automatically. Seeley's mind wasn't on the class action. He was thinking of Cobb, his forgetfulness about *Spykiller*, the crossed arms. What was Cobb hiding?

"What kind of research does the alliance have on the blacklist?"

"That's Julia's department," Devlin said. "She teaches film over at USC. She has all the files."

"And she'd have a list of every writer who used a front?"

In the 1950s, if a writer was blacklisted, some studios would buy his script from him but put another person's name on it; for the use of his name, they'd give the front a percentage of the writer's fee.

"It wouldn't surprise me if Julia had a list like that." Devlin paused as if Seeley's question had a meaning he hadn't caught, then let it drop. "I was serious before. Would you be interested in trying the case for us? I promise you, United will waive any conflict. We're going to file here in the Central District. We figure whatever district judge we draw, the Ninth Circuit will get it right on appeal. We're interviewing counsel next week, but I'm sure you'll be everyone's first choice."

"In the early days, when the alliance was starting out, did you ever meet a guy named Bert Cobb?"

"The fellow who wrote *Spykiller*?" Devlin appeared to think for a moment and slowly shook his head. "No, I don't think I ever met him."

"He's not a writer. He's a studio photographer. I think he was a front."

If Devlin represented blacklisted screenwriters in the fifties, that meant he also helped them find fronts for their scripts. And if Bert Cobb was a front, he didn't own the rights to *Spykiller*. The writer who actually wrote the script owned the rights. All this time, the studio had been talking to the wrong man.

"As I said, if anyone knows, it would be Julia. She just finished writing a book about Hollywood in the forties and fifties." Devlin removed a business card from his wallet and scribbled something on the back. "Here's her number." He relaxed comfortably into his chair, hands clasped across his belly. "Now, listen to what's coming. Short and sweet."

On the dais, perspiration streamed down Hardesty's face. Spittle flew from his lips. He paused for breath. "If we are to honor authorship, if we are to salvage the genius that sustains

this industry, we must be willing to destroy the very founda-
tions of this damned and damnable corporate culture."

"That's pretty strong," Seeley said.

"No one takes Hardesty seriously. No one's even listening.
The alliance has a great sense of humor. Do you know how it
got started? There was an outfit called—you won't believe
this—the Motion Picture Alliance for the Preservation of
American Ideals. Everyone you'd expect was in it. John Wayne,
Gary Cooper—oh, and Hedda Hopper. When I moved out
here from New York, I got some work from the guilds, and
that's how I got hooked up with their battles against this Motion
Picture Alliance. We called our organization an alliance, too,
just to rib them. After all this time, that's the only thing I can tell
you about this group that's a hundred percent constant. Their
sense of humor." Devlin looked around the room. "Do you
know why they have their fund-raiser here every year?"

Seeley figured they held the lunch at the Biltmore to incon-
venience the studio executives by making them travel downtown from their offices on the west side or out in the valley.

"No, I mean *here*, in the ballroom." Devlin thumped the
tabletop. "They started holding it downtown around fifteen
years ago, and when they needed more space, someone came
up with the brilliant idea of having it where the subcommittee
held its hearings to investigate subversives in the movie industry. Right here in the Biltmore. That's when—"

There was a movement behind Seeley, and when Devlin
looked up, Seeley did, too. It was Jack Elm. He looked only at
Seeley, ignoring Devlin.

"Can we have a few minutes of your time?" Elm nodded
in the direction of a table across the room where Hersh was sitting alone.

Seeley told him he would come over in a few minutes

Devlin waited for Elm to leave. "I'd like you to talk to my
board next week about heading up the class action for us."

"I told you, I already have a client."

"I don't like to speak ill of your client, Mr. Seeley. In ordinary circumstances they are not bad people, but this business with *Spykiller* is, as I am sure you have seen, driving them to extremes. I would advise you to walk away from your project there and come see us next week about our lawsuit."

Seeley pushed his chair back. "This is between my client and me."

When Seeley rose, Devlin gripped his wrist. "You're the kind of man who, if someone twice your age gives you sound advice, you won't take it. Just on principle. The one thing you won't admit is that you're in trouble and you need help."

"Is that it? Are you finished?"

Devlin looked over the wreckage of the table—half-eaten rolls, soiled napkins, silver in disarray. "It may surprise you, but we're very much alike, you and I." The old man's eyes were remarkably clear under bristly eyebrows that rose and fell with his gestures. "You know, when I come to a feed like this, the first thing I do is turn over my wineglass so they don't fill it up. That way the waiter doesn't make a mistake, and neither do I."

Hersh reversed his chair so that he faced Seeley over the back. He started in at once quizzing him about the meeting with Cobb, demanding a minute-by-minute account. Cobb hadn't looked well the two times Hersh was there. How did he look this time? Did you say anything that made him anxious? Did he take your picture? What about the Joan Crawford double portrait? And after that? After he told you about Crawford? The questions came rapidly, like an amateur's idea of cross-examination, and Hersh didn't seem to notice that Seeley was making no effort to answer them.

Bermann arrived at the table and, when Hersh introduced them, gave Seeley a brisk handshake, but otherwise was silent during Hersh's one-sided interrogation, watching through gray eyes hooded beneath lizard-lids. The creased, unnaturally pink face was robust and vital.

Seeley had been close to great wealth before, both old and new. A former client in the music business possessed a fortune that dwarfed Bermann's. Seeley had been next to power, too, representing the mayor of New York in litigation that had arisen out of the publishing contract for his autobiography. The studio chairman in repose exuded the same potent energy as these men.

Hersh persisted. "Did he tell you why he wouldn't sign over the rights?" Hersh had the easy physicality of a college athlete—basketball, maybe, or tennis—and while he spoke his hands constantly touched the silverware, a glass, the tablecloth, as if to assure himself he had everything under control. "Did you tell him why we need the rights?"

It occurred to Seeley that Hersh didn't care about the answers; this was a performance to impress Mayer Bermann.

At the entrance to the banquet room, where Seeley had first seen Bermann and Hersh, three men stood, talking. Two were in the black suits, white shirts, and black ties of limousine drivers. The third man, medium height and stocky, had on a brown leather windbreaker over his shirt and tie. There was something about the way the man held himself, shoulders back, chin tucked in, that made Seeley think of a prizefighter, a boxer. Seeley had seen the man two or three times in United's underground parking garage, at an exit not far from the assigned space where Seeley parked. He thought he had also seen him in Santa Monica, on the bar and restaurant side of Ocean Avenue.

To Hersh, he said, "Do you know the guy standing over there? The one in the leather jacket."

Hersh looked toward the entrance. "Sure. He's one of our drivers. We have three of them."

"He looks more like a bodyguard," Seeley said.

"Driver, bodyguard—they're the same thing these days." Hersh looked at Bermann, who gave him no response. "You have to be careful."

To Bermann, Seeley said, "I want to know why Bert Cobb won't sign a transfer of rights. He wouldn't tell me, but he said you knew why."

Bermann said, "That is completely ridiculous. How could I possibly know such a thing?"

If he was forced to choose one of these men to believe, Seeley decided he would pick Cobb. The old photographer was holding something back, but only because it wasn't in him to tell an outright lie. The curious feeling of kinship with Cobb returned, and with it the sense that the man was in danger of some kind.

"I think if you went out to see Cobb, he might change his mind."

"Mr. Landau said the same thing to me. However, I am not a man given to futile gestures. I would go if I thought it would accomplish something. But it will not. Most definitely, Mr. Seeley, it will not."

The words had a German inflection but were a world apart from the guttural accents of Seeley's parents and neighbors in Buffalo's far east side. The manner was light and cultivated, urbane Vienna, perhaps, or Zurich. *Fines herbes*, not pork shanks and bread dumplings.

"It would depend on what you said. How you said it."

"You mean I should go there, a penitent on bended knee, like Henry at Canossa?" Bermann allowed a small smile. "As you know, Mr. Landau was already there. He told me the story of the bent-over moguls. No, I can assure you that will not work. Mr. Cobb, whom I remember well, is a genuine mischief maker, a rascal of the first degree. He will lead you on—and Mr. Landau here, too—and have you believe that a nod from me to him will achieve the result we all want. But, trust me, it will just feed the flame. My going there will only make the man more intransigent."

"Because he didn't write the script?"

The question didn't appear to surprise Bermann. He studied Seeley, but managed at the same time to look across the room. "What are you suggesting?"

"Was Bert Cobb a front for someone else?"

Elm, across the table, said, "That's ridiculous. We have all the papers from the guild and the copyright office. You saw the files. Bert Cobb wrote *Spykiller*."

A wave of applause rolled toward them from the back of the room where the writers were rising from their chairs. Hardesty had finished his speech and returned to his place. The people at the head table, taking a signal from the silver-haired alliance president, rose and extended their hands in applause toward Hardesty. After some embarrassed chair shuffling, everyone in the place got up except Bermann and, across the room, his old enemy and pinochle partner. Bermann's ovation was a slow *clap, clap*, one cupped hand moving, the other level and still, as if marking time.

Hardesty stood and bowed, his face working frantically at the appearance of humility. He raised his hands, making Seeley think he was going to speak again, then clasped them over his head, pumped his arms in victory, and, as quickly, dropped them. The applause ended abruptly, like a radio being turned off, and the buzz of conversation resumed.

People swarmed to the exits. Bermann gave no indication that he noticed. "What did you think of our speaker's remarks just now?"

"It was a little showy, but he makes a valid point. The studios should respect the integrity of a writer's or director's work."

"No editing of films for television? No colorization of our black-and-white library?"

"Not without the director's permission, or the writer's."

"Then we will make sure that these people give us their permission to alter and edit their works when we sign our contracts with them. If they refuse permission, we will sign with someone else. There are plenty of writers and directors looking for work. We will not pay an extra dime for the rights, either. In the end, these rights will give the writers and directors nothing but false expectations."

"When high-school kids copy your movies off the Internet, you might ask them if they would respect your interests more if they knew you paid greater respect to your authors' interests."

Bermann looked at him for a few moments and finally decided to smile. "That is an interesting point. Do you feel the same way about the author's right to be credited for his work?"

"After the blacklist, I'd think that's not even an issue."

Hersh looked at a slip of paper Elm had handed him, crumpled it, and put it in his jacket pocket. "This is entertaining, but it's got nothing to do with what we're paying you for."

"The studio engaged me to provide my opinion on who owns the rights to *Spykiller*. Yesterday I gave my opinion to Jack here. If Bert Cobb wrote *Spykiller*, he owns it, and the studio has no claim to the script. If you want me to put that in writing and send it to your insurance company, just let me know. If Cobb didn't write *Spykiller*—if he was a front for someone else—then you need to get the real author to sign over the rights. But that's not what you hired me for."

Bermann said, "I'm sure your schedule is crowded, Mr. Seeley, but I hope you will consider staying in Los Angeles for another day or two—of course, entirely at our expense. Pursue this theory of yours about Mr. Cobb, if you like. We hope we can impose on you to stay for just another two days. No more."

Hersh shot Bermann what Seeley interpreted as a puzzled look. If Bert Cobb was a front, Mayer Bermann, whose grip on the studio was even tighter fifty years ago, knew that he was.

Perhaps this was why Bermann was avoiding a confrontation with Cobb. Whatever Bermann's motives were, if Bert Cobb didn't write *Spykiller*, someone else had, and—if he or she was alive—still owned the rights to the script today. Why hadn't Mayer Bermann sent Hersh to talk with the real author, or gone himself? Harry Devlin's class action could wait.

"Two days," Seeley said.

"Fine," said Bermann. "We are agreed, then." He rose and, followed by Hersh, strode toward the departing crowd. Elm followed at a distance.

Seeley looked over to Devlin's table, but he was gone. The old lawyer, with his obtuse banter about soul not heart, had been a disappointment. Still, Devlin knew things about the studio that he shouldn't know. Then another thought occurred to Seeley. If there was no good reason for Harry Devlin to have this information about United's business, why was he letting him, United's lawyer, know that he had it?

SIX

When she answered his knock at her office door, Julia Walsh greeted Seeley as if she had been expecting him.

"Did Harry Devlin tell you I was coming?"

"He said you were asking about the blacklist. You want to know if Bert Cobb wrote *Spykiller*."

It interested Seeley not only that Devlin had called Julia but that he had been so specific in remembering his question about Cobb.

Julia said, "I can tell you, categorically, Bert Cobb wrote *Spykiller*."

"What makes you so sure?"

"All the research says he wrote it." Julia tapped the keyboard of her computer. The screen came to life, filled with lines of data, and she turned it toward Seeley. "His name is on the script, the script's registered with the Writers Guild, and there's no record that anyone else ever claimed an authorship credit.

There's not a single document that even suggests he's not the author. Bert Cobb wrote *Spykiller*."

"How do you know your files are complete?"

"A committee at the guild did the research years ago. They hired investigators, read scripts, interviewed all the writers they could find. I went over their data and filled in the holes. They'd missed some names, and I added them. I know every script that has a front's name on it and who the actual writer was. I interviewed all the people I could find who worked on the studio lots. If you think there's a big mystery about this, you're wrong. Everyone in Hollywood knew who the real writers were. You'd be surprised how many of them are still around."

"You talked to Bert Cobb?"

"A couple of years ago."

"He's not a writer. He's a photographer."

As much as Seeley admired him, Bert Cobb was a man of surfaces, a collector of shapes and texture, light and shade, not words and ideas. Seeley doubted the man ever had an introspective thought. "He took pictures of glamour girls," Seeley said. "He never had his name on another film."

"You'd be surprised how many people have just one script in them, the single burning flame of their lives."

Julia ran elegantly tapered fingers through the short haircut, a nervous gesture Seeley recognized from the lunch. Her outfit was a notch or two above what you'd expect of a film school assistant professor, even in Los Angeles. The faint but eloquent fragrance hadn't been purchased at a drugstore counter.

The office was standard issue for a junior faculty member— a narrow, shelf-lined room with a large window at the back looking onto a leafy plaza—but Julia had brightened it with home-magazine touches: a spindled rocking chair, a brightly colored throw on the wooden floor, a porcelain tea set on a small table. Open file boxes crammed with papers filled the shelves. Hanging from a hook on the door, a framed poster for the film *All Quiet on the Western Front* was sufficiently worn from folding and refolding to be an original. There were two cups and saucers in the tea set, but the office had a feeling of long and solitary hours.

"There weren't as many fronts as people think. Most of the blacklisted writers just used pseudonyms. The inside joke at the Academy Awards was when the best screenplay award went to one of them. It happened a lot. Sometimes I think the Academy used the blacklist itself as a ballot. Just to rub the industry's face in it. The producer would have to go up and say how sorry he was, the guy was sick and he'd been asked to collect his Oscar for him. There were a lot of bedridden screenwriters in the fifties. A few of the studio bosses like Disney and Jack Warner played it straight and never touched a script by a pink writer, even with a pseudonym. But most of the studios looked the other way."

"What about Mayer Bermann?"

"Mayer Bermann embodies all the evils of capitalism, but he stood behind the blacklisted workers when no other studio head would."

Seeley thought: Evils of capitalism?

"If you haven't discovered it already, this is an industry of sheep. In 1947, after the Hollywood Ten refused to testify about their membership in the Communist Party, all the studio heads flew off to New York City. Everyone thought they were going to issue a statement supporting the Ten. They got together at the Waldorf-Astoria. Sam Goldwyn pounded the table and made a pretty speech about how they had to take a stand against the investigations. After he finished, a couple of the others said that was a noble sentiment but, as practical businessmen, they'd be crazy to go up against the committee. So what did these brave men do? They were the ones who came up with the idea of the blacklist. They signed an agreement that they wouldn't hire anyone who refused to cooperate with the committee. Only Mayer Bermann refused to sign, and he let everyone in the industry know it. I spent a whole day interviewing him."

Julia sparkled. She was getting a kick out of lecturing at him. "That's another reason Cobb couldn't be a front. Bermann didn't need fronts."

"Whose word do you have other than Bermann's?"

"Harry Devlin. And he likes Bermann even less than I do. But don't think Bermann did it because he's a saint. He didn't reject the blacklist on principle. He was just smarter than the rest of them. The other studio heads thought it was all about politics, but Bermann saw from the beginning that the investigations were about just one thing: economics. He's your client. Ask him about it."

"You tell me."

"I will if you drop your patronizing attitude."

Seeley raised his hands in mock self-defense. "Mea culpa." He thought it was she who had been patronizing him.

"In the seven hours I spent with him, it was the only time Bermann showed any real emotion. You'd think he'd be pleased about it. Here he was, just getting started in the industry, and of all the studio heads—most of them were twenty, thirty years older than he was—he was the only one who saw that the investigations were a sham. But all he felt was anger at how blind the other studio heads were to what was happening."

"He couldn't have been more than thirty years old."

"Twenty-six. People grew up a lot faster then. Particularly if you were a refugee."

Julia crossed her legs, but made no effort to rearrange her skirt where it had slipped up her slender thighs. There was nothing seductive about it; just an academic's indifference, but the effect on Seeley was electric. Apart from Clare, how long was it since he had been this close to an attractive woman? That he had been close to Clare?

"What Bermann understood, and what none of the others did, was that it wasn't the politicians who were behind the investigations. It was Wall Street. The politicians were the bankers' pawns. From the 1940s until the late fifties, Wall Street orchestrated everything that happened in Hollywood. The committee hearings, the blacklist, the boycotts. Even the guilds and the unions."

"The alliance?"

"Nothing direct. Wall Street worked through fear. That was the bankers' big weapon. Most of the studio heads were Jews, and they were still terrified by what almost happened in America in the 1940s. If you believed Father Coughlin, Lucky Lindbergh, and Gerald Smith—and a lot of people did—the movie industry was the advance guard of the international Zionist conspiracy that got us into war."

"And on the wrong side," Seeley said.

"What infuriated Bermann was that the Wall Street bankers who were behind the investigations—'these white-shoe anti-Semites,' he called them—presented themselves to the studio heads as their saviors. The deal was, the grateful moguls—*moguls*, can you believe they actually called themselves that?—would give Wall Street control over their studios and Wall Street would protect the studios from all of America's Jew-haters. Rejecting the blacklist was Bermann's way of telling Wall Street it wasn't going to get its hands on United."

The story sounded to Seeley like an academic's paranoid fantasy, with just enough authentic detail to get her tenure. Still, he had to work to find a hole in it.

"The studios were nothing in the forties. Sure, they were making great movies, but they were seat-of-the-pants operations. The bosses ran them the way you'd run a kid's lemonade stand. The Wall Street bankers saw television coming. They'd already invested in it. But they needed content. Their plan was to create another American industry, like steel or automobiles, with an assembly line that churned out a popular product for the masses as uniform and inoffensive as bars of soap. But to do that, they had to get the troublemakers out of the industry. No strikes. No stoppages. That's why they started the investigations and the blacklist. It's how they wrecked the unions. Without the blacklist, not a single one of the entertainment conglomerates would exist today. Bermann saw it coming. That's why he wouldn't give in to the bankers."

"Until they outsmarted him," Seeley said. "It just took them some time."

Seeley remembered how tenaciously Bermann had fought Beau Callaway's acquisition of his studio, the countless trips Boone, Bancroft lawyers, representing Intermedia, had made to federal court to fight United's attempts to enjoin the takeover of the studio.

"The irony," Julia said, "is that, after all his posturing, Mayer Bermann never hired anyone on the blacklist or anyone else named by the committee. He always managed to find someone hanging around the lot to write his screenplays for him, people like this guy Cobb." She glanced at her watch, which she wore like a politician, the face on the inside of her wrist.

"Are you expecting someone?"

"Here? No. Why?"

"I got the impression you were hurrying me out."

"I just don't think there's anything else I can do to help you."

Seeley thought, You can help me understand how it is that Harry Devlin, who likes Mayer Bermann even less than you do, knew about United's attempt to bribe me, right down to the figure Bermann had authorized.

"How does Harry Devlin fit into your Wall Street con-spiracy?"

The question caught Julia off guard. She swiveled to the bookcase, started to remove an open file box, then pushed it back onto the shelf.

"Harry's been the alliance's lawyer since the 1940s. He rep-resented most of the members who were in trouble with the committee. Not just writers and directors. Composers, cine-matographers, even the lighting guys. At first he instructed his clients not to testify, but by 1951 everything changed. The party leaders were in prison and the committee had no interest in locking up anyone else. All they wanted was to humiliate the left-wingers who were still around. The deal was, if you wanted to get off the blacklist and go back to work, you had to inform on your friends. Harry showed them how to name names so no one was hurt—people who were in jail or who'd left the country, or people who'd already been named a dozen times. Most of this went on in closed sessions."

"You're telling me he sold out."

Again, Julia hesitated before answering. "The committee didn't care about identifying Communists anymore—it proba-bly never did. It just did what the bankers told it to do: break the will of everyone who works in the motion picture indus-try. Harry was an honest broker. He got people back to work."

"How do you know he won't do the same thing with the class action he's going to file against the studios?" Seeley thought he had left his feelings in New York, but his anger at Gary Minietello's eagerness to settle the lawsuit still boiled in-side him. "What's to stop him from selling out and settling?"

"How do you know about the case?"

"He asked me if I wanted to work on it."

"Harry won't let the alliance settle. It's an important prin-ciple."

For the first time, Seeley noticed the fine dusting of freckles, light as nutmeg, high on Julia's cheeks. One, of the same faint color, was the shape and size of a teardrop. For a moment, that's what Seeley thought it was, or the pale stain left by one.

Julia said, "Cutting up a film to make room for television ads or to sanitize it for the airlines is just another Wall Street tactic to separate laborers from the product of their labor."

Seeley didn't know people still talked like this. He thought this kind of warmed-over Marxism had disappeared in the fifties, the sixties at the latest.

"Don't be so confident about Harry Devlin. A lawsuit like this can go on for a long time. Six, seven years. The alliance writers and directors aren't going to be any more patient than the ordinary run of plaintiffs. In a couple of months they're going to start putting pressure on him to settle."

Julia said, "Why does Harry want you to work on the case?"

"It's like a case I already had."

"Did you win?"

"It never got to trial."

"You settled?"

"My client did. I probably knew he was going to settle even before I took the case."

"But you took it anyway because he was paying you."

"I took it because I believed in the principle."

"So you were using him."

"You like working close to the bone, don't you?"

Julia smiled, but it wasn't the smile Seeley remembered from the alliance lunch.

"You could say we were using each other."

"Your client—was he someone famous?"

"Is that important to you?"

"No. Just curious."

"Most of the artists I represent you'll never see in *People* magazine. They're going to struggle for recognition their whole lives."

"And that's why you want to know who wrote *Spykiller*. If it wasn't Cobb, you want to get credit for some unknown writer."

Julia was smart, but she was way off.

"It's so I can get a client off my back. My partners, too."

"Then why do you work for artists? The ones who'll never be famous?"

"They're great at stirring up trouble, but when they wind up in court, they're helpless."

"And you take their cases so you can stir up a little trouble, too."

"I hadn't looked at it that way."

"You use them the way you were using that guy who settled his case."

"Is there an extra charge for the psychoanalysis?"

"No." Julia dismissively waved a hand that took in the bookshelves and the computer. "It comes with the basic service." Then she surprised him with the smile she had given Devlin at lunch.

It occurred to Seeley that he had come to see Julia Walsh as much for that smile as to find out who wrote a screenplay. He had been waiting for it.

"I hope you decide to work with Harry on the case."

She came off the chair and thrust out her hand. "Stop by whenever you want. You're fun to talk to."

Fun, Seeley thought. A real California word.

As Seeley let go of her hand, their fingers touched for a moment longer than was necessary.

"Sure," he said, "I'll do that."

Seeley was returning to the Vista del Mar from a late lunch, still thinking about the encounter with Julia, when he saw reflected in a shop window the image of the man in the leather windbreaker. It was United's driver, except that no limousine or town car was in sight. The man was following him, and he had to know why.

Seeley crossed the street at midblock, dodging traffic, quickening his stride. The man looked over his shoulder and increased his pace, too, and when Seeley broke into a run, so did he; it was as if they were connected by a wire, one pulling the other, Seeley moving around the pedestrians on the sidewalk, the man ahead pushing through them. Not breaking stride, the man made an abrupt turn onto a walkway and moments later disappeared behind the double glass doors of a low building.

A sign identified the redwood building as a senior center. At its far end was a bulky, windowless structure, a story higher than the building itself. An oversized plywood cutout of a tripod and camera dominated its façade and, in a loopy 1950s script, was the word CAMERA on one side of the cutout and OBSCURA on the other.

The lobby opened onto a bright room busy with foursomes at card tables and old men playing billiards, all oblivious to the picture-window view of the rolling Pacific below. But the stalker was nowhere in sight. Seeley went down the hallway leading off the common room. At the end was a door with an alarm and a lit exit sign above and, on one side, a narrow staircase. Seeley took the stairs two at a time. The door at the top was locked, but Seeley could hear movement from behind it. The door was solid and well secured, and when Seeley pounded on it, the wall shook. After a few seconds, the door opened.

A blinking, moon-shaped face said, "Is there a problem?" The man was in shorts, sandals, and a flowered Hawaiian shirt. A boy and a girl, each with the same moon face, looked out from behind him.

"No problem. I was looking for someone."

"Well, it's just us pilgrims from Nebraska."

"I'm sorry to bother you."

"No problem." The man's sunburned face beamed as he pushed the children ahead of him. "The kids and I were just picking up and getting ready to go."

The place was empty; the stalker had somehow gone through the downstairs door without triggering the alarm. The room was smaller than Seeley's bedroom at the Vista del Mar and, when the door shut behind him, it became musty and close. A round table, its surface painted in mottled colors, occupied almost the entire space. Alongside the table was an old-fashioned ship's wheel connected to a post. The wheel, the closeness, the brackish scent of the ocean—together they conjured the pilothouse of some seagoing vessel.

Then Seeley saw that what he thought were formless colors on the tabletop were in fact reflected images from the street outside. As he turned the ship's wheel, spoke by spoke, a small cupola revolved at the apex of the ceiling, and the image on the table revolved with it, so that from his hidden prospect Seeley could survey all 360 degrees of life below—palm trees framing beach and surf, the edge of the beachside park, the grassy park itself, the shops on Ocean Avenue. People, cars, even pets on leashes, surfaced with an oddly dimensional acutance, and the harsh colors outside dissolved. The figures on the table appeared rounder, more fully human, than did the pedestrians in the scorching light outside. It could have been a projection room, the way the colors and frames of vision moved more slowly than in life. It took some time before Seeley realized that the image on the table was the reverse of the world outside. It had a familiar reality of its own, but it also unsettled him.

Seeley stared at the scene until it became mottled colors again. He thought of carefree summer evenings he had spent during his first year as a lawyer in Buffalo. Twenty years had passed, and the time seemed as distant as the reflected scene outside. Neither he nor the other young associates at the firm had their own cases yet, or any real responsibility, and they regularly gathered on the leafy patio of a downtown bar to share pitchers of beer and gossip long into the night about partners and clients and the imagined trajectories of their own careers. After that year, though, Seeley began getting cases of his own, and soon enough he fell into an irreversible pattern of trying one case, then another, with no break between, winning cases the way a machine gun fires bullets. First in Buffalo, then in New York, he arrived at the office before dawn to review depositions of witnesses who would be on the stand that day; returning from trial, he would study the day's transcripts until long after everyone else had left the office. Unable to sleep when he finally got home, he pounded down as much alcohol as he could as fast as he could, until he passed out on the couch or in an easy chair; any place he happened to be.

At some point—he couldn't remember when—he started taking drinks in the morning to clear his mind for the work ahead. It amazed him that he could go for hours, even whole days, executing the most demanding tasks, engaging in complicated negotiations, and the next day remember nothing of what he had said or done. He'd be downing cocktails with a client in Manhattan and wake up the next morning in a hotel room in Westchester, with no idea of how he got there. One morning, a few months after he met Clare, he awoke hungover to find her on the phone giddily informing her sister that he had proposed marriage the night before.

As he thought about it now in the darkened room, it frightened him how completely he had let the drinking and the cases cut him off from the currents of his life. If he could do that to himself, what had he done to others? A sudden panic rushed through him. Clare. If he didn't call her at once, Seeley knew she would be lost to him forever.

On the round table, the image of a solitary figure stopped him. The boxer. Directly across from the senior center, leaning against the display window of a shoe store, the man in tie and leather windbreaker was set apart from the tourists in shorts and open shirts. On a street that throbbed with movement, the figure was entirely still. Seeley spun the ship's wheel as if to erase the scene, then sped out of the room and down the stairs. When, moments later, he walked out the double doors of the senior center, the man was still by the store window. But the instant he saw Seeley, he moved onto the sidewalk and rapidly strode away. Seeley had the impression that the man did not mind being seen—he *wanted* to be seen; that was his purpose in being there.

Seeley's insides churned as he lifted the telephone in the sitting room of his suite at the Vista del Mar. The Manhattan number was his own, but he felt like a teenager calling for a first date. Clare's voice, when she answered, sounded tentative, as if she had been expecting the call.

"It's me," Seeley said.

"What do you want, Mike?"

"How are you?"

"I'm getting by. What do you want?"

"You're not making this easy."

"This isn't a good time."

"I quit drinking. I haven't had a drink in more than a week."

There was a muffled sound of conversation as if Clare had put a hand over the receiver. Call back later, Seeley told himself.

Clare came back on. "This isn't going to work. I talked to a lawyer—"

"I'm a lawyer. Why don't you talk to me?"

It occurred to Seeley, as it had that afternoon at the Frick, that when the jokes become forced it's a good sign that a relationship is over. He knew what was coming and he didn't want to hear it.

Clare's voice was strained. "I talked to a lawyer about a divorce."

Seeley wanted to hang up and start over or, better, just forget, blot this out. Instead, he said, "Are you with someone?"

"I already told you, it's none of your business. This isn't about anyone else. It's about me. I have to stop worrying about you and start taking care of myself. I've been talking to a therapist."

Seeley felt betrayed. "You could have talked to me."

"Do you ever listen to yourself? I've been trying to talk to you forever."

"We can do this, Clare. We used to talk. You said if I stopped drinking we could get back together. Well, I stopped."

"This isn't about the drinking."

"You said if I quit I could come back."

"I never said that. It's what you wanted to hear."

He had kept his part of the bargain; she had not. The injustice of it tore at him.

Clare said, "Face reality, Mike. You're not someone who's built for a relationship."

This was new ground for her.

"Think about it. Have you ever had a real relationship with anyone?"

The question had never occurred to him, and it shook Seeley more than anything Clare had said, or could say.

Clare said, "I care for you, Mike."

"I don't want pity."

"That's not what I meant."

"Then drop this thing with the lawyer," he said. "I love you. I want to be with you."

Even as he spoke the words, he wondered if they were true. He did know that he couldn't stand for her to leave him.

"That's another thing you have to learn—just because you want something doesn't mean you get to have it."

"You're telling me the door's closed."

There was silence at the other end, and then the sound of a small girl. Clare was weeping.

"You're crying—"

"Yes." She heard where he was going, and cut him off. "Yes, I'm crying, and yes, the door is closed."

The silence was longer this time, until at last Clare hung up. After a while there was the harsh warning signal of a receiver too long off the hook, and after that the telephone in Seeley's hand went dead.

Seeley remembered little of what happened next. He did remember the elevator's painfully slow descent to the lobby and a bartender measuring out two miserly jiggers of gin. There were more such doubles, ordered even before he touched the one in front of him so that the alcohol would flow uninterrupted. Something in the bartender's increasingly sour expression reminded Seeley of Judge Randall Rappaport in the doorway to his chambers. Seeley's only other memory was being in a taxi, but he had no recollection of where it took him.

He came to on the floor of his sitting room in the Vista del Mar, his head propped against the edge of the sofa and an ancient black-and-white movie playing on the television. A near-empty pint of Bombay gin was on the floor next to him. The pale sun of early dawn leaked through the blinds. An awareness of loss overwhelmed him. He tested its edges gingerly, as he might explore the dimensions of a painful bruise. To his surprise, though the loss felt bottomless, the ache was not for Clare but for the brief respite of sobriety he had forfeited, a mere handful of days that, in retrospect, were as frail and precious as anything in his life.

SEVEN

Through the tinted windows of the studio's office tower, the glare of the morning sun raked the papers scattered on Seeley's borrowed desk. Vacantly, he sorted the time notes he'd kept over the past several days, his life measured out in six-minute increments, so that Boone, Bancroft could send a bill to the studio. He was empty, depleted from the night before, hollowed out. He had no desire to drink, as on other hungover mornings, but he had no particular desire to go on living either.

The ringing of the telephone scraped across his brain like a rasp. The voice, breathless and strained with anger, was Bert Cobb's.

"What did you tell those bastards about my pictures? The portraits I showed you."

Seeley imagined the thick hands and blackened nails clutching at the phone, the thin face and worn eyes. "I didn't talk to anyone about your pictures."

"I don't know if you did or you didn't, but those pictures are none of their business."

"What happened?"

"Last night, I'm working in my darkroom. With the water running, you can't hear anything. But when I got out, the front door was open. I go into my office and the pictures were all over the floor."

Seeley thought of the neatly stacked yellow boxes, the stunning black-and-white portraits. "Is anything missing?"

"I'm not finished looking in my files."

"Is there a particular picture someone might want?" He remembered Cobb stopping partway through a box, even though Seeley had asked to see more.

Cobb ignored the question. "The police said it was kids. They said this happens all the time. What they didn't say is they think I'm an old man that makes things up. This wasn't any kids. I know who's behind it, and so do you."

"What makes you think it wasn't kids?"

A strangled noise came from the other end. Cobb had lost his patience for questions.

Seeley said, "What do you want from me?"

"Help." The way Cobb spat out the word, it could have been an obscenity. "I need to talk to you."

"We're talking. That's what we're doing."

"I mean face-to-face."

"Where are you?"

At the door to Seeley's office, Elm appeared, and Seeley gestured for him to wait.

"I'll come to you," Cobb said. "But not anywhere near that damn studio."

"Can you get to Santa Monica?"

"Tell me where to be."

Seeley gave him the name of a place on the pier. "Meet me there in an hour and a half."

At Cobb's end, the phone clicked off.

"I can't make lunch," Seeley said, answering Elm's look. "I have to see a friend."

"I thought we were going to talk about the opinion."

"I already told you, Jack. There's nothing to talk about." He got up from the desk.

Elm glanced at the time notes on the desktop. "I hope you're not planning to leave us."

"The firm likes to get its bills out every month."

"You can't just walk away from this. Hersh will want to talk with you. Maybe Mayer." Elm nodded in the direction of the desk. "Your bill's not going to be paid until you finish what we hired you for."

Seeley was halfway out the door. "I told Bermann I'd stay two more days. But that's it."

Cobb was at the farthest table in the back of the Sea Breeze Café. Seeley stopped at the counter to pick up a cup of coffee. At one of the tables, three teenage boys flicked lit cigarettes at one another under the flat, harsh light of a fluorescent fixture. A tired-looking family of four was at another. In front of Cobb was a plate of chili dogs, sodden with gravy and beans, and, to the side, a legal-size manila envelope.

"What took you so long?"

"Take it easy, Bert. Tell me what's going on."

"If you're going to say this was just kids, you can go back to where you came from." He took a napkin from the metal dispenser, crumpled it, and rolled it onto the Formica tabletop. He remembered the manila envelope. "Here. This is yours."

Seeley unsealed the flap with his thumb. Inside were two five-by-seven prints the size of a high-school senior portrait. Of the exposures Cobb had taken in his den, he had picked one to print. In it, Seeley stared straight ahead, as in a mug shot, but the plane of light from the single lamp left a third of his face in shadow. He studied the portrait. It was not the hungover face he had seen in the mirror this morning. The eyes were steady, even direct, and there was no puffiness beneath them. This was someone he no longer knew. In the lower right corner of the portrait, in an old-fashioned script, white against the dark ground of Seeley's suit jacket, was printed: PHOTOGRAPH BY BERTRAM COBB.

"This is good work," Seeley said. "Thank you."

Cobb had started on the second chili dog and just nodded.

"Let's say it wasn't kids. Who do you think would want to go through your photographs?"

"I don't *think* who did it. I know! Someone your employer sent, the great Mayer Bermann. That's why I phoned you. You've got to call him off."

"Why would Mayer Bermann want to scare you?" Seeley knew why. They were trying to frighten him into signing. But he wanted to hear the answer from Cobb.

"I didn't say they were trying to scare me. You did." Cobb's meal had left a thin chili mustache above his lip. "If they were trying to scare me, they would've given me some message why. No one's told me anything."

"Of course they have. The studio president has already been out twice to get you to sign. It doesn't get any clearer than that. Think about it, Bert. Say you're right and the studio was behind the break-in. The rights to a script aren't worth getting yourself hurt for. Give me a figure, and I'll bring it to the studio. If you want, I'll come up with a number for you. Forget your pride or whatever it is that's holding you back and sign the agreement."

"I can't," Cobb said. "I know it looks like the smart thing to do, but I can't."

The profound bleakness in the man's expression told Seeley his instinct had been right from the start.

"You didn't write the script, did you? You're a fine photographer, but you're not a writer. You put your name on the script for someone else."

Cobb unballed one of the several napkins he had crushed and delicately wiped his mouth with it.

"That's why you didn't remember about Natalia. What her lines were. I can't help you with Bermann unless you tell me."

He didn't enjoy badgering Cobb. The studio only wanted to scare him into signing. But the next break-in, or the one after that, could misfire and do some real harm.

On the other side of the café window a crowd had gathered around a man painting scenes on white dinner plates. But it wasn't the crowd that caught Seeley's attention. Across the boardwalk, his back to the ocean and a leg bent on the sea rail, was the boxer, still in his tie and brown leather windbreaker.

Cobb leaned into Seeley and lowered his voice. "Do you know what it's like when someone wants you to do something that goes against your principles?"

Seeley hesitated. "Sure. The studio's been pressuring me to sign a letter saying it owns the rights to *Spykiller*."

"Are you going to?"

"Not unless the guy who wrote the script signs over the rights."

"And if he doesn't?"

"I won't sign."

"Because it's against your principles," Cobb said. "That's why I won't sign either."

"What's the principle?"

Cobb shook his head. "Don't you think I want to tell you? I can't."

Seeley placed a hand over Cobb's. "There's a guy who's been following me since I got here. He's out there now. I want to find out why."

Seeley waited for the boxer to look away from the café,

then half rose and moved quickly to the kitchen's swinging door. A lone grill cook taking a cigarette break by the sink stared as he walked past him to the rear exit. Seeley stayed low and scrambled behind the buildings to where the narrow alley ended. Edging against the wall of the corner building until he was almost to the boardwalk, he cautiously peered out. Small knots of tourists scuttled along the boardwalk, pausing at souvenir shops, pushing into the video-game galleries. In the distance, a few of the locals were at their usual places against the railings, baiting lines or adjusting tackle, watching the plastic floats that bobbed in the surf below.

The boxer hadn't moved from his place on the rail. He was watching the restaurant entrance. Seeley kept the crowd of tourists between himself and the man for as long as he could, taking long, easy strides across the pier.

At the edge of the crowd a couple drifted off, exposing Seeley. The boxer saw him at once and in the next instant turned and vaulted the rail. Seeley raced to the edge of the boardwalk, but the man had disappeared. Seeley plunged down the stairs, taking the steps two and three at a time, finally hitting the hard-packed sand. The air under the boardwalk was heavy with the brackish stench of seawater. Kelp and garbage had collected in mounds the size of automobiles. Seeley worked to catch his breath, searching for the man in the dense maze of trunklike supports. On the other side of the pilings, in a gray splinter of light, a figure moved. Seeley leaned back to draw one clean breath, and in that instant something hard pummeled his side with such force that even a gasp was impossible. As he collapsed against the piling, a palm, cold and stiff, pushed against the side of his head so that he toppled sideways onto the sand.

Seeley didn't know how long he had been there. What he at first thought was his blood pounding was the throb of foot-

steps on the boardwalk. On the beach beyond the pilings, people moved as if in slow motion; it could have been a silent
black-and-white film. Even if he could summon the strength to
cry out, it would be futile. Here and there around him, pools
were forming from the incoming tide. What would it mean
just to let the cold water anesthetize and finally submerse him?
How many times, blind, senselessly drunk, had he fallen into
bed, his only conscious thought the blessed release it would be
if by some good fortune he never awoke.

When Seeley moved to prop himself with his elbows, an ex-
cruciating pain shot through his ribs. After lying still for some
time, collecting his strength, he found he was able to move a
small distance by pressing his heels into the sand and shrugging
his arms and shoulders backward. He continued, advancing in
inches, until finally the back of his head struck the piling. He repeated the movement, but now shrugging upward, slowing,
stopped by the jarring pain, recovering, inching upward again,
until he had raised himself to a half crouch. Then he used his
hands to move himself up the damp, splintery piling.

Soundlessly, an arm like a steel bar clamped his neck in a
stranglehold. The boxer had been watching all this time. A
hand grabbed his wrist and wrenched it behind him around the
piling.

From the first blow, Seeley knew he was in the hands of a
professional, a man who had studied holds and jabs the way a
lawyer studies cases and trial technique. Seeley was in reasonably good shape, and he scrapped regularly as a boy and played
football in college, but there was no possibility he could repel,
much less defeat this man. Yet even as the searing pain beneath
his chest told him to escape still more injury by going limp, he
instinctively strained and fought the boxer's hold on him.

"Easy now, friend." The voice was soft and the man's breath
was warm against his ear. "You move real good for a lawyer.

Just take it easy now, and listen to me." The man gave off the spicy, cloying smell of a common brand of aftershave.

"What's this about?" Seeley's heart hammered against his chest.

"Does this look like a courtroom?" The voice remained calm. "Does this look like the kind of situation where you get to ask me questions?"

Seeley's breath returned. "You know, you've got to do better than that silly outfit if you want to do surveillance. You have to be a real rube to dress like that."

The man grunted, and the steel bar eased a degree. "They told me you're an expert at pissing people off. If my job was surveillance, you can be sure you wouldn't see me."

Seeley was wary of the loosening in the man's hold. "*Who* told you?"

"Just be quiet and let me give you some advice. You know about giving advice, right? Go home, Mr. Seeley. There's nothing for you here."

If United had asked him to stay on in Los Angeles when he told Hersh and Bermann he was going to leave, why was their man now telling him to go home? "It was you who broke into the photographer's house last night, wasn't it?"

"Like I said, Mr. Seeley, go home."

The steel bar swung away and Seeley gripped the water-logged post so that this time he wouldn't fall. When he looked around, the man had disappeared into the pilings and only the faint scent of aftershave mixing with the sour smells of still sea-water gave any evidence he had been there.

Cobb, Seeley thought. He's going after Cobb.

Cobb was still at the table in the café, the envelope with the photographs under his arm.

"What happened to you? You look like hell."

"My conversation was more one-sided than I expected. He didn't come after you?"

"I didn't see anyone," Cobb said.

Seeley tried to connect what had just happened under the boardwalk with the break-in at Cobb's home. *Go home, Mr. Seeley.* His spending time with Cobb was bothering someone. If Bert Cobb didn't write *Spykiller*, Mayer Bermann knew that; and if he knew that, Bermann also knew who the true author was. Why, then, was the studio pursuing Bert Cobb's signature? For that matter, why had they tried to pressure Michael Seeley into writing a fraudulent E&O opinion? Why didn't they just get the real author to sign? Because they couldn't find him? Because he was no more ready to acquiesce than Cobb was?

"They're not going to stop, Bert. They're going to keep after you until you sign over the rights."

"You've got to talk to Bermann."

"It doesn't work that way. You have to let me know what's going on. If you don't, I won't talk to him. And, from the tangle I just had, I don't think you have much time to decide."

Cobb's thin chest widened as he drew an exaggerated breath, but the eyes rested evenly on Seeley's.

"I lied to you. The script isn't mine." As he exhaled, he seemed visibly to shrink. "I put my name on that damned script as a favor." His head jerked back. "Some favor! Back then, everyone thought the studios owned the scripts, so it didn't matter who the author was. The studio had all the rights. But I knew it was wrong when I did it. They paid me the money and I wrote a check to the fellow that wrote the script. I didn't take a dime commission either, like some of them did. Then the Supreme Court decided that goddamn case, and everything changed. Just like that"—Cobb snapped his stained fingers—"I'm an author, and everybody thinks I own the rights to the whole damn series." The narrow face clenched with frustration. "That's why I can't sign over the rights. I'm not the author. I can't say I wrote something I didn't."

"It wouldn't be considered a crime if you signed," Seeley said. "There wouldn't be any civil liability either."

The words made him feel cheap, like the kind of lawyer he despised. He knew it wasn't the threat of legal sanctions that was stopping Cobb. "If it mattered so much, why did you put your name on the script in the first place?"

Cobb pushed the accumulated wads of paper to the side and rested his hands flat on the table. The black nails lay like dull jewels on the speckled white Formica. "Like I said"—the response was quick, as if he had been thinking about this for a long time—"the way the law was then, the studio owned everything anyway, so it didn't matter whose name was on the script. They could put anyone's name on it they wanted. Why would it matter that they used my name?"

Seeley could see that the legal nicety didn't satisfy Cobb.

"The guy that wrote the script was in a fix, a real fix. I helped him out." He sucked on his lower lip for a while before continuing. "But, if you want to know the truth, I've been sorry ever since the day I put my name on that damned piece of paper. It's over fifty years ago, and I'm still sorry. It's a bum thing to put your name on another man's work."

"Who wrote the script?"

Cobb pulled a napkin from the dispenser and balled it around the one already in his fist. "He wrote a few films a long time ago, but you never heard of him."

"If I'm going to help you, I need to know."

"His name is Max Kanarek."

Somewhere, Seeley had heard the name before. "Tell me about what went on between you and Max Kanarek."

Cobb's demeanor relaxed and the nervous twitching

stopped, as if simply speaking Kanarek's name, shrugging off the encrusted lie of false authorship, had released a burden.

"It was George Hurrell that introduced us, at one of those parties that crowd was always having. There was a famous Hungarian photographer, a refugee, that was visiting from back East and George knew I'd like to meet him. The Hungarian didn't show up, but there was lots of food and cake and wine— that crowd was really big on sweets—so I stuck around. George had already met Kanarek somewhere else. They were friends. George was a real social type, always meeting and greeting, chatting people up at parties, looking for business in my opin- ion, so he pretty much left Kanarek with me. To tell you the truth, Max Kanarek was not a pleasant man, someone that made friends easily. He wasn't a Jew, like most of them were, so maybe that made a difference. He was always putting the other writers down, as if he was better than them. He wrote novels, he said. Big ones. Screenplays were just a way to make a living."

"So Kanarek was a Communist, he got blacklisted, and you were his front."

"He'd never let another writer take credit for his work. I could understand that. I'd never let another photographer put his name on one of my pictures. That left Hurrell and me, and George was too busy as a photographer for anyone to buy that he wrote a script. I was safe because I never got mixed up in politics. When the boys at the alliance started talking all their nonsense about solidarity and oppression and this and that, I'd head out of there."

Seeley thought of Julia's research, the exhaustively docu- mented computer entries. "But he wasn't on the blacklist."

"The federal boys never called him to testify," Cobb said. "They didn't know anything about him. That was the funny part: none of these guys who testified were still Communists—

if they ever were—and here's Max Kanarek, a practicing Communist, and the feds never caught on to him. He told me he worked behind the scenes. The guys that got caught were show-offs. He called them amateurs. Kanarek knew how to keep quiet when he had to."

"But he got caught."

"Not by the federal boys. It was the California investigators that caught up with him. They were a lot meaner than the federal boys. After that, Kanarek couldn't even give one of his scripts away, but that's what he finally did. He gave it to Bermann for peanuts—remember, I'm the fellow that cashed the check—and Bermann let him put anyone's name on it he wanted, as long as it wasn't his. Kanarek told me Bermann made a big thing about what a favor he was doing, making that picture."

"Why would Mayer Bermann do a favor for a Communist?"

Julia told Seeley that Bermann refused to sign onto the blacklist, but she also said he never hired anyone who was on it.

Cobb pondered that for a moment, then shrugged. "I wouldn't know. Like I said, you wouldn't call us friends."

"Where's Kanarek now?"

"He left the country after the movie came out. For all I know, he's dead. If he's alive, he wouldn't be a young man. Somewhere in his eighties, I'd guess."

"What about his friends? Someone who would know where he is."

"I already told you. He didn't know anyone except George and me. Oh, and Carlotta. Carlotta Reyes."

The actress who played Natalia in *Spykiller*.

"She was Kanarek's girlfriend. A real knockout. I had her sit for me once. She worked as a maid in one of the German's houses."

"Did Kanarek ever sit for you?"

"Sure. The same day as Carlotta." He anticipated Seeley's next question and shook his head. "The picture's still there. Whoever broke in didn't get it."

"Who else besides you knows Kanarek wrote the script?"

"Bermann. Carlotta, I suppose. I don't know who else. Look, I've told you everything I know. You've got to tell Mayer Bermann that if he doesn't call his people off, I'm going to the trades. *Variety*, *The Reporter*. It's no skin off my keister to tell them about Max Kanarek."

Cobb was bluffing. He could tell Seeley about Kanarek, but he was not going to tell the world he had put his name on another man's work.

"I'll make a deal with you. You hold off telling the studio you won't sign, and I'll talk to Bermann. Buy me some time. You don't have to make any commitments. Just tell them you're thinking about it."

Cobb stared at the wall and said nothing.

"Look, Bert, I'm trying to help you. Tell them you need to talk it over with your wife."

"I'll think about it." His voice was a depressed whisper.

"That's not good enough."

"Okay. But I'm not calling them. They have to come to me."

If Bermann knew that Max Kanarek wrote *Spykiller*, why didn't he just get a declaration from him saying so—there was a simple copyright office procedure for recording such declarations—and then have Kanarek sign over the rights? Money would have to be paid, but the studio had already tried to buy off Cobb. It would be easy. *If* Kanarek was alive, and *if* he was willing.

EIGHT

It was evening before Julia returned his call.

"I found the file on Kanarek." She was out of breath, as if she had just run up a flight of stairs. "Don't go anywhere. I'll bring it over."

She hung up before Seeley could tell her that the next morning was soon enough. He had already decided that the best he could do to help Bert Cobb would be to get Max Kanarek to sign over the rights to *Spykiller*. Cobb wasn't going to sign a piece of paper transferring rights that weren't his, and United wasn't going to stop pressuring him until he did. The break-in had been a warning to let Cobb know how vulnerable he was. He was a tough old bird, but United's hired man, the boxer, would crush him. The studio's bankers and insurance company wouldn't care who executed the assignment—Cobb, who they thought was the author, or Kanarek, who they would soon enough learn was the real one—as long as the assignment gave the studio full rights to the script.

Through an open window, Seeley watched the night life surge below him. On the ribbon of grass and palm trees that separated the beach and dunes from Ocean Avenue, Latin music blared, charcoal glowed in portable grills, kids on skateboards careened into the darkness.

He heard the car before he saw it, an ancient Porsche, the model in which James Dean ended his life, top down, flying past the Vista del Mar, gears whining and thrashing as the driver double-clutched into a U-turn a block down from the hotel. The car had passed in an instant, but Seeley recognized the driver, her short hair flattened by the speed. Unconsciously, he moved a hand inside his shirt, probing the sore place over his ribs where the boxer's blows had fallen. Above the dull, throbbing pain, the flesh was numb and felt oddly thick. He could have been exploring the bent contours of his soul, the moral pummeling that the alcohol had inflicted the night before.

The file folder Julia handed him was as light as if it were empty.

"This is it?"

"I checked every possible source. This is all the government had on him."

She was still out of breath, but Seeley saw that she had stopped to comb her hair.

"Where'd you learn to drive like that?"

"A boyfriend taught me in high school." She seemed pleased that he had observed the performance. "Do you have something to drink?"

For a confused moment, Seeley misunderstood and looked stricken.

"Juice? Water? Something cold?"

"Oh," he said, and showed her where the refrigerator was.

The file contained a single typed sheet, and there was little on it that Bert Cobb hadn't already told him: Max Kanarek, writer, arrived in the United States, New York, New York, Port of Entry, on November 3, 1949, and departed on March 16, 1952, San Diego, California, Port of Embarkation. During his twenty-eight months in the United States he wrote four screenplays that had been made into films. One of the scripts possessed manifestly subversive content, but this had been eliminated in the motion picture. There was a reference to a confidential report from an unnamed informant that Kanarek had conspired at the highest levels of the American Communist Party, Los Angeles branch, but no copy of the report itself. The only names that appeared as acquaintances—"known associates"—were those of Bertram Cobb and George Hurrell. Somehow the investigators had missed Carlotta Reyes. Acronyms were typed along the bottom of the page—FBI, INS, OSS, CIA, HUAC—and, next to each, in pencil, a single zero with a diagonal line through it.

Julia returned to the sitting room with a glass of water.

Seeley said, "How did you miss him?"

"Look at the bottom of the page. I'm not making excuses, but Kanarek was as close to invisible as you could get in those days." The words came out rapidly, intensely. "None of the federal agencies knew anything about him. The sheet was in the Writers Guild files, but it never made it into mine. For all I know, somebody made up a story to get him in trouble. The federal investigators weren't after him. It was the Burns Committee."

"The California investigation."

"The California Senate Fact-Finding Committee on Un-American Activities. It had a lower profile than the federal operation, but it was a lot more tenacious. What did Cobb tell you?"

"Nothing that's not in the file. Why didn't Harry Devlin know about Kanarek?"

"Maybe he did," Julia said, "but if he knew him, he never told me."

"Wasn't Kanarek in the alliance?"

"There's no record that he belonged. He may have had a lawyer from out of town handle his case, someone Harry didn't know. If he was working class he probably didn't have a lawyer." She looked up at him. "Why are you smiling?"

"I was thinking, the outfit you have on would cost a member of your working class a couple of weeks' wages."

"Don't let the get-up fool you. Or the degrees. I'm state schools and scholarships all the way. Berkeley, UCLA. I grew up in San Pedro."

Seeley had driven through San Pedro, a blue-collar town that was home to the Port of Los Angeles.

"Your father worked the docks?"

Julia smiled, though not the complicated smile from the alliance lunch. "That shows how much you know about what workers make. There are dockworkers on the port who make $150,000 a year. My father laid flooring. He could cut quarter-inch plywood with a linoleum knife like he was peeling an apple. He used to make play dolls for me that way. He's where my politics come from."

Julia took a chair by the window, sitting on the edge of the seat. "You're going to go looking for Kanarek, aren't you? That's why you told Harry you wouldn't take the class action."

"I haven't decided about the case. But, you're right. I want to find Kanarek."

"You don't even know if he's alive."

"It's worth trying."

"Why?"

Seeley told her about the pressure United was putting on Cobb, and that it was only going to increase; getting Kanarek to sign over the rights would make a transfer from Cobb unnecessary. As he spoke, he felt an affection and concern for Cobb that was deeper than he expected it to be. He didn't tell Julia about his encounter under the boardwalk.

"And that's your only reason? To help Cobb?"

"Why else would I need to find Kanarek?"

"I think you like challenging authority—the alliance for letting Kanarek down; United for not squaring things with him after fifty years."

"You have a good memory."

"As academics go, I'm not all that smart. But I learned that paying attention to details can go a long way to make up the difference."

Julia was wrong about his motive for going after Kanarek, but Seeley was surprised to find that he was enjoying himself. Being close to an attractive woman, talking about things that were serious but not sad, it was almost possible to forget the drinking disaster of last night, the calamitous day he'd just been through, and the disbarment proceedings waiting for him in New York.

"What happened to your boyfriend from high school? The one who taught you to drive like James Dean?"

"He's an eye surgeon in San Francisco."

"And now?"

"Me? No boyfriends, no husband. No men in my life."

"You don't like men?"

"Men are okay," she said, "but not the ones I get to meet. The university types, even the left-wingers—no, *especially* the left-wingers—are all seedy and self-congratulatory. My politics scare off the men who work at the studios. They're poorly educated, celebrity struck, and incapable of a single rigorous thought. If you mention the Fabian Society, they think you want to talk about the fan club for a fifties teen idol."

Seeley wondered how Julia pegged him and, if he had gotten over her first hurdle, whether she was calibrating him as a friend or as a lover.

"A therapist I saw told me I had a pattern of abandoning

men before they got the chance to abandon me. I told him I dropped them because they weren't particularly bright or interesting. The therapist was pretty dim, himself. I stopped seeing him after two sessions. Anyway, right now my work takes all my time. Research. Teaching. Helping Harry with the class action." As she lifted the glass of water, she glanced at her watch. "What about you?"

Seeley thought he heard something more than curiosity in the question. "Married. Just barely."

He was still trying to understand why the last conversation with Clare had so completely unhinged him. If he was honest about it, they had been living apart long before he moved out of the apartment. Why, then, couldn't he handle the thought of severing their last, legal tie?

"I wouldn't think you had a wife. No wedding band. You seem like a loner, the kind women of a certain type throw themselves at."

"What type is that?"

Julia said, "What's your wife like?"

"What is it about people in California that they think they have the right to ask any question they want?"

Julia laughed. "Maybe it has something to do with living on the edge of the world."

"It could get you in trouble some day."

The smile disappeared. "Relationships aren't what the movies make them out to be, are they?"

"It's hard to be romantic without a hundred violins playing in the background," Seeley said.

"And you don't think a Marxist can be romantic."

"I think Marxists are nothing but romantic."

"That's your secret, isn't it? Underneath all those layers, you believe in romance. It's why you represent all those unknown artists."

Seeley frowned, and Julia said, "You think I'm being simplistic."

"When I was in grade school," Seeley said, "we had a class trip to the local art museum. Picture a couple of nuns dragging thirty noisy sixth graders past walls hung with Kandinsky, Kline, Pollock, Rauschenberg, and all the time some poor docent is trying to explain to these kids what they should make of them."

"But you were different. You cared about the pictures and the artists."

"Not at first. Not for a long time. But that weekend I went back to the museum. It was a half-hour bus ride—two buses—from where I lived, and I went week after week. I don't know how long I did that. In the summer, I'd go two or three times a week."

"But not for the art," she said.

"For the silence. Outside of church, I had never seen rooms that big or ceilings that high. They were all white, and when you left one room, there was another one the same size. And, it was quiet. There was that unwritten rule in museums that no one talks above a whisper."

Seeley had the uncomfortable feeling that to say more, to describe to this woman he barely knew the circumstances that had compelled him to seek out the solace of an art museum, would be cheating on Clare. He had told Clare some of the story, although never more than she pressed him for. It was as if the darkness of his past, distant as it was, would contaminate the life he sought with her.

"I didn't realize it until later, but I had been looking at the pictures all along. After a while, I got to know the paintings. I started with the ones that were easy and accessible, and gradually worked my way up to the hard ones. I'd skip an afternoon of school just to stand in front of de Kooning's *Gotham News*. I could get lost in those paintings. In a way, they were like the museum itself, a quiet place I could go to. There was a danger of losing myself in some of them. But, even with these, I always felt safe. Everything was under control."

"Art can be a great teacher," Julia said. She thought for a moment, then shrugged at the pretentiousness of the remark. "I majored in art history when I was at Berkeley. I guess it shows."

"How did you wind up in film?"

"Art has no political traction. The last time it even got close to being relevant was during the Depression. When I was deciding about graduate school, I thought film was where art and politics met."

"You don't sound convinced."

"There's more culture in a cup of yogurt than there is in the entire film industry. The politics are even more ridiculous. The industry's idea of social revolution is throwing fund-raisers to get a Democrat into the White House."

"What about the speech you wrote for Hardesty?"

Julia's fingers, long and cool, tented over the rim of the half-filled tumbler, a gesture so innocent that its potency astonished Seeley.

"The only way you can get the studios to do what's right for the workers is to threaten their bottom line. A speech can do that, especially if you follow up with a lawsuit."

She set the glass down and nodded at the file in Seeley's hands. "What will you do if you can't find Max Kanarek?"

Seeley knew where Julia was heading.

"If he's alive, I'll find him. If he's not, I'll find his widow or his next of kin."

"We can do this together," Julia said. "Pool our efforts."

"You don't know where Max Kanarek is any more than I do."

"But I have better sources. I know every writer and director from the fifties who's still alive. I've interviewed every one of them. People in the studios, too."

"What's in it for you?"

"You can't be serious! This is my field."

"Your book's finished."

"You never finish this kind of research. Max Kanarek is the last blacklisted writer. Nobody knew about him. Mayer Bermann said he never hired a front, but now it turns out he did. Maybe this isn't a lost Shakespeare sonnet that fell out of an old recipe book, but in my field, a discovery like this counts as important. I've got a lot of questions for him."

"It may come to nothing. What if he won't talk to you?"

"That happens in research. Like you said, it's worth the risk."

"What about your classes?"

"I can get a colleague to cover for me. You're not thinking about my research or my classes. You think I'm going to get in your way."

"I work better alone."

Seeley had another reason for not wanting Julia along: her connection—whatever it was—to Harry Devlin. He wanted to trust Julia, but Devlin knew things, including the most intimate details of United's operations, that he had no reason to know, and Seeley had no idea where he got his information or who he shared it with.

Julia left the chair and came to within inches of his face. "Did you ever ask yourself why you're such a loner?"

It may have been a shadow, but the tear-sized freckle beneath her eye seemed to darken. The pain beneath Seeley's chest throbbed. More than anything else at this moment, he wanted to touch her, but too many people stood in the way: Clare, Bert Cobb, Mayer Bermann, Judge Randall Rappaport.

When he didn't answer, she turned and walked away.

At the door, she said, "You have a choice. I'm going to find Max Kanarek before you even get the chance to tie your running shoes. If you want to come along, that's fine, but you have to decide now." Her hand was on the doorknob. "Now or not at all."

"Thanks, but I'll go it alone."

Julia started to say something, but stopped and turned, angrily rolling a slender hip as she let the door slam shut behind her.

Seeley went to the telephone. If Julia knew every writer from the fifties, so did Harry Devlin, who had introduced her to them.

NINE

In his rental car, driving to Harry Devlin's office in Century City, Seeley thought about what he had not told Julia, or even Clare. His escape to the quiet of Buffalo's Albright-Knox Art Gallery was from a house where the racket never stopped. A television or radio, sometimes both, was always playing at top volume. When, at unpredictable hours, his father came home—from work, from a bar, from the social club where he drank with his friends—a maelstrom descended. He would tear into Seeley or his younger brother for some wrong he thought they had done him, or he would chase Seeley's mother through the racketing rooms with the revolver from his dresser drawer, firing rounds of live ammunition into the ceiling. Seeley's mother would lock herself in the bedroom and Seeley, with his brother, would hide behind the living-room couch. When no one was left to terrorize, Leonard Seeley would slam doors, maybe light a fire in the garbage can, hurl more complaints and insults at the empty rooms, and leave.

But as unrelenting as the noise had been—the one time Seeley visited a client in state prison, he found the echoing din familiar—what truly clung to his memory was the encompassing darkness of his parents' house.

When Lothar Seelig came to the United States in 1951, he rented a room in a German neighborhood on Buffalo's far east side and, on a tip from a man he met in a bar there, found a job on the assembly line at the Chevrolet plant. He discovered the Germania Hall social club and, through another drinking friend, met a woman who was put off neither by his rough manner nor his erratic courtship. Margaret Hubbell was the last unmarried daughter of aging parents, with no career and no interest in acquiring one. She knew she had little bargaining power, but she set one non-negotiable condition: if she was to take her husband's name, he had to change it legally, as her own father, Wolf Hueber, had done years before to deflect the wartime hatred of German Americans that boiled outside their little community. When she told Michael the story years later, she said, war or no war, for a family to survive it must fit into society. Seeley had no idea how Lothar—now Leonard—conducted himself in society, but with his family he spoke only German. Of the resentments that filled his perpetual rage, one invariably rose above the others, that his wife had rendered him nameless and unknown: *namenlos und unbekannt.*

Growing up, Seeley never knew what shape his father's drunken shadow would at any moment assume: storming room to room, the revolver swinging in his hand; hidden behind a German-language tabloid in his massive black recliner, pulsing with anger; passed out on the couch in his underwear, reeking of whiskey, snoring violently. Usually the stuporous tirades started in longing: rambling evocations of the homeland, a fairy-tale kingdom of snowcapped mountains, dense shadowy woods, sturdy honest workers. To Seeley's repeated astonishment, the eyes of this brutish man actually filled with tears.

Then longing would turn into rage. Once, when his father had passed like this from revery to inconsolable fury, Seeley had tried to draw him back to the fairy tale by asking what he remembered best of his village. The shadow stared down at him fixedly, as if he were sighting down a rifle. "Mud," his father said. "Barbed wire and mud." Over time, Seeley's efforts at placating his father ceased, replaced by confrontation. Of all the challenges he hurled at the man, most of which ended in beatings, there were two questions he never asked, for he feared the answers just as, when he was younger, he had feared knowing what lay in the dark recesses of his parents' closet: Why did you leave Germany? Why have you not gone back?

At about the time Seeley's confrontations with his father had escalated to where it was necessary for him to move out, shuttling between his Catholic high school, part-time jobs, the local Y, and friends' pullout sofa beds, the television news was carrying the story of a federal court proceeding in Cleveland, three hours away, to revoke the citizenship of a local autoworker for concealing in his immigration papers that he had been an SS guard at two death camps in Poland. In the mind of a fifteen-year-old boy not accustomed to ambiguity, the implications of the prosecution were irrefutable; it was the only sense he could make of Leonard Seeley's otherwise senseless behavior. The two autoworkers—his father and the Cleveland defendant—had arrived in America in the same year, and who but a concentration-camp guard would brandish a revolver inside his own house? It explained the Hansel-and-Gretel fantasy of the homeland, the dazed silences, and, above all, his father's misery and rage. Even the absence in the house of any physical evidence of Lothar Seelig's previous life in Germany confirmed his complicity. To the two questions Seeley feared to ask, he now added a third: What did you do there?

Seeley called the federal courthouse in Cleveland and, after being directed from one office to another, all the time dropping quarters into the pay telephone at the Y, he got the number of the Justice Department office in Washington that was prosecuting the case. No, he was told, the Justice Department was only now beginning to organize its files on European immigrants suspected of falsifying their entry papers. Did he have someone he wanted to report? If he wanted to put his request in writing, the Berlin Document Center in Germany had the most complete information on SS personnel. Did he want the address there? To Seeley, Berlin might as well have been on another planet and so, disappointed, he dropped his quest.

By the time the Justice Department set up its own Office of Special Investigation four years later, Seeley was in college and the question of informing on one's father had taken on a moral nuance he had previously missed. He despised the man but, still, he was his son, and what would be gained by a prosecution for crimes, however heinous, committed forty years ago? *If* Lothar Seelig had committed any crimes. What more did Seeley have than a young man's suspicions? He would have given up his father's name if the office promised him that it would only investigate, not prosecute. But the investigators wouldn't do that; as soon as they had his father's name, the course of inquiry would be out of his control. Once again, he dropped the matter. Leonard Seeley died of liver failure in 1984, just as Seeley was finishing law school, and the question of what his father had done in Germany, though it persisted for him, had lost any consequence in the world.

From the doorway to Harry Devlin's office, Seeley watched the lawyer's back, rocking gently in a desk chair, illuminated by the glow of an old-fashioned desk lamp. Devlin had a telephone receiver to his ear and for long, silent stretches listened intently. It was well past eleven, but one of the buttons on the telephone was lit and another was flashing. Observing unnoticed like this, Seeley had the same uneasy sense of apartness he'd experienced in the Camera Obscura. He knew he should knock or walk in, but he couldn't move. He had only just met Devlin, but the image of the man—the newsreels, the cameos in the 1950s movies—had occupied a corner of Seeley's thoughts for years, and the result was an uncomfortable, one-sided intimacy.

Devlin swiveled and, seeing him, mumbled something in French into the telephone to end the conversation, then pressed the flashing button and in English told the waiting caller he would get back to him.

"What a happy surprise," Devlin said. "I've already told some members of the board that you've agreed to think about taking the lead on our class action."

"That's not why I'm here."

The room was large, but sparsely furnished. There was a worn oak desk, some wooden chairs, a battered cabinet; they could have been purchased at Goodwill. The office was on the top floor of a glass-and-steel tower, and the lights of Los Angeles filled the floor-to-ceiling windows. On the inside walls were autographed pictures of Devlin with movie stars and directors, mostly men and women who had won their fame in the forties and fifties. Invariably a highball glass was in Devlin's hand and his companion had an arm over his shoulder. The overall effect was corny, like the boyish pompadour Devlin still coaxed out of his thin, silvery-white hair.

"An old man's souvenirs," Devlin said. "The consolations of memory. But I don't expect you came up here to chat about the giants of the silver screen."

"Not a giant. A small-time screenwriter. Max Kanarek."

"What's your interest in him?" There was no warmth in Devlin's smile.

"Did you know him?"

"You didn't answer my question."

"I'm looking for him. He wrote *Spykiller*."

"I thought this fellow Cobb wrote the script. Kanarek may have been on the government's list, but that doesn't make Cobb a front."

"You talked to Julia."

Seeley hadn't been able to get through on Devlin's busy telephone, but evidently Julia had.

"Take a seat." Devlin indicated the client's chair next to the desk. "I'm getting a crick in my neck looking up at you."

When Seeley took the chair, Devlin leaned over the desk and brought his face close to Seeley's, studying him for some time. "What makes you think Cobb didn't write the script?"

"Apart from the fact that he told me he didn't?"

"Kanarek's never even claimed a co-author's credit. How long has it been, forty-five years, fifty—"

"Fifty-three years."

"The statute of limitations runs out after three."

"Except in cases of fraud, and then it doesn't run at all," Seeley said.

"In all this time, has anyone come forward and said: Bert Cobb was a front, I wrote *Spykiller*? The witch hunts are over. Writers started coming forward in the sixties to claim their work. If Max Kanarek wrote the script, why hasn't anyone heard from him?"

The eccentric rhythms of Devlin's speech struck Seeley as they had at the alliance lunch, errant inflections and practiced verbal tics that could seduce a jury. There was a story about the time Devlin represented a convicted child molester seeking damages against one of the television networks for broadcasting a thinly fictionalized version of his life. According to the story, Devlin bet the network's lawyer a thousand dollars that, within the first five minutes of his closing argument, he would bring at least one member of the jury to tears on behalf of his client, this miscreant. With forty seconds to go, a retired telephone lineman in the second row of the jury box lifted a handkerchief to his eyes.

Seeley said, "Did you know Kanarek?"

"He was a small-time writer, a refugee. His English wasn't the best, but good enough for B movies. He kept pretty much to himself. I understand he was a lot more political than the writers who made the front pages back then. He was a political operator, a provocateur."

"That's what Cobb said."

"Don't misunderstand me: he was as misguided as the rest of them but, from what I hear, he was a hell of a lot smarter. One big mistake the public makes is thinking that writers are more intelligent than the rest of us, maybe because they make their living out of words. None of these fellows was particularly bright. And I can tell you—I knew every one of them—for all their wisecracking, there wasn't a cynic in the lot."

"You buy Julia's line about Wall Street?"

"She's a hundred percent right about that. Don't short-change Julia Walsh because of her politics. She's one smart cookie. The politics are in her genes. Her father used to be an organizer for Harry Bridges's union on the docks. He got disillusioned when automation came in and the guys who ran the local traded layoffs for higher wages. So he quit. He went to work in construction, I think."

Seeley thought of the man cutting quarter-inch plywood like he was peeling an apple. "Flooring."

"It seems unlikely, doesn't it, that if Kanarek wrote the script he would have left the pot of gold sitting in the hands of a greedy capitalist like Mayer Bermann?"

"What reason would Bert Cobb have to say that Kanarek wrote *Spykiller* if he didn't?"

Devlin said, "How many clients have you had who didn't lie to you about something important?"

"Nothing Cobb said or that Julia showed me adds up to a lie. I won't talk to your board about taking the class action until I've found Kanarek."

"Don't be so impressed with yourself. You're a talented litigator, but so are a dozen lawyers we can retain."

"I need to find Max Kanarek."

"You don't have the remotest idea of what you need. I was watching you at the alliance lunch. The way you stared at that wineglass, it could have been filled with all the melancholy in the world. You looked like a prince in exile from his kingdom. I didn't know who was going to win, you or the wine."

Devlin leaned forward and, in a reflex, Seeley pulled away.

"If you have any doubt what side I'm on, I was pulling for you."

"I don't know what you're talking about."

"I think you've got a problem with alcohol."

"It's nothing I can't handle."

"Do you really think you can control your drinking?"

"It's never been a problem."

"Over the past couple of years, what's the longest you've gone without a drink?"

It was none of the man's business. Seeley said, "More than a week. Nine days."

Devlin studied him from under thick eyebrows. "And you're going to tell me that all that time you were in control. That's very impressive. How would you like to prove it to me? You just have to do one small thing, something that requires no particular physical or mental skill. If you can do it, I'll help you find Max Kanarek."

Devlin pulled out the center desk drawer partway and searched through it with his fingers until he found what he was looking for.

"What's that for?"

The object Devlin had taken from the drawer was a golden cylinder that could have been the casing for a large-caliber bullet. A light flashed on the telephone, but he ignored it.

"A ten-year-old could do this without breaking a sweat." Devlin walked across the room to the cabinet, absently whistling a few trite notes. He knelt in front of it and called out over his shoulder, "What will it be? You're too far gone to be a wine or beer man. I've got scotch, bourbon, rye, gin, vodka. I even have an old Cognac in here."

For the first time since he came into the office, Seeley relaxed. This would be easy. Devlin, whatever his motives were, would put a drink in front of him and challenge him not to take even a sip. Seeley had done as much every night when he walked past the bars on Ocean Avenue.

"What's yours?"

"Gin," Seeley said.

"I don't have any ice, but I'm sure that never stopped you. One martini coming up, hold the vermouth, hold the olive, hold the ice."

Devlin returned to the desk with a tumbler and a bottle of a better-quality English gin, three-quarters full. He grasped each end of the slender gold cylinder with his fingers and, as he pulled it apart, Seeley saw it was a woman's lipstick, garish cherry red. Devlin twisted the cylinder and, turning the tumbler as a glassblower would, applied the lipstick to the glass, drawing a thick red line around the circumference, halfway down from the rim. When he finished, he put the tumbler on the desk and filled it from the gin bottle right to the top, letting the liquid swell above the rim.

The juniper fragrance was strong and the foretaste was where it always was, at the back of Seeley's tongue.

"So," Devlin said, "all you have to do is drink your martini here down to the red line—no less, no more—and I will help you find Max Kanarek. But if you drink the whole thing down, you're on your own. The same if you don't touch the glass at all, just walk away from it."

"I'm not drinking anymore. I stopped."

"Then you shouldn't have any trouble stopping again. It just has to be at the red line. Anyone who can control his drinking could do that. I'm betting you can't."

Seeley cursed himself for falling into the trap. He knew he couldn't stop at Devlin's red line. Once he took the first sip, he would not stop drinking—from this tumbler and all the tumblers to follow—until he passed out.

There was a complicated interplay between Devlin's eyes and mouth, each challenging the other, it seemed, to break into a smile. He rotated the glass carefully.

"Some things are impossible for people like us. One of them is drinking down to the red line. Other things aren't impossible, just hard. Like asking for help. I think that's why you came to see me."

"I'm not like you," Seeley said. "To hell with you!" With a sweep of his arm, he backhanded the glass off Devlin's desk. The sweet juniper fragrance blossomed like a flower.

Devlin shrugged.

"Trial practice isn't for sissies. For a long time I kidded myself that I used alcohol to fight the tedium of trying cases—and to get to sleep at night. I don't know about you, but at some point I discovered that I had it backward: I was in fact using work as an excuse to drink."

It may have been a trick of the light, but Devlin's eyes looked moist.

"You drink, Michael, for the same reason I did. Because it's in our nature. Normal people don't drink because their work is exhausting or because their mother has a mustache or their father wears a dress. You drink because you're a drunk."

Seeley was tired of Harry Devlin's pieties. He didn't need a lecture. What he needed was to find Max Kanarek.

"The only way I can protect Bert Cobb is to find Max Kanarek."

"Protect him from what? That nonsense you told Julia about United arranging a break-in at his house? Maybe Cobb's just decided it's not safe anymore to be the author of this particular movie script. Whatever's going on, why should it be any of your business?"

Why was Devlin trying to steer him away from Kanarek? Seeley remembered Bert Cobb's odd complaint about the alliance's closeness to the studios, and wondered what that implied about the alliance's lawyer.

"What I'm telling you is, I'm not going to be the one who aids and abets this foolish quest of yours. Say that somehow you find Max Kanarek and he says, 'You're absolutely right, Michael. I wrote the script, not Bert Cobb.' So you ask him to sign over the rights. There are only two things he can do. He can sign your piece of paper, or he can say, 'No, I won't sign.' Either way, you're going to take a drink, and this time you may not be lucky enough to stop."

"I think you know something about Max Kanarek you're not telling me." Or, Seeley thought, he knows something about you.

"There's a fellow I knew once, a lawyer just like you, except he didn't get lucky and manage to quit the booze until he had lost everything—job, family, house, bank account. He got sober living under a bridge. Five, six years go by without a drink and he puts his life back together. He goes to work for a big corporation, remarries, starts a new family. Everything's just hunky-dory. Then, one fine spring morning, the thought occurs to him that the drinking hadn't really been all that bad, it was just circumstances that had brought him down. So that day, on the way home from work, he stops into a bar for a cocktail—just one—and the next day he does the same. Again, just one. By the end of the month, he's got the drinks lined up on the bar and he's drinking just the way he did before, from the moment he got up in the morning until he passed out at night. Inside of a year he was dead."

The way my father died, Seeley thought. He had not gone to see him then, but his brother, who had just started medical school, told him it was the worst—most violent and exhausting—death he could imagine. If Seeley had been there, he knew he would have felt nothing other than relief. But he wasn't there, and he felt nothing at all.

Another light flashed on Devlin's telephone, like a beacon's warning.

Devlin said, "Did you get Bert Cobb into this mess? You weren't even alive when he put his name on the script." His manner had all the earnestness of a highway patrolman directing motorists away from an accident. "Stay in Los Angeles. The interview for the class action will just be a formality. The work's yours if you want it."

Seeley shifted in the hard chair. His head had finally cleared from the night before, but his ribs still ached where the boxer had crushed them. He got up. He'd taken enough abuse.

Devlin leaned back to look up at him. "I'm not kidding myself that anything I said is going to stop you from chasing after Max Kanarek. I'd tell you to stay away from Mayer Bermann, too, if I thought you'd listen. But if you ever feel like talking, I want you to know you can call me night or day."

"I'm doing fine on my own."

"Don't sell yourself short. The last time I got sober I was locked up in a drunk ward—it wasn't the penthouse suite at Cedars-Sinai, it was a sad, one-story place out on Pico—and I unloaded to the guy on the bed next to mine, told him all my secrets, all my shame. I was in a straitjacket and he wasn't, so I figured he knew something I didn't."

A sudden tightness in Seeley's throat made it impossible for him to answer. He had to get out of Devlin's office. He gave Devlin a half salute and left.

TEN

Mayer Bermann's receptionist was telling Seeley that the chairman was tied up in meetings when Hersh Landau came into the reception area.

"He's out with the hunt," Hersh said. "Every Monday—can you believe it?—he rides with the Malibu Hunt."

Seeley checked the receptionist for a reaction, but got none. He had a vision of red jackets, black hats, and fast horses vaulting through bikini-crowded beaches in pursuit of a rust-colored creature.

"No foxes," Hersh said. "They use a scent. The dogs chase the scent, Bermann chases the dogs. Come into my office a second. There's something I want to talk to you about."

"I came to see Bermann. I can wait."

"He won't be back for a couple of hours. I just need you for a few minutes. Whatever you have to say to Mayer Bermann you can say to me. Talking to me is like talking to him."

The boast was groundless, but Seeley followed Hersh through the doorway into a smaller reception area where another secretary sat, hands crossed on an empty desk, then into a high-ceilinged office filled with glass surfaces, hard steel edges, and an abundance of black leather. A rectangular black rug positioned in front of the desk looked at first to be an open trapdoor. The single window in the room, a narrow strip of glass from floor to ceiling, looked out on a checkerboard of tarred roofs cluttered with utility equipment and giant exhaust fans.

An amplified voice from behind the credenza announced a telephone call, and while Hersh murmured into the phone, Seeley inspected the framed snapshots he had come to expect in Los Angeles offices. These people had to be the most ardent members of their own fan clubs. There was one of a beaming Hersh in tennis clothes, holding his racket before him like a shield; Hersh at the net, eyes tense, racket poised; Hersh serving; Hersh with three exhausted-looking players, himself radiant in victory. Behind the smaller photographs and lit by recessed lamps was a black-and-white blowup, almost life-size, of a slender, youthful woman with the looks of a fashion model. She was in a one-piece bathing suit, and an abundance of wavy dark hair cascaded onto her shoulders; the rolling surf was fashionably out of focus in the background.

"Recognize her?" Hersh had finished with the phone.

Seeley didn't.

"Gretchen Wyler. The supermodel. We're releasing her first film next month."

As at the alliance lunch, Seeley's eyes went to the single grotesque element of Hersh's getup. The well-cut navy suit and striped shirt open at the neck were the usual costume for a Hollywood executive, as were the gold wristwatch and gold cuff links that shone discreetly inside the jacket sleeve. It was the shoes. Thick-soled, of a black material that could have been leather but looked more like some dull synthetic, they were wide and oafish, bulbous at the toe, with brass grommets for the laces. These were clown shoes, clodhoppers, something you might buy on sale at an army surplus store.

A secretary who could have been the less-stunning younger sister of the supermodel brought in a tray with china and a silver carafe. She set the tray on a table by the leather couch and Hersh poured coffee, handing a cup to Seeley. There was no cream or sugar.

"What do you think of her?"

Seeley decided he meant the model. "Is she Method, or does she do traditional Stanislavski?"

"Sure," Hersh said, frowning, "and I do Shakespeare at the Royal Globe." He meant it to be mocking, but there was a sour edge to his voice. "We want you to wrap up whatever you're doing and have your firm send us their bill. You're not going to make any headway with this fellow Cobb."

"What about the opinion letter?"

"Forget it. We have the financing."

"Without an E&O policy?"

"Banks don't have a monopoly on money."

Hersh was lying. No lender would hand over $80 million without insurance, not even the tax shelters that courted the orthodontists and car dealers who invested in movie projects, and United didn't have the cash to finance the film itself. That left only one source of funds, and Seeley knew that in the circumstances it would offer no help.

"Intermedia's not going to finance *Spykiller*. Callaway's using every dime he has for acquisitions."

"You haven't seen what happens to outsiders like Beau Callaway when they buy a movie studio. They fall in love: the history, the tumult, the celebrities. They fall in love with all of it."

Seeley thought of the one time he had seen Beau Callaway

in the offices of Boone, Bancroft: the chill breeze, the streak of quicksilver. This was not someone who fell in love with anyone or anything.

"Go home, Mr. Seeley."

"That's funny. A guy underneath the Santa Monica boardwalk told me the same thing."

"It's good advice. You should take it."

"So I don't get between you and Bert Cobb?"

"Me?"

"Someone broke into his house." Seeley watched Hersh for any sign that he knew of the break-in, but saw none. "He said Bermann's behind it, but he meant the studio. You."

Hersh moved to the other side of the office where a single framed canvas hung on the wall. "What do you know about Mayer Bermann's art collection?"

"I was talking about Bert Cobb."

"So am I. When he said Bermann was behind the break-in, that's exactly who he meant. Mayer Bermann. Not the studio. Not me."

The portrait on the wall was the head and shoulders of a plump young woman, her eyes demurely closed. She had on a straw hat that sported a silly blue-and-white ribbon, and a black cloak that occupied half the painting. The image, almost somber except for the ribbon, was in sharp contrast to the glamorous black-and-white photograph on the credenza. The signature, in shaky red letters in the lower left corner, was E. Vuillard.

"Bermann calls the pictures his beautiful children," Hersh said. "I don't know if they're any good, and I don't think he does either, but he pretends he does. The important thing for him is they're unique. Authentic. They can't be replaced. What else in this town can you say that about? He thinks they're as much his as if he painted them himself."

Seeley waited to let Hersh make his point about Bermann

and Cobb, whatever it was, in his own way. "How many are there?"

"Dozens. He keeps some here and some at his house. About half are in the LA County Museum, in the wing he gave them."

Seeley was still studying the painting and Hersh waited for him to turn back to him before continuing.

"At one time, a Jewish art dealer in Amsterdam owned them. Then they belonged to Hermann Göring. Göring himself visited the man's shop and carted off all the best works, even the Rembrandts, for his own private museum. Later, he sent his art dealer, a man named Miedl, to take whatever was left, including this one and the others that Bermann owns now. After the war, the paintings disappeared, and so did Miedl."

"How do you know this?"

"Bermann hired an art expert to determine the paintings' province—"

"Provenance."

"The insurance company required an expert's report before they would cover them against loss."

"Which means he paid the expert to write a fraudulent opinion."

"That's not the point I'm trying to make."

"Bermann dealt with Miedl?"

"There were intermediaries. Europeans. A gallery in New York got involved. But their only purpose was to launder the works. So you could say the works came from Miedl. Or, if you want to press the point, from Hermann Göring."

It seemed unlikely to Seeley that a refugee from the Holocaust would buy stolen art from Hermann Göring's art dealer. "When did Bermann leave Germany?"

"Germany?" Hersh scowled. "The first time he was in Germany was eighteen years ago, when we started making distribution deals there. Bermann was born in Poland. He went from there to Canada and then to New York."

"I thought—"

"The name? It's made up. God knows what it was in Poland. Something unpronounceable. By the time he landed in Canada, it was Meyer Bernstein. Later, he changed it to Berman. When he moved to California, he had his lawyers change it again. This time it became Mayer, and he added an extra *n* to Berman. He said it was a more appropriate spelling in the circumstances, whatever that means. It was all sleight of hand. No one saw it happen."

Seeley thought about the duplicity of names. While Meyer Bernstein was burnishing his persona into that of a German Jewish industrialist so he could better fit into Los Angeles society, Seeley's father had gone to the Erie County courthouse and changed his name from Lothar Seelig to Leonard Seeley so that the woman he had decided on for his wife would marry him.

Hersh was craftier than Seeley gave him credit for. "Your little lecture is to tell me this is how Mayer Bermann arranges things. Through intermediaries. Art purchases, name changes. Break-ins."

"Cobb obviously knows Mayer Bermann a lot better than you do. If he says Bermann is behind it, you should believe him."

Hersh was close enough for Seeley to smell the tobacco on his breath. A secret smoker.

"For this kind of thing, you need to hire thugs, lowlifes. I don't figure Bermann for that. If I had to choose, I'd say it's you who arranged it."

The remark didn't appear to offend Hersh. "You're thinking an eighty-four-year-old man who collects art, gets dressed up like an English lord, and rides to hounds isn't capable of having someone's knees broken? How do you think he built this studio? If he wasn't willing to do business with criminals, he'd still be selling popcorn in Albany, New York. But popcorn wasn't good enough for Mayer Bermann. When the movie house where he had the snack concession went into the toilet, he borrowed money from an uncle, bought the business, and made a deal with the local union bosses. He cut them a slice of his profits and they paid him back by shutting down the other theaters in town, one by one. He'd wait a few weeks, and when the competitor's house was about to go broke, he'd buy it for a nickel on the dollar. Like magic, the shutdown ended. By the time he finished, Bermann owned a circuit that covered all of upstate New York and parts of New Jersey."

"You weren't even alive when this was happening."

"Bermann told me some of it. Olive, too. His daughter. I was an entertainment lawyer on the west side. After I married Olive, I came to work here. When the studios put their own distribution chains together and began stiffing Bermann on product, he got into the studio business. He bought a couple of one-reel outfits in New Jersey, and some out here. Do you know what set him apart from all the other studio heads? He had absolutely no fear. He wasn't afraid of the racketeers and he wasn't afraid of Wall Street. You have no idea how important this studio is to him. It's almost sixty years of his life. Mayer Bermann is an emotional man—that surprises you, doesn't it?—but he's also extremely practical. He'll do anything to keep the studio going. He wouldn't think twice about hiring someone to scare this photographer into signing over the rights to *Spykiller*."

Seeley's first thought was that Hersh was making this up. His second was, Why? What did Hersh have to gain by telling him this? The origins of Bermann's art collection, the movie-house racket, his refusal to support the blacklist—all had a common thread of recklessness to them. Nor was Mayer Bermann the sort of man who stopped to count his victims.

A secretary Seeley hadn't seen before, an older woman with carefully coiffed silver hair, came into the room.

"Mr. Bermann is in his office." She looked at Hersh, then Seeley. "He would like to see you. Both of you."

Hersh waited for her to leave.

"So far," Hersh said, "I don't particularly like you or dislike you. That could change. I don't know what Bermann's up to, but I don't want you to be part of the mess I have to clean up when he's finished. Sure, I know. He told you to stick around. Sooner or later, he's going to ask you to get involved in one of his little projects. Don't. You're way out of your depth here. Forget about Cobb signing over the rights. It's not going to happen. Forget about the opinion letter. Show me how smart you are. Go home."

"I'd think your interests would be the same as Bermann's."

"I'm just an employee here. My job is to keep the studio going, whether we make another *Spykiller* or not. If we don't meet our profit targets, I'm out of a job. Bermann's out of a job, too, but he owns enough stock that he'll land on his feet and I'll land on my *tuchas*. If you're smart, you'll stay away from Harry Devlin, too."

"Why?"

"I saw you talking to him at the alliance lunch. Harry Devlin is no friend of this studio."

"If you really want to get rid of me, why don't you tell me how I can find Max Kanarek?"

Seeley didn't expect Hersh to offer help in finding Kanarek. But he also didn't expect the answer Hersh gave.

Hersh said, "Who is Max Kanarek?"

ELEVEN

"You made a serious error in judgment, Heshy. Mr. Mendelson told me you left instructions to terminate Mr. Seeley."

Mayer Bermann came around from behind a massive carved desk, every bit the horseman in starched white shirt and high-waisted riding pants, leather-crotched, blousy at the top and narrow at the calf. Seeley found himself comparing Bermann's finely crafted boots with Hersh's bulky orthopedic shoes.

Bermann motioned Hersh to the low couch across from the desk, but Hersh ignored the gesture. Seeley saw the power play at once. Take that seat, with Mayer Bermann perched above you on his desktop like a raptor, and give up any hope of escaping with a splinter of dignity. Seeley propped himself on the arm of the couch.

"Fortunately, Mr. Mendelson had the good sense to consult with me first. Sit down, Heshy. You are not afraid, are you, that an old man can intimidate a big-shot film executive like you?"

Hersh eased himself onto the couch. "Mr. Seeley is no longer of any use to us, but"—he looked at Seeley—"this is not the time to talk about it."

"Mr. Seeley is our lawyer. You can speak freely in front of him. Anything that is said here remains in confidence. Is that not so, Mr. Seeley?"

"As long as it relates to the reason you hired me."

Bermann's office was twice the size of Hersh's, a collection of browns and burgundies, carved wood, and well-creased mahogany leather. Somber canvases in heavily figured gilt frames lined a wall. Behind the desk, a brass canister sprouted a profusion of leather riding crops and walking sticks, their handles worked in silver: horse heads, stirrups, beaked hunting caps, simple crooks and knobs.

Hersh said, "Even if he signs the E&O opinion, it's too late. This has been in the works for a month. The insurance company knows there's a problem. The only way they'll write a policy is if we give them Cobb's signature on an assignment of rights."

Hersh had been right to try and resist the low couch. Craning to face Bermann, he could have been a child called into the principal's office. He said, "If Seeley goes out there again, Cobb's only going to dig in his heels."

"I am sure Mr. Seeley will correct me if I am wrong, but I believe he is the kind of man who, if we fired him, would pursue Mr. Cobb on his own time."

Bermann turned to Seeley. "I think you are like my Jack Russell terriers. Once one of them sinks his teeth into prey, nothing can make him let go of it. Shoot him in the leg, he will still hold on. Only if you kill him will he drop it, and maybe not even then. I believe you will not let Mr. Cobb go until he has signed a transfer of rights, or gives you a good reason for not signing." Bermann paused. "Perhaps he has done so already."

When at the alliance lunch Seeley suggested that Bert Cobb was a front, Jack Elm objected, but Bermann had said nothing. Bermann had been counting on his Jack Russell terrier to wrest the truth from Bert Cobb, and now that Seeley had—and Bermann somehow knew that he had—Bermann gave him an approving smile.

Seeley had told Hersh nothing about Max Kanarek, and evidently this was what Mayer Bermann wanted. If Bermann had wanted his son-in-law to know about Kanarek, he would have told him. For Seeley to bring Kanarek up now seemed a small matter, but if that was so, why did the decision seem so laden with consequence? He knew that by saying nothing about Kanarek, he was allying himself with Bermann; but allying himself against *what*? For now, he decided, Max Kanarek would remain a secret between Bermann, Bert Cobb, and himself. As to his own irrational sense of foreboding, what was there to do?

Bermann reached behind him and, from a crystal ashtray the size of a dinner plate, lifted a cigar that had already been started. He trimmed the barrel of ash with a fingernail. While Bermann rotated the cigar over the flame from a heavy gold lighter, Hersh said, "I've been talking to the finance people at Intermedia. I think we can get them to pay for the new picture out of cash reserves. We won't have to go to the banks."

Bermann said, "You let them mislead you, Heshy. Mr. Callaway will never pay for a film out of his own pocket."

Seeley had told Hersh the same thing.

Hersh said, "How many opportunities does he have to make back $250 million, guaranteed, on an $80 million investment?"

"Mr. Callaway does not have the $80 million to spend. He needs leverage, not margins."

"But you don't," Hersh said. "You could lend the studio the funds yourself."

"Why should I put my money into a project for which, as Mr. Seeley has made painfully clear, we do not own the rights?" Bermann drew with satisfaction on the cigar. "It is unfortunate, Heshy, but your mind is not on the business."

Seeley regretted being present at Hersh's humiliation. He didn't much care for the studio's president, but seeing him demeaned like this gave him no pleasure. And, having witnessed it, he had become Hersh's enemy forever; to come to his defense now would only make it worse.

"Look," Seeley said, rising, "none of this concerns me."

Bermann swiveled on the desk to face Seeley. "I understood you told Mrs. Frybarger that you wished to speak with me."

"It can wait."

"Good. Permit me to continue my thought." Bermann drew on the cigar again, taking his time. "When a man reaches middle age, and his family is grown and no longer requires his attention, he can move in one of two directions. He can focus on his business life. With all the years of experience he has behind him, if he devotes himself single-mindedly to his business affairs he can achieve a level of excellence that is attained by only a few. These are the men who lead their companies. This is true not just of business, of course, but of excellence in the professions, the arts and sciences.

"Or—you understand this, do you not, Mr. Seeley?—our subject can take a different, far more common path and allow himself to be distracted by a life of self-indulgence and material dissolution. Mr. Landau here has, sadly, taken the more common path. He thinks that, like his hero, Mr. Callaway, he can enjoy both a business career at the highest level and a life of sensuality as well. But Mr. Callaway—a whoremeister if ever there was one; he bought this studio so he could sleep with starlets—is the unusual case. Regrettably for him, Mr. Landau is not an unusual case. I told my daughter when she married him that he is an ordinary man, but of course she would not listen to me."

Hersh struggled to lift his tall frame from the couch.

"Sit still! You are surprised, Mr. Seeley, that I know of Mr. Landau's little dalliance? But you have already been to his office. What kind of man places a photograph of his mistress—not just a photograph, a life-size mural of the woman—in his place of business?"

Seeley wondered when and how the occasion would arise for Hersh to take revenge on him for witnessing this.

"Mr. Landau and I have an agreement. He will not tell my daughter about his girlfriend, and I will not either.

"How long do you think she will stay with you, Heshy?" Bermann spoke quietly, but the ferocity in his voice was shattering. "You buy a condominium in Brentwood for this woman, you pay for her dressmakers, her masseuse, her trainers. What has this bought for you? How long will her loyalty last? I will tell you. When Mr. Callaway fires you—and if you continue as you are, he certainly will fire you—that very day this girlfriend of yours will change the locks to the condominium and you will never see her again."

Hersh said, "You should be careful about getting yourself excited, Mayer. When was the last time you saw the doctor?"

As quickly as Bermann's anger had risen, it disappeared. "Weinbaum?"

"Bergstrom, the cardiologist."

"Months ago. He retired. Can you imagine he did that, Mr. Seeley, a man in the prime of his life shutting down a million-dollar practice, just like that?" Bermann snapped his fingers abruptly. "It was not enough to be a top heart man. He had to be a stand-up comic playing dumps in hick towns! Getting booked into big-time venues. Fullerton! Costa Mesa!"

Hersh said, "Just because you have a contract doesn't mean you can't retire early."

"There is no need for me to retire. I may not be here day and night, but I am still in control. Your responsibility is to be this studio's chief operating officer, not its chairman, no matter how desperately you desire my job. And you are forgetting, Heshy, I am the only protection there is between you and Mr. Callaway. You have no idea what this fellow is like. Without me here, Mr. Callaway would eat you alive. That is what rednecks like him do with flat-footed Jew boys like you. They do not even stop to kill them. They eat them alive."

Seated on the edge of his desk, Bermann could have been a kid on a swing, pumping his legs happily. "I saw Bergstrom's partner, the Indian. He says I have plenty of tread left on me. That is exactly how he put it. Plenty of tread. So you see, Heshy, just do your job, and you have nothing to worry about. Everything is right with the world. Your little love nest is secure. I may be an old man, but my health is sound and I have taken care of everything. You just have to trust me. Everything is under control. I am not going to die. Not anytime soon." He beamed. "I will not throw you to Beau Callaway."

Seeley rose. He'd had enough. Mayer Bermann had called him to his office not to do business but to demonstrate the absolute power that he wielded over the studio he created.

"Again, Mr. Seeley, I must apologize. Too often, the urgent"—he nodded in Hersh's direction—"takes precedence over the truly important. And it is very important that we speak. Please come to my home this evening. My driver will pick you up at eight. Where are you staying?"

Seeley felt a wave of relief pass through him. Mayer Bermann knew where to find Max Kanarek, and after tonight so would he.

"The Vista del Mar. In Santa Monica."

"The Vista del Mar is not at all suitable." He turned to Hersh. "Who is responsible for booking Mr. Seeley there?"

Hersh shrugged.

"It seems, Mr. Seeley, that I must apologize for your accommodations as well. But we will make up for that."

Agilely, Bermann lifted himself off the corner of the desk and offered his hand. "If our discussion this evening progresses as it should, I believe the remainder of your stay in Los Angeles will be very brief." He placed his free hand low on Hersh's back. "Mr. Landau will show you out."

TWELVE

After several blocks, the cheap storefronts on Pico gave way to garden apartments and bungalows elbowing into spaces between the high-rises. Cramped front yards overlaid with improbably green artificial turf sprouted plastic daffodils. As the big Mercedes climbed into the hills, the landscape changed again, this time dramatically. Trees lined the narrow streets, so umbral and verdant that their taproots had to be drainpipes. Lawns, where Seeley could see them in intermittent glimpses between the hedgerows, undulated like fairways. Dusk stained the surrounding hills in greens and purples.

At the top of a rise, the car turned into a gated opening in a low stone wall. The driver, who had not spoken during the trip from the Vista del Mar, reached up to a button on the visor and, after a moment, the double gate opened out slowly, like a hesitant gesture of welcome. For a quarter mile, the white gravel drive wound through acres of perfect lawn. A pond glistened in a grove of willows. Lights from the house, three stories of fieldstone and white shutters with a gabled roof, poured golden pools onto the lawn. The car stopped at the foot of a stairway cut into the embankment and Seeley let himself out before the driver could get to his door.

Off in the neighboring hills, a dog howled. Other than that, the stillness was impenetrable. As Seeley took the flagstone path to the house, there was a crunch of gravel and, when he turned, the car disappeared behind a bend at the rear of the property. He was partway up the stairs when the heavy double doors moved a crack, then swung inward, pulled open by a gray wisp of a man of indeterminate middle age. As he led Seeley into the house, the man murmured that he was Hobday, Mr. Bermann's secretary.

The foyer was lit by sconces and hung with tapestries of hunting scenes; a staircase at one end circled to the second floor. Seeley was again struck by the quality of the silence. It wasn't a momentary absence of sound. Rather, it was as if a bell jar had long ago been lowered over the place so that all sound and movement had ceased forever. Hobday motioned Seeley to follow him down a hallway studded with more hunting scenes and, after a turn, they came into a high-ceilinged room lined wall to wall with shelves of leather-bound books and the occasional brightly colored art book. The weak, late light filtering through mullioned windows gave the place a sepulchral feel, saved only by floor lamps that ignited deep jeweled colors in the rugs scattered about.

"Mr. Seeley." The voice came from behind him. "I greatly appreciate your taking the time to see me, particularly on such short notice."

From what Hersh had told him, Seeley knew the precise good manners were as phony as the German accent. Bermann was dressed informally in a tweed sport coat and slacks; a dark paisley cravat was tucked into the luxurious tattersall shirt. Cordovan loafers, bench-made and nicked with age, showed layer on layer of careful hand polishing, their rich burgundy deepening into darker shades.

"May I offer you a drink?"

Bermann went to a glass-paneled cabinet set into the open bookshelves. Lit from within the cabinet, the bottles glittered like diamonds, like gold and silver: single malt whiskeys, ancient Armagnacs, red-tinted bourbons and ryes, fine Russian and Polish vodkas, crisp English gins. As Seeley's eyes passed over the fifth of Bombay gin, he remembered the bottomless misery of his last drunk and a gorge of nausea rose inside him. On a shelf of their own were the specialty drinks in every possible color, even the straw-colored Akvavit and a dark green bottle of the wretched, medicinal Jägermeister. There wasn't a drink here he hadn't sampled. Chilled sparkling aperitifs waited in a refrigerated compartment. Seeley's heart shuddered at the sight and he dismissed Bermann's offer with a brisk gesture.

Bermann ran a hand spotted with age along one side of the antique cabinet. "Biedermeier," he said. With a blunt index finger, he identified one after another piece of furniture in the room. Biedermeier . . . Biedermeier . . . Biedermeier. For some reason, Bermann was showing off to him. Most of the pieces were Biedermeier, but a few, such as an ornately turned side chair, he proudly identified as Jugendstil. In the openings between the bookshelves were more paintings from the Nabi school, like the Vuillard Seeley had seen in Hersh Landau's office.

Seeley said, "I appreciate the tour of your possessions, but it's not why I'm here."

"I understood you are a student of German culture."

"Culture? No."

"It is nothing to be ashamed of. Or do you subscribe to

what Hermann Göring said: 'When people talk of culture, I reach for my revolver'?"

"I know the language, not the culture." Unless a couple of pewter-lidded beer steins qualified, there had been no German culture in his parents' house. "Where can I find Max Kanarek?"

"Ah, yes. I have also been told that you are very direct. That is sometimes a virtue, sometimes not."

Bermann took the corner of a tufted leather couch and motioned Seeley to the other end. "You are a man who presses hard. This is why I am counting on you to persuade Mr. Kanarek to do what is right."

"Where is he now?"

"Starnberg. It is a small lake town half an hour outside Munich. He traveled around for some time after leaving this country, but it is where he finally settled down. It had the best golf course in Germany, perhaps in all of continental Europe. Of course he no longer plays. But he still writes. I speak regularly with his girlfriend."

"Girlfriend?"

"I am living in the past. She has been his wife for many years. You saw her in the movie. She played the part of the Russian agent. Carlotta Reyes. Quite a beauty. I cannot imagine what she sees in Max Kanarek that she has stayed with him this long. He is not well. He suffers from a wasting disease and she tells me it has become worse. Over a year ago, his doctors—doctors I paid for—told him he had less than a month to live. I believe this will be the only chance we have with him."

Bermann's eyes became set and cold. "So you see, this is why it is necessary that you travel to Starnberg immediately to see him."

Seeley knew that he was going to go to Starnberg, with or without Bermann's support. But if it was to be for Bermann, he had to know why. "Why don't you send Hersh or your general counsel?"

"Mr. Landau, as you have already seen, is incapable of thinking one step ahead of where he stands. Mr. Mendelson, let us say, lacks what I believe are called people skills."

"What about you?"

"I would go if I thought it would accomplish the result we all desire. Unfortunately, Mr. Kanarek will not meet with me. If I did succeed in seeing him, it would be certain to achieve only a negative result. It is not unusual for a dying man to have second thoughts about how he has lived his life, but if Max Kanarek saw me, any doubts he might have would immediately disappear. You, on the other hand, will be a stranger. Also, you are not only tenacious; you are one of those rare individuals who comes across as genuinely sincere."

The hazard, Seeley thought, of preparing himself for too many jury trials.

Bermann returned to the liquor cabinet, selected a popular midpriced brand of scotch, and poured an inch of it into a short crystal tumbler. Seeley liked that he had picked this brand for himself and not one of the twelve-year-olds or single malts. He guessed that it was the scotch Bermann drank as a struggling young businessman, and he was staying loyal to his memories.

"Did you know I paid for his passage to this country? That was back before I had any money to spend. But the money I had, I sent to him so he could escape what was left of Poland at that time. I made all the necessary arrangements here. I saw to it that he always had work, until he made it so bad for himself that no studio would give him work. I should tell you, Max Kanarek is a willful, ridiculous man. He could be a character from Dostoyevsky. Even then, what did I do? I produced his little masterpiece for him. I did that for him when no other studio would touch it."

And, Seeley thought, with the sequels, you made a fortune from the film.

"But you wouldn't put his name on the picture."

"Don't talk about what you don't know!" Bermann's voice was at once cross and condescending. "Thanks to me, Max Kanarek is financially well-settled today."

"You're telling me he won't see you, but it isn't about the movie."

"This goes back to the old country, to another time."

Bermann sipped meditatively at his drink, then abruptly drank it all. His pink face turned a shade deeper. "You have no idea what kinds of constraints there were in wartime for the population of an invaded country."

Seeley said, "If I go and see Max Kanarek, it has to be on my own terms, with no interference from the studio."

"That is an unusual request from a lawyer who is in my employ."

"It's not a request. It's a condition. I agreed to review the files on *Spykiller*, but I didn't agree to sign a fraudulent errors and omissions opinion. I did what I could to get Bert Cobb to sign over the rights, but now that I know Max Kanarek wrote the script, that would have been fraudulent, too. The way I see it, I don't owe you anything."

"What do you think of this Vuillard?" Bermann gestured toward an ornately framed canvas between the bookshelves.

The painting was no more than two by three feet, and in the half-light of the library was as dense and alive in its concentration of nature as sparks ricocheting off the interior of a dark gemstone. The sun coming through the painting's sketchily flowered curtains at first seemed to make a silhouette of the seated woman, but as Seeley drew closer his eyes adjusted to the painting's own tonalities and he made out the umber details of her cloak and gown. In the foreground, the paint was built up, layer over layer, the brushstrokes thick and vigorous; the background, by contrast, looked unfinished, revealing patches of raw canvas.

"Hersh told me your collection came from Hermann Göring."

Seeley thought he saw a breach in Bermann's stony condescension.

"Mr. Landau has the most extraordinary imagination! You are thinking of my small joke about Göring and his revolver. The paintings were acquired after the war, of course, but only through the most reputable channels. There is no stolen art here. Do you really think that the Los Angeles County Museum would have accepted my gift—they have most of the collection now, and I have promised them the rest in my will—if they had not engaged the finest experts to examine them, investigate their provenance?"

"Why would Hersh say you bought them from Göring's agent . . . What was his name?"

Bermann waited, a small smile on his lips, refusing to fall into the trap.

"Miedl," Seeley said. "Why would Hersh make something like that up?"

Bermann said, "I can assure you, I have no idea." He moved closer to the painting and idly traced the gilt frame with a finger.

"Just for the sake of discussion—I am told lawyers enjoy hypothetical propositions—let us say Mr. Landau is right, and this painting is Nazi treasure trove. Should the taint in ownership in any way impair your appreciation of the work? Why should it matter whose hands the painting passed through?"

"Your hypothetical owner wouldn't be the owner if the art was stolen."

"True. He would not be the owner, but what difference

would that make to one's appreciation of the work itself? Indeed, what difference would it make if it was not the seller of the painting who was a war criminal and thief, but the painter himself?"

Bermann seized Seeley's hand and drew it to the canvas. "Go ahead, touch it."

When Seeley hesitated, Bermann pressed his fingers first into the thick impasto and then onto an almost bare spot of canvas. "Can you feel the struggle in every brushstroke? The conflict the painter experienced?"

"Such an artist," Seeley said, "a war criminal, would be unable to hide his misery. It would be a repellent work."

"That is the difference between you and me. I believe in art and you believe in justice."

"I hadn't thought there was a difference," Seeley said.

Bermann stared at him. "An interesting notion," he said. "Do you know Mahler's Second Symphony? The *Resurrection* Symphony."

"I don't listen to music much."

"A most remarkable event occurred in Berlin in 1941, on an evening late in February. You can imagine, of course, what it was like to be a Jew in Berlin at that time. Nonetheless, a group of Jewish musicians, an orchestra and a chorus of sorts, somehow came together in a concert hall that night and performed this symphony by a Jewish composer for what was left of Berlin's Jewish community. More than a thousand men and women came in silence, and departed the hall in silence, and in the interval between those two silences they heard—no, they breathed in, assimilated into their flesh and spirit—music of such sublime beauty and nobility that they were for that moment lifted far above the pain and humiliations of their daily existence. Would it have mattered to them to know that Mahler himself was a petty household tyrant?"

Bermann's pleasure at his argument was a child's—preening, self-indulgent. "Suppose," he said, "our art collector dispenses his fortune with extraordinary generosity to all of the best charities—museums, hospitals, universities. Should the recipients turn these gifts back because they originated in the worst sort of economic crimes and mayhem? Not of a war criminal but of the donor's ancestors, or of the donor himself?"

"I think the charities should accept the gift, however corrupt its sources are."

"Even if the effect would be to relieve the donor of his guilt?"

"Nothing can relieve a man of guilt," Seeley said. "If the man has a conscience, he will get no relief, and if he has no conscience, he will feel no guilt, one way or the other."

And Mayer Bermann, what did he feel?

"Why do you say the donor is different from the artist? Why is the art corrupted but not the gift?"

"Because art is different. You cannot separate its morality from the artist's."

"Then you are an idealist."

Seeley said, "Only about art, not about ownership. If Mahler's publisher wanted, he could have shut down that performance, just as you can decide who gets to see these paintings—assuming you own them."

"So," Bermann said, "we have been talking about the same thing. For good or for ill, we must respect the rights of the true author. I believe you have the moral bearing and the skill to persuade Max Kanarek to take credit for his work."

Seeley, himself so adept at maneuvering witnesses, knew that he had just been manipulated by a master.

Bermann went to a window seat with framed photographs arranged in rows. Some were of Bermann with American presidents going back to Truman. Others showed him in riding garb, posed with horse and hounds, still others on horseback leaping fences. There were pictures from the forties and fifties of Bermann in business attire with actors and actresses, a few of whom Seeley vaguely recognized. In a more recent picture in the front, he was with a stunning blonde in riding gear, standing before an alert horse, a dense blur of forest in the background. The blonde could have been one of Bert Cobb's glamour girls, except there was no artifice of light or makeup here, just a beautiful woman outdoors, with sunlight stroking her thick golden hair.

"Mrs. Bermann?" Seeley was sure it wasn't.

Bermann took it as a joke. "That is Heather Hobday, the English actress." He lifted the frame and studied the picture from arm's length, as if he might learn something from it. "She is my protégée. Mr. Hobday, my secretary, is her brother."

The show-and-tell was becoming tedious, as were Bermann's continued evasions.

Seeley said, "If I go to Germany, I travel alone. I don't want any of your men following me."

"That was Mr. Landau's mistake, for which I must apologize. I have spoken to him."

Bermann drew close enough for Seeley to smell the scotch. "The studio has become a large organization, larger today than it was even a year ago. Mr. Callaway's business-school boys are everywhere. I am not always aware of everything that is done in my name. Come"—he took Seeley's arm—"let me show you a picture you will find interesting."

From outside, there was the sound of tires on gravel and a car door slamming.

It had become clear to Seeley what purpose these possessions and their allusions to power served for Bermann. The Biedermeier, the books, the pictures with politicians, the Vuillards and Bonnards. Like Bermann's humiliation of Hersh Landau earlier in the day, these were not vain conceits. They were the emblems that enhanced power. Which, Seeley wondered, did Bermann value more, the beauty of the paintings or the black rumor that they had passed through the hands of the second most powerful man in the Third Reich?

From a hidden drawer beneath the window seat Bermann removed a heavy, rose-colored folder. He opened the folder and handed Seeley a glossy black-and-white photograph. It showed Bermann seated at a piano keyboard, and standing behind him, his hands on Bermann's shoulders, playacting for the camera that he was singing along, Senator Joseph McCarthy. Bermann, in a double-breasted jacket with wide lapels, couldn't have been more than thirty-five when the picture was taken, but looked older, as men did in those days. The senator's watery eyes had a liquorish glitter; the five o'clock shadow and corrupt leer were unmistakable.

"I thought you were the one studio head who opposed the blacklist."

"For the senator, it was always about politics, nothing more."

"And for you?"

"Principle. First and foremost, principle." Bermann watched Seeley carefully. "He was a boozer, you know."

The word sounded odd coming from Bermann. It was a Harry Devlin word.

"In any event, the senator pretty much hit the mark. Of course, he was wrong on some of the details, mostly about people. But he was one hundred percent right about the big picture, that there was a Communist conspiracy in this country."

"Here? In Hollywood?" Seeley didn't think that someone as worldly as Mayer Bermann could actually believe that.

"Hollywood?" Bermann laughed. "No, not Hollywood. The committee came here because it was starstruck, just like everyone else in this country. When they had the hearings here in the fifties, they were living out the fantasy of every kid in America. Every grown-up, too. Come Saturday, they would be in the newsreels. Nixon was as bad as the worst of them, a celebrity hound if ever there was one. Of course, he and I were strangers then. I only got to spend time with him on the golf course later, when he was president."

"You're saying the hearings at the Biltmore were just a show?"

"Of course they were. But, whether it intended to or not, the committee did us a great favor. They wounded our enemy, some would say mortally. The investigations cleaned out the left-wingers from the unions, and they were really the only talented leaders the unions had. The guilds never recovered from the investigation. They have been weak at the top ever since the fifties. That is why we own the alliance today. The organization is run by kids from the seventies. Lightweights. Some of them are smart, but they lack the shrewdness of the old left-wingers. They lack any feeling for subtlety."

"Is there a point to this?"

"Ah, one grows old, and the tendency to digress grows, too. My point is that art transcends politics. What I have accomplished at this studio will last far longer than these politicians, and even far longer than their politics. I am not blind. The new *Spykiller* films have no claim to being art. But this studio has been responsible for a decent amount of serious work. I am sure you will agree that, by any measure, the original *Spykiller*—Max Kanarek's film—is a work of art."

Footsteps from the hallway stopped Bermann, and then he continued.

"It is important that you get Max Kanarek's authorship of the script established and recognized—"

Bermann looked to the doorway and Seeley turned.

Bermann said, "Do you know my old friend, Harry Devlin?"

Devlin was in slacks and an open sport shirt. Playing on his lips was what looked to Seeley like an embarrassed smile.

After a moment, Seeley said, "Not as well as I thought."

THIRTEEN

"Please come in, Harry. Would you care for something to drink? Fruit juice? Sparkling water? We were just discussing your Golden Age. The 1950s. The blacklist."

Seeley quickly sorted through the implications of this "old friend's" presence in Mayer Bermann's library. Bermann wanted Seeley to go to Germany to get Max Kanarek's signature. Harry Devlin did not. Bermann had plied him with art, charm, and philosophy. Devlin had warned him that the studio was getting reckless.

"You are surprised, Mr. Seeley, that my adversary should come to visit me at my home? Mr. Devlin and I have been acquainted for a great many years. Our relationship dates to when I was making my start in the industry and Mr. Devlin was trying to put a law practice together by representing labor unions."

When, Seeley thought, you owned a single, failing movie theater in Albany, New York, and Harry Devlin was the bag man who carried your payoffs to his bosses in the rackets.

Seeley said to Devlin, "Why are you here?"

Devlin gave him a bland look. "When I told Mr. Bermann of your interest in finding Max Kanarek, he kindly invited me to join the two of you. But"—Devlin glanced at the empty glass on the bar—"it looks like you started without me. You misled me, Mayer. You said your driver wasn't picking Michael up until nine."

"You should take your vitamins, Harry." Bermann placed a hand on Devlin's shoulder. "I specifically told you eight o'clock. But, yes, Mr. Seeley and I have been speaking. He will be traveling to Germany to secure Max Kanarek's statement that he is the author of *Spykiller*."

Devlin said, "Fifty years is a long time. Why is it suddenly so important for Kanarek to acknowledge his authorship? Why hasn't he come forward already? Why don't you go after him yourself?"

Seeley was certain that Devlin knew the answers to his questions. Why was he baiting Bermann?

"I have already told Mr. Seeley that Mr. Kanarek will not speak to me."

"Why would Max Kanarek refuse to speak to the man who has shown him such consideration? The man who has been sending him money all this time?"

Devlin wasn't expecting answers. The questions were to make Seeley understand that a trip to Germany to get Max Kanarek's signature would be futile. This was why Devlin had come.

"Mr. Seeley will tell you that I have already explained how difficult Max Kanarek can be. But Mr. Seeley is an accomplished lawyer and is accustomed to dealing with such people."

"Did you tell him about Max's novels? What number is he up to now? Seven? Eight? As soon as he completes one, Michael, he puts it on the shelf and starts the next one. He won't show them to publishers. Can you imagine that? All that work and no one gets to read the book."

Bermann said, "I could never understand why someone would do that. If a director spends two, three years making a movie, he wants to release it. He *fights* to release the film."

Bermann's evasion didn't distract Seeley. If in fact Max Kanarek wrote books only to leave them on the shelf, unread, why would he want to take credit for a movie script he wrote half a century ago?

"Why won't he publish his books?"

Seeley's question was to Bermann, but Devlin answered. "If I had to guess, I'd say it has to do with something in his past. History can be a heavy burden."

"The problem with lawyers is, you are all wrapped up in the past, these old cases, what do you call them . . ."

"Precedents," Devlin said.

"These precedents you worship. The past is a sickness, a disease. A man cannot live in the past and remain healthy. You should understand that, Harry. Better than anyone." To Seeley, he said, "I gather that you have met Mr. Devlin's good friend, Professor Walsh."

"We've met."

"What is your impression of her? Professionally speaking."

"She's smart," Seeley said. "Serious about her work. Why?"

"I have the same impression. Would it surprise you to know that, when it comes to Mr. Devlin here, this very competent professional has a blind spot a mile wide? She thinks he walks on water. You know, Harry, you should have been here when she interviewed me for her book. Any time I suggested that you were less than vigorous in your advocacy for the alliance and your other clients, she rose to your defense. It would be unfortunate if she heard something to make her change her mind about you. I have the feeling that behind that grown-up pose is a sensitive little girl. Do you understand what I am saying?"

"Rest assured, Mayer," Devlin said to Bermann's back, "your concerns have never been far from my thoughts."

Behind the banter were deep shadows, but neither man was going to give up any secrets about the other.

Seeley said, "Is this what the two of you do to kill time? You sit around and blackmail each other?"

Devlin laughed and the tension broke.

Bermann smiled. "There is no one in this town with any success who is not a blackmailer. It is the single stabilizing force in the industry. How do you imagine I have held my studio together all these years? One makes arrangements with one's adversaries. I once told this to Dr. Kissinger at a benefit at the Beverly Wilshire. He understood immediately. The principle of mutually assured destruction, he said."

Devlin said, "I hope you won't forget what we talked about, Michael."

Which did Devlin mean: The offer to represent the alliance in its class action? Or the glass with the circle of red lipstick? Seeley thought of Devlin's story about the lawyer who came out from under the bridge, only to drink himself to death.

"Your fabled rhetorical skills have failed you, Harry. I believe that Mr. Seeley has made up his mind on this matter."

Seeley said, "What makes you think I can get Kanarek to acknowledge that he wrote *Spykiller*?"

"Because you already believe you can. That is why you asked to see me. You are a resourceful man, Mr. Seeley. I am sure you will find a way."

Seeley was not as sure as Bermann was. But compared to the danger that was awaiting Bert Cobb, Devlin's warnings were a lawyer's empty hypothetical. If Seeley didn't do everything he could to get Max Kanarek's signature, and if harm came to Cobb, he knew he couldn't live with himself.

Seeley said, "We haven't talked about compensation."

Devlin's narrow shoulders slumped, and his body bent as if he had taken a blow.

Bermann noticed, too. "You look tired, Harry. Mr. Seeley and I will be finished, and then you and I can talk about our business together. Pull up a chair in the philosophy corner. I just acquired a first edition of Santayana's *Life of Reason*. You will find it on the third shelf."

Devlin reached down a glass from the bar cabinet and a bottle of mineral water from the refrigerator, and took them with him to an easy chair away from Seeley and Bermann.

Bermann said, "What did we agree to pay you if you persuaded Mr. Cobb to sign?"

"We're not talking about driving half an hour to see a portrait photographer in Pacoima."

"Nor are we talking about obtaining an assignment of rights—only a declaration of authorship. All I desire is for Mr. Kanarek to acknowledge that he is the author of *Spykiller* and for you to attend to the necessary formalities."

"A declaration won't be enough for your lenders. You also need an assignment of rights."

"Please, Mr. Seeley, I appreciate your concern, but there is no call for you to tell me what I need."

"What will a declaration from Max Kanarek get for you?"

"What were we talking about before Mr. Devlin arrived?" Bermann watched Devlin settle into the easy chair. "We were speaking of the value of authorship. Mr. Kanarek's acknowledgment will restore his name to his work."

"But he'll still own the rights."

"That is perfectly acceptable. He can dispose of the rights as he wishes."

This made no sense. Seeley remembered Hersh's warning not to get mixed up in Bermann's "little projects."

"You are probably thinking that I have lost touch with reality. Let me assure you, this is not so. Permit me also to remind you that when Intermedia acquired my studio, I became that company's largest individual stockholder. I own more stock in Intermedia than even Mr. Callaway. I have a seat on the board and I control two other seats. Five hundred thousand dollars should be a more than generous fee, don't you think? Of course, we will cover your expenses."

"One million dollars."

Seeley had already decided that, if he had to, he would go after Max Kanarek without being paid and at his own expense. But if the studio was going to pay, it was going to pay him a sum that had some proportion to his needs. While Bermann had been treating him to a tour of his photo gallery, Seeley had been calculating what it would require to set up a solo practice and run it for a year, maybe two if he was careful, without having to accept every client who came through the door. No more Gary Minietellos. No more Mayer Bermanns, either.

Bermann said, "Seven hundred and fifty thousand."

"One million." He would accept no less. If Bermann wouldn't pay a million, he would go on his own, for nothing.

"That is a substantial sum of money for three or four days of work."

"I didn't volunteer. You asked me to do it."

"Why do I have the impression, Mr. Seeley, that you have been playing me from the start? That you came up here so committed to the idea of finding Max Kanarek that you would do it without my paying you a single cent?"

"Maybe it's your idealism."

"One million dollars," Bermann said. "*When* you get Mr. Kanarek to sign."

"Plus expenses."

Bermann made a small movement under the table with his hand.

"I hope that when you get to Germany you will not forget where your loyalty lies."

The caution seemed unnecessary. "I don't expect to be there more than a week."

"Do you have any idea how much a person can change in a single day?"

The library door opened and the gray secretary came in. Bermann instructed him to prepare a letter covering the fee and to give Seeley Kanarek's address in Starnberg, as well as Bermann's private telephone numbers at home and at the studio.

"Reserve a room—no, a suite—for Mr. Seeley at the Königshof in Munich." As he spoke, he was already moving to where Devlin was. "Mr. Hobday will have a fee agreement and the air ticket delivered to your hotel first thing tomorrow morning."

Seeley had seen Munich only in advertisement for one of the Bavarian brands of beer, but if the pictures were anywhere close to reality, the broad gray boulevards, Gothic towers and golden church domes, the deep park meadows and groves of trees would be a blessed relief from California's bright, abrasive edges. If he tried, he could even imagine the malty scent of the place. Before Bermann reached the corner where Devlin was sitting, he turned. "When you see Max Kanarek, be careful of your sympathies. As I told you, he is a difficult, willful man, but in his own way charming. It would be a mistake for you to fall in love with him."

Devlin gave Seeley a halfhearted wave. "Take care of yourself, Michael. Call me anytime if you want to talk."

Unexpectedly, Seeley choked up as he had the night before in Devlin's office. Even if he could find the words, he couldn't speak them.

Outside, it was absolutely still and the sound of the door latch locking behind Seeley could have been a crack of thunder. The dog's howl from afar again broke the stillness. When he arrived at Bermann's property an hour earlier, Seeley had not stopped to look over the edge of the hill. Now he did.

Cloaked in a deep, inky blue, the city stretched out below him like a cascade of diamonds on a wash of coal. The lights of the silently moving traffic mirrored the lights in the jet-black sky. When had he ever seen stars like this? A faint scent—a whisper of citrus or some tropical flower—wafted by, stirring echoes of memory. It made him think of Julia—not the scent itself, for hers was different, but its evanescence and what it left him with, an unanticipated melancholy and longing. There was a current of sound beneath the silence, a rushing of air that could have been the Pacific surf or the thousands of cars moving below. For a single transcendent moment that felt as if it would never end, a tide of complete well-being flooded over him such as he had never before experienced.

The moment faded, and the lights of the black Mercedes swung out from behind the house to take him away.

FOURTEEN

Starnberg, where Max Kanarek lived, was a clean-swept, sunny town a half-hour train ride southwest of Munich. Set on the shores of the Starnberger See and surrounded by centuries-old forests and country estates, the town had the insouciant laziness of a lakeside resort. Along the main street leading out of town, aproned waiters unfolded chairs and opened table umbrellas on freshly hosed terraces. The taxi taking Seeley from the train station continued on through meadowlands dotted with small houses and finally down a steep grade into a wooded area close by the lake. When the driver let Seeley off, the grass was still damp with dew and the sun had begun to burn the mist off the Starnberger See. The white cottage was at the bottom of a weed-choked drive under a dusty tile roof. A scrawny ramble rose halfheartedly climbed a trellis over the doorway.

There was a moment's confusion in the doorway before Seeley realized how foolish his expectation had been. The image in his mind during the train ride from Munich to Starnberg had been of Natalia, the young Russian spy, pensive and hopeful, gazing out from the television screen in his suite at the Vista del Mar, and this was who he had been expecting to find at Max Kanarek's door, as if half a century hadn't passed since *Spykiller* was filmed.

Age had refined Carlotta's features. Fine lines etched the corners of her eyes and mouth and her complexion was darker than he remembered. But whatever else had changed, the eyes were the same: black as coal, holding that same wistful light. Being in her presence, Seeley felt a quiet thrill.

Before he could speak, Carlotta said, "Max is gone. I don't know where he is. But, please, come in." She pulled the door wide and with her foot brushed aside a yapping dog, as long and brown as a wurst.

In the parlor, snapshots with sun-filled backgrounds of palm trees, beaches, and adobe structures filled an entire wall, the framed pictures hung so close together that the effect, as Seeley inspected them, was of looking through an intricately partitioned window into the past. The facing wall was a picture window, and beyond it the lake.

Carlotta returned with cups and a pot of coffee on a tray. The Mexican girl who once played a Russian spy was now an elegant Bavarian hausfrau in beige riding breeches, with a dark knitted shawl over her shoulders. She positioned herself carefully on the couch so that the gray light coming off the lake revealed a handsome profile. She patted a place next to her, and when the dachshund jumped onto it, said, "Not you, Pepita," and pushed the dog off.

"Come sit by me," she said to Seeley.

From the coffee table she lifted a fat volume tied with a worn pink ribbon. "You said on the telephone you wanted to know about the movie. I don't know what I can tell you, but here are some photographs. I looked for this after you called."

Setting the album between them, she gestured for Seeley to open it. "The whole story is in here."

Seeley turned the vellum pages. On each page, precisely fastened with gold mounting corners, was an eight-by-ten photograph of a scene from the movie. Instead of following the film's narrative, the pictures were grouped around individual actors. For the first several pages, all the photographs were of Carlotta. The old-fashioned lettering embossed in the bottom right corner was familiar: PHOTOGRAPH BY BERTRAM COBB.

"Did it bother your husband that Bert Cobb got the credit for writing the screenplay?"

Carlotta's body stiffened. For the first time, Seeley noticed the dark wooden crucifix hanging from a gold chain around her neck.

"That was one of Mayer Bermann's ideas, letting a production photographer take the credit for the script." She turned the album toward herself. "Max put the pictures of me in the front. Let me show you some of the other actors. We were like a family."

The mist had lifted from the lake. A few sailboats scudded across the water and, in the distance, a tourist steamer idly traced the shoreline. Less than two hundred yards from the cottage, a compact wooden cross rose through the lake's surface. The taxi driver had told Seeley to look for the cross, which marked the point where Ludwig II—Mad Ludwig, Ludwig the Dream King—having escaped his imprisonment in nearby Berg Castle, marched into the Starnberger See to drown, taking with him his custodian, the head physician of the Munich asylum. Seeley expected a more dramatic marker, something taller and wider, a gleaming white cruciform, not a modest assemblage of unfinished two-by-fours anchored in a concrete piling.

"You think I'm living in the past, don't you?" Her voice was light, almost coquettish. "A real screwball, like our poor friend Ludwig out there."

She switched on the table lamp and Seeley could see every line and wrinkle in her face.

"I was still a girl when I took up with Max in 1951. I was eighteen years old. Go ahead, you can add it up. I made one movie in my life. Max sent me to acting school—it wasn't really a school, just an old stage actress from the east who came to Hollywood to coach actors. If you want to know the truth, it was Max who taught me. He showed me how to carry myself, how to speak. And don't think I gave up my career for Max. I didn't have a career. I was no actress. I was a serving girl and Max wrote that part for me so that, just one time, I could know what it was like to be famous, to have every single person in theaters all over the world stare up at me on the screen."

Carlotta closed the album. "You came because you're interested in Max, I think, not the movie. You should have known him then. He was a different man. He was melancholy, yes, but it was only later that he became so bitter, the way he is now. I fell in love with him the first time I saw him. I was doing maid's work for one of the émigrés, helping out in the kitchen. The people in that crowd were nice enough, but they were stuffy and taken with themselves, the way writers are. They did nothing but talk and, of course, they didn't know I existed. But Max stood out like there was a spotlight on him. And you could see, all night, he couldn't take his eyes off me. The rest of them knew their doctrine. Lenin, Trotsky, all that theory. But Max was the only real man there. How could I help falling for him? The minute I saw him, I knew something would happen between us." She nodded in the direction of the picture-filled wall. "We lived in Los Angeles first, later in Mexico."

Seeley said, "That's a long way from a resort town in Germany."

"I have my swimming. I'm a Pisces. Every morning by six I'm in the lake. And I ride. I instruct Munich housewives in dressage. I read a few hours every day, but none of your modern trash. Max taught me how to read the classics. And, of course, I have my music." She gestured in the direction of a low cabinet that held what must have been more than a hundred cardboard sleeves of old-style 33s. "It is a solitary life, yes, but not a bad life."

"How is Max?" The instant Seeley asked the question he realized that, coming from a stranger, it must have sounded cruel.

Carlotta's shoulders slumped. For the first time, she looked like an old woman. "What do you know about that?"

"Mayer Bermann told me he was ill. I'm sorry."

"Max is dying." She lifted the picture album off her lap and slipped it heavily onto the coffee table. "You didn't come all the way to Germany to hear me rattle on about my life. What is it you want from Max?"

"I would like to talk with him about signing a declaration that he wrote *Spykiller*."

"The studio already owns the rights. They paid this photographer, Cobb, and he gave the money to Max."

Seeley considered the impossibility of explaining how, in the U.S. Supreme Court's way of making law, a studio can own rights one day and someone else can own them the next. "The studio doesn't want an assignment of rights. It just wants Max to acknowledge his authorship."

"Max would never do anything for Mayer Bermann."

"The studio will pay him—both of you—a substantial amount."

It puzzled Seeley that, while agreeing to give him a million dollars to bring back Max Kanarek's signature, Bermann had said nothing about what he would give Kanarek to get him to sign.

"One dollar or a million dollars, it makes no difference. Max will accept nothing from Mayer Bermann."

"I thought Bermann sent him money."

"He did, but Max always sent it back. Now Bermann sends the money to me. Max doesn't know about it. As you can see, we do not live extravagantly. Max thinks our income comes from my teaching."

Seeley glanced at the pink-ribboned album on the table. Kanarek must have rearranged the photographs and placed the pictures of Carlotta first in order to obliterate the narrative but preserve his memories.

"A declaration will get Max the recognition he's entitled to. The studio will restore Max's name to the script. They'll give him a credit on the negative." Seeley was making this up, but he was confident he could get the studio to do it. "He'll get credit on all the sequels, too."

"You're talking about the blacklist?" Carlotta moved the album so it lined up squarely with the table's edge. "The investigations? The committees? That's not what this is about. Mayer Bermann is why Max won't sign your piece of paper. Do you know that in the three years Max lived in California, Mayer Bermann agreed to meet with him only once? The rest of the time Max got as far as the great man's secretary, or an assistant. The one time he got in to see him was to beg him to produce his script."

When Bermann told him he paid for Kanarek's passage to America, Seeley had the impression they were friends.

"No, Mr. Seeley, this goes back to before Max went to America. To when the two of them were boys in Poland. But it will do no good to talk about that time." She rose from the couch. "Would you like something instead of coffee? A glass of Riesling? Maybe some spirits? Do you think it's too early for a glass of wine?"

Seeley shook his head, thinking that, for him, it was too late. "The coffee is fine."

"Well, I think I'll have a glass of wine."

Carlotta went off to the kitchen and a few minutes later Seeley heard a cork pop from a bottle. He was thinking about the distances Max Kanarek had traveled, from a wartime childhood in Poland to refuge in America and then, forced from his home a second time, to Mexico, finally settling in this rustic German town. How deeply had his travels worn him? How thick a carapace had he formed? Seeley's own short journey now seemed foolhardy. The very idea that he would be able to impose his will on this man was preposterous.

When Carlotta returned to the room, she carried two clear green goblets, each half filled. At the scent of the wine, the dachshund rose on its hind legs and crossed its front paws as if in prayer.

Carlotta said, "Are you sure you won't have some?" When Seeley shook his head, she knelt and placed the goblet in front of the dog. "Max taught her that. She won't let me alone if I don't give her a sip."

Carlotta returned to her place on the couch. "You didn't know, did you? That Max and Bermann were boys together in Poland. I'm telling you this so you will understand that Max will do nothing to help Mayer Bermann in any way. If Mayer Bermann was dying of thirst, Max wouldn't turn the faucet to give him a glass of water."

"When is he coming home?"

Carlotta sipped at the wine. "I can't let you see him. You wanted to know about the movie. I showed you." She nodded in the direction of the album. "I'll answer any questions you have about the movie, but I cannot let you see Max."

"I understand he won't see Bermann, but it's the studio that's my client, not Mayer Bermann."

"I said *I* won't let you see him. It's not up to Max."

She had taken just a small amount of wine, and Seeley didn't think this could explain the sudden chill.

"I told you. Max is ill. He is going to die. Talking about the past will only upset him."

"All I want is to put a piece of paper in front of him. There won't be any pressure. I won't do anything to disturb him."

"That is just what she said. The American girl. Those were her exact words: I won't do anything to disturb him. And then . . . well, it happened."

"The American girl?" Seeley already knew. The anger rising in him tasted like gall. "When was she here?"

"Yesterday. When I came home from church, she was waiting at the door. Max was still asleep, so I let her in. I made coffee, then Max came in and they talked."

"What did they talk about?"

"She asked Max about the script. She said she wanted to be sure he wrote it. That was fine. But then she wanted to talk about the committees, the party, all of that. She's writing a book, she said."

Seeley decided not to tell Carlotta the book was already written.

"What did he tell her?"

"I don't know. By the time they got talking, I was back in the kitchen. If you knew anything about Max Kanarek, you would know his affairs are for him alone."

"And then?"

"I told you, I don't know. After they'd been talking for some time, the girl raised her voice at him and a minute or two later I heard the door slam. When I came in, she was gone and Max was sitting right where you are. He was stunned, like someone had punched him in the face, but he wouldn't say anything. Later, when I was out, he must have called a taxi. He was gone when I got home. He could be anywhere."

"Has he gone off like that before?"

"Many times. But this was different. That's why I'm worried. He's never been this sick. And he didn't take his notebooks with him."

"Why should that matter?"

Carlotta drew erect. "Max is a writer. He writes four hours a day, every day. It is like a religion for him. He writes novels. He works on them even when he is traveling. He always takes his notebooks."

"When he left like this before, where did he go?"

"To the mountains. Munich, sometimes. I told you, he could be anywhere."

"Mayer Bermann said that when he finishes a novel he just puts it on the shelf and starts the next one."

The thought of her husband's disappearance had distracted Carlotta. She nodded.

"What are they like?"

"The novels? Every one of them is an important work. They are not beautiful; none of them. They are deeper than beauty. If people read them, they would say they were sad. But they are profound. Always they tell a human story."

"Why doesn't he publish them?"

"At first, I asked the same thing. This is a great work. Why don't you publish it? And always he said there is no reason to publish. Publishing is not why he wrote these books. After a time I stopped bothering him about it. He is stubborn and nothing I could say would change his mind."

"And you don't think Max should be recognized for the work that's already been published? For *Spykiller*? Shouldn't he make the studio acknowledge it as his?"

"How can you ask that? Of course I do. But not if it means upsetting him."

"I only want to talk with him. If he doesn't want to sign, I'll leave."

"Three times the girl called last night, until I told her to stop. Then again this morning. She wants to see him."

"I'll make sure she leaves you alone."

"Do you know her?"

Seeley nodded, although it occurred to him that, as with Devlin, he didn't know her as well as he thought he did.

"If Max signs your paper, everyone will know he wrote *Spykiller?*"

"I promise. But you have to help me."

Carlotta said, "All my life, I've trusted people too much."

Seeley wrote down his number at the Königshof and asked her to call when Kanarek came home. For a long, unembarrassed moment they studied each other. Being with Carlotta like this, the image of the eighteen-year-old actress still vivid in his mind, Seeley had the sense of observing a life compressed into a single moment. The dark eyes that on the movie screen conveyed such a flood of warring emotions now communicated only fear. When she rose to see him to the door, the dog stayed behind at the foot of the couch, flattened, snoring. Passed out, drunk.

In the lobby bar of the Königshof, Seeley picked at a small plate of charcuterie. It didn't surprise him that Julia had found Kanarek so quickly—after all, she worked with Harry Devlin—or that she had kept Kanarek's location to herself. But what had happened between her and Kanarek?

Seeley found himself staring at an oversize trench coat hanging off the column in the center of the lobby. The coat had been there when he arrived at the hotel the day before. It was twice the size of a normal garment but, other than that, was identical in every detail to a British-style trench coat, with epaulets, shoulder flaps, and a casually tied belt. The brim of a similarly oversize fedora rested on the collar and lapels. Beneath that, a plaid woolen scarf was tucked into the breast. An issue of the *International Herald Tribune*, also jumbo-size, was carelessly folded in a pocket. The shoulders of the garment swooped out from the column; the sleeves were raised, as if in benediction. Overall, it gave the impression that the lobby and its occupants were in the care of a rakish but well-tailored angel, a phantom, a spirit.

Seeley left some change on the table for the waiter. As he rose to leave, the concierge bustled toward him, a large, silver-haired man in cream flannels busy with gilt buttons and yellow braid. Only an innate reserve saved him from appearing comical.

"Good afternoon, Mr. Seeley. You are enjoying your stay?"

"Ja, Herr Schreiner. Danke. Ist schön."

Seeley and the concierge had sparred since Seeley's arrival: Seeley wanting to practice his long unused German, Schreiner insisting on English.

"I hope you are taking time from your business to see the many wonderful sights of our city."

Seeley thought to ask about the trench coat, but before he could remember the German word, Schreiner was talking again. "Already, you must visit Oktoberfest. It closes in four days. Yes, you are astonished. All of our foreign guests are astonished. It is still September and Oktoberfest is almost finished. Oktoberfest should start in October! This is like a joke, yes? I promise you, it is very touristic. Not only the variety of drink and food—of course, you don't care for amusement rides—but to savor the authentic Bavarian spirit." The concierge inhaled extravagantly, as if setting off on a brisk hike. "There is no better place than Oktoberfest to take in the Bavarian spirit!" Schreiner clapped his hands, letting an express mail envelope slip from under his arm.

Seeley pointed at the envelope. "*Ist das für mich?*"

Schreiner examined the envelope, as if for the first time. "How could I forget! Yes, of course, it is for you."

The return information on the cardboard mailer was United Pictures' address in Burbank. Schreiner waited for Seeley to open it.

"*Danke schön, Herr Schreiner,*" Seeley said, heading for the elevator.

In the suite, Seeley opened the mailer and lifted out a business envelope on which his name was typed. Inside this was an article clipped from a newspaper that, by the typeface of the headline, he recognized as the *Los Angeles Times*: PHOTOGRA-PHER DIES IN HOME BURGLARY.

As Seeley rapidly scanned the article, the accumulated jet lag, the countless cups of coffee he had consumed, the strangeness of being in a foreign place severed him from any connection to where he was or what he was reading. He could have been floating above the earth. It took some time for him to absorb the words.

According to the article, late on the evening of Monday, September 26—the night before Seeley boarded the plane for Munich—Bertram Cobb, a professional photographer, surprised an intruder in the Pacoima home that also served as his photography studio. Cobb had been clubbed to death with a heavy object, from preliminary indications a tire iron or length of rebar. The police said drawers and closets were ransacked, and there was evidence of a struggle. Police had found the door to Cobb's photography darkroom ripped from its hinges; the photographer's body was on the darkroom floor.

Clipped to the article was a buff card on which the silhouette of a centaur was engraved in the upper left-hand corner. The handwriting was as neat and elegant as the man himself. "Dear Mr. Seeley," the card read, "You will now understand the great importance of obtaining Max Kanarek's signature. M.B." Not a word of condolence, regret, or responsibility, only an order to repair the omission.

Seeley's first reflex was to get drunk. The next—the image of it fixed in his brain—was to put a revolver to his ear and blow his head off. At the moment, oblivion was all he desired. He lifted the telephone, as if to call someone, but not knowing whom to call, replaced it.

To someone looking into Seeley's hotel room from across the courtyard, what he did next might have appeared to be evidence of insanity. In fact, as Seeley later realized, it is what saved him.

Concentrating on the herringbone pattern of the beige carpet, he carefully placed one foot in front of the other, and then the other foot in front of that one, so that, proceeding this way, he traveled with measured steps diagonally across the room, taking a jog to the right where the hallway led to the door. When he came to the door, he turned and followed the same invisible line across the carpet, back to the table with the telephone. He repeated this trajectory, back and forth, one foot placed precisely ahead of the other, but with no consciousness of his movement across the room.

By the fiftieth or sixtieth circuit—he was not counting— superficial distractions slipped away, leaving him to contemplate only the most essential facts and the connections between them. When the reason for Bert Cobb's death finally revealed itself to him, like a bolt slipping into a hasp, there was no shock of discovery, only a dull thud of recognition, as if he knew it all along. He no longer felt the need for a drink, or to blow his head off, or for oblivion. The impulse had passed.

He picked up the telephone again, waited for the international dial tone, and dialed the main number for the U.S. Copyright Office in Washington, D.C. He asked for the Records

Division and when the records clerk came on told her what he needed. A simple search in the Records Division's files would tell him whether his suspicion was correct.

"How will you be paying for this?"

"Let me give you my credit card number."

"This isn't a restaurant."

"I'm sure it isn't. But I'm calling from Munich. In Germany. I need this information as soon as possible."

"We take cash or check. Or if you have a deposit account, you can use that."

"Look, I'm sure you have the information right in front of you, on your screen. You don't have to send me anything. Just tell me what it says."

"I'm sorry, but we can't do that. To provide you with any information, we have to open a file number, and we can't open a file number without payment. If you had a deposit account it would be real easy."

He had a deposit account—or Boone, Bancroft did—but he didn't want to risk anyone at the firm finding out about his inquiry. Still, there seemed to be no choice, and it occurred to him that by the time the copyright office charge got to the firm's accounting department, this would all be over. He gave the firm name to the clerk.

"If you hold, I'll confirm that with your law firm."

"You've never done that before."

The clerk made no effort to hide her distrust. "I've never had this long a conversation about payment before."

Before Seeley could decide whether to cancel the order, she put him on hold.

Five minutes later, she came back on the line. "They authorized the charge for you." Skepticism still echoed in her voice. "How do you want us to send this to you?"

"Can't you give it to me over the phone?"

"Mister, it's 8:45 in the morning here, and I've got a pile of orders from yesterday I still have to do."

"Fax it to me," Seeley said, looking through the pile of hotel information for the fax number. "As soon as you can." He gave her the number and hung up.

Only five hours had passed since he boarded the train for Starnberg to see Carlotta, but it seemed like days. The juniper taste of gin rolled onto the back of his tongue and, just as quickly, evaporated. He imagined the jolt and rush of alcohol to his brain, but this time no hand gripped his shoulder to hold him back, and that unsettled him. When he was six or seven and learning to ride a bicycle, his mother recruited an older boy in the neighborhood to run alongside, holding on to the seat so he wouldn't fall. Pedaling furiously, hands frozen to the handlebar, Seeley hadn't thought to glance to the side for approval or encouragement, and when he finally did look around, his guide was at the far end of the street, waving to him. He was on his own. He missed Bert Cobb, this man he hardly knew. Inside him, a hole had opened so wide that the wind could blow right through it.

FIFTEEN

Unable to sleep, Seeley dozed fitfully, shuffling and reshuffling possibilities, testing out assumptions, backing out of dead ends, Bert Cobb always at the edge of his consciousness. Briefly he considered the possibility that he was wrong about Cobb's death. It wouldn't be the first time a homeowner surprised an intruder or that the intruder repelled his victim with more force than was necessary. But too many people had conspired for him to be far from Pacoima on the night Cobb was attacked. Go back to New York, Hersh told him; the boxer, too. Come meet me at my home, Bermann said. Seeley imagined Cobb falling, dying even as he and Bermann exchanged deep thoughts on the morality of art. Come to my home and meet my surprise guest. Only Harry Devlin seemed to be indifferent to where Seeley went, so long as he didn't go chasing after Max Kanarek.

When the room finally grew light, Seeley dialed the hotel

operator yet again. No, a sleepy voice told him, no fax had arrived for him from Washington. He dressed, looked over the newspaper from the previous day, flipped through the few television channels that had started broadcasting, and, still restless, took the elevator to the hotel roof.

The outdoor bar was shuttered and the deck chairs were stacked at the edge of the terrace. A breeze sent ripples across the blue-green swimming pool. Seeley surveyed the rooftops of the slumbering city: shingles of gray slate in gingerbread shapes; sheets of crenelated copper, tarnished green; dormers peeking out of red tile; the whole mosaic interrupted by an occasional onion dome or Gothic church spire. Across the alley, the empty beer garden of the Hofbräuhaus seemed still to reverberate from the carousing of the night before. Next to the beer garden, and three stories up on a flat graveled roof, a play area was fenced in with child-size tables, brightly colored beach umbrellas, and a wading pool. A maid in a white uniform, followed by a small child in white shorts, emerged through double doors and dumped a bucket of water into the pool. At ground level, a man stood inside a glass door, smoking, looking out.

There was an obscure familiarity to the scene, but also something awry, like the trench coat in the hotel lobby, identical in every detail to how reality should appear, but foreign in its proportions. Seeley had experienced the same sense of dislocated memory the afternoon he arrived in Munich. The after-lunch strollers on Maximilianstrasse—the men thick-shouldered and robust in their double-breasted blazers, the women as lacquered, buffed, and polished as any Mercedes or BMW—could have emerged from a forgotten corner of his life to gather on the expensive shopping street. Like a memory or a dream, the pink sandstone façade of the Maximilianeum floated above the far end of the avenue. He felt an inexplicable surge of nostalgia for this place he had never been before.

What had kept him from coming to Germany all this time? Seeley had turned down business meetings and invitations to conferences, pleading other obligations. Asked to speak to a Berlin gathering of an international artists' rights society on how American courts protect authors' rights, Seeley declined with the truthful observation that there was little to be said, and certainly not enough to justify the trip. As he reflected now on the familiarity of the scene that lay about him, the possibility startled him that a child's fears of what he would find in the dark corners of his parents' closet, or of his father's past, could deform the course of his life so many years later. Had he in fact come to Germany to put these fears to rest? For a moment he considered calling Berlin to see if the Nazi documentation center there was still in operation.

The thought of Bert Cobb stopped him. He had come to Germany to save Cobb's life, and no amount of daydreaming could dispel the fact that he had failed his friend completely.

Two gray hotel envelopes had been slipped under the door while Seeley was out. He tossed the lighter one on the desk and opened the other. Inside was a photocopied document with the seal of the U.S. Copyright Office rubber-stamped across a corner. The text of the document started a quarter of the way down the first page under the caption DEED OF TRANSFER. It was the standard instrument United Pictures used to obtain an assignment of rights from a writer or other copyright owner, and was identical to the form Seeley had brought to Pacoima for Bert Cobb to sign.

After the "Whereas" clause and the preamble, in the space provided to indicate the rights being transferred, was typed, "Exclusive rights, in perpetuity and throughout the world, to reproduce, and distribute one or more motion pictures, including sequels, from a script entitled 'Spykiller,' written by Bertram Cobb." Below that, "United Pictures, Inc." was printed in the space for the buyer and, handwritten on the line provided for the seller was "Verna Cobb."

Seeley turned to the second page. There was an indecipherable signature over the name of the studio and, next to it, Verna Cobb's signature in a neat secretarial hand. Below that was a notary's seal and the signature of a witness even though, since the conveyance was executed in the United States, neither formality was necessary. Whoever had overseen the deed's execution was taking no chances. There was no mistaking the fussy but legible signature: Jack Elm had served as the witness when Verna Cobb signed over the rights to *Spykiller*. The deed was dated September 23, the day after Seeley's first meeting with Bert Cobb and three days before the photographer's death.

The deed confirmed what Seeley had pieced together pacing the carpet in his hotel suite the day before. Bert Cobb's death was premeditated and United Pictures was responsible. What Seeley remembered as he put one foot in front of the other on the herringbone pile was the frilly apron hanging from the kitchen door. Bert Cobb had a wife. Once she became his widow, Verna Cobb acquired any copyrights Bert owned at the time of his death. That she had signed over the rights to the studio before Cobb died made no legal difference. Upon her husband's death, Verna at once became the owner of the copyright in the script, and any earlier transfer that Verna made of the copyright—such as her transfer to the studio— would automatically take effect. So far as the paper record went, United Pictures now owned the rights to *Spykiller*.

Seeley filled in the gaps. Someone from the studio—the fact that it was Jack Elm was predictable—visited Mrs. Cobb and informed her that, as the result of a recent and unexpected Supreme Court decision, a small technical question had arisen about the copyright ownership of some old movie scripts. The deed of transfer was just a minor formality to fix the problem. The studio would, of course, ask Bert to sign a deed, too, but since Elm was in the neighborhood, he thought he'd stop by to get her signature. Naturally the studio would be happy to pay her a modest consideration for her trouble. Seeley turned back to the first page of the document. The recital in the opening paragraph contained the standard formula that lawyers use to hide the true value of a transaction: "For ten dollars and other valuable consideration . . ." Doubtless the studio had paid Verna Cobb more than ten dollars. But did she have any idea that, by signing the deed, she was setting in motion the sequence of acts leading to her husband's death?

Seeley opened the other envelope. In it was a telephone message from Carlotta taken by the hotel operator at 6:15. Max had still not come home. He had not telephoned either. Make contact, Seeley whispered to the empty room. Meet with me before it's too late for you. Save yourself, Max. Save me.

SIXTEEN

It took Seeley one visit to the front desk and three telephone calls to locate Julia. From the pearls and expensive perfume, he figured she would stay in Munich, not Starnberg, and there weren't more than a handful of five-star hotels in the city. The room clerk at the Königshof told him she wasn't staying there, as did the clerks at the Bayerische Hof and the Platzl. The telephone operator at the Vier Jahreszeiten put him through to her room at once.

"I can't talk to you." Julia's voice was faint, the words clipped. "I'm packing. I'm leaving."

"What happened with you and Max Kanarek?"

"Nothing."

"You ran out of there. Kanarek left right after you did. He hasn't been home for two nights."

Julia said, "I took your call. I didn't agree to be cross-examined."

"Harry Devlin sent you to Munich. He told you where to find Max Kanarek. He had you scare Kanarek off so I couldn't get to him."

"Has the possibility occurred to you that, whatever happened, it's not about Michael Seeley?"

"Then tell me what it is about. You had Kanarek's file all along, didn't you? There's something about Kanarek that you and Devlin are covering up."

"Harry Devlin is the last person in the world who would want me to find Max Kanarek."

"I need to know what happened, Julia. Please." Seeley drew in a breath. This was hard. "I need your help."

Seeley waited. Finally, Julia said, "I'll be in the lobby in fifteen minutes."

As he replaced the receiver, Seeley was certain he was missing something—a fact or consequence that had eluded his shuttling back and forth across the herringbone carpet—that would change everything he believed was true. Whatever it was, he had no hope of discovering it in the fifteen minutes it would take to walk to Julia's hotel on Maximilianstrasse.

Julia was at a corner table in the hotel lobby, so still in the subdued light that she could have been a portrait. When she looked up, her eyes were blurry, as if she had been crying, and the flesh beneath them was swollen and discolored.

"Are you okay?"

"Sure. A little jet lag." The smile was forced; as on the telephone, the voice was hollow, inert.

"What happened with Max Kanarek? Carlotta said you walked out on him."

"She's exaggerating. We talked about how he got blacklisted. What he knew about the other writers. She wasn't even in the room when I left. How did you find him?"

"I didn't," Seeley said. "I told you. He left right after you did. He hasn't come back."

"I meant how did you know where he lived?"

"Bermann told me."

"It was Crowe who found him for me."

"Crowe?"

"James Crowe Hardesty. Our lunch speaker. He got Kanarek's address from a friend at the Cinémathèque." She ran a hand through her short hair. "Crowe's waiting for me in Paris. We're talking to the people at the Cinémathèque about getting their support for the class action. There's not a head of an American studio who isn't intimidated by the French. The French love Crowe. They think he's the real thing."

Julia looked around the grand lobby, as if for the first time. Only an occasional muffled cough or the genteel clatter of a serving fork against a pastry tray broke the hush of conversation in the golden-hued space.

"I'm sorry Kanarek disappeared. I know you thought that seeing him could make things easier for Bert Cobb."

"Bert Cobb is dead."

Fragile as Julia already was, her face went white. "I'm sorry. You really liked him, didn't you?"

Seeley nodded. He gave her the newspaper details, but told her nothing of his suspicions about the studio's part in Cobb's death. Julia had too many secrets for him to trust her with his own.

"When I called you, why did you say Harry Devlin was the last person in the world who would want you to find Max Kanarek?"

"Did I say that?"

Seeley nodded.

"If you look back at the forties and fifties," Julia said, "it was the good guys, the people in the guilds and the unions—the alliance, too—who believed that the ends justified the means." The words were tense, rapid, evasive. She was hiding something. "It's not fair to judge them with hindsight."

"Can you tell me what you're talking about? I asked you why Harry Devlin wouldn't want you to see Kanarek."

Small red blossoms rose on Julia's cheeks. "Did you know that Harry's devoted his whole life to defending workers against the system? During the investigations, he represented more writers and directors than anyone. If you were in trouble with the committee, he was the man to see."

"Julia. Look at me." Seeley reached across the table and grabbed her wrists. "Tell me why you won't answer my question."

Frantically, her eyes searched the lobby, as if seeking rescue. Her pulse pounded beneath Seeley's hands. All at once, she began to sob, great racking heaves.

A beige jacket materialized at the table. "Is there some way in which I can assist you?"

The voice, East Asian, was gentle, but the eyes that bore into Seeley were not. Seeley withdrew his hands.

Julia looked up at the bland, dark face. "It was just a misunderstanding. There's no problem. Everything's all right."

The man hesitated.

"Really," Julia said.

He gave Seeley a warning look and left.

Seeley said. "Look, don't try to tell me everything. Just a small corner of it. You can stop whenever you want."

For a moment, Julia closed her eyes, as if in thought or prayer. When she opened them, she said, "It was Harry who informed on Max Kanarek."

After Devlin's unexpected appearance in Mayer Bermann's library, the information didn't surprise Seeley. Still, he felt a sudden stab of loss. He pictured Harry Devlin with a highball glass in hand and a celebrity's arm around his shoulder; Harry Devlin in a straitjacket unburdening himself to a fellow drunk;

Harry Devlin carrying Bermann's payoff money to his racketeer bosses in upstate New York. Harry Devlin was a man of many parts, most of them hidden.

Seeley said, "That's why you came to Germany, isn't it? When you found out about Kanarek and the script you thought Harry was involved."

Julia shrugged. Then the words spilled out. "Max Kanarek was a Communist. A real one. Not like the Hollywood dilettantes. He didn't belong to the alliance. He was in the Writers Guild, but he wasn't active. He'd already worked on a couple of scripts for Bermann. He heard rumors and he thought he was in trouble. He got Harry's telephone number from another writer. Kanarek told me he went to Harry's office three times before he trusted him enough to tell him about his work with the party."

"Harry Devlin signed on as Kanarek's lawyer and then turned him over to the state investigators."

"He told Harry he was working with the top party leadership in Los Angeles—not the Hollywood crowd, *Los Angeles*—and he thought one of them was getting ready to talk to the FBI. For an immigrant, that meant jail time and deportation. Harry said he'd do what he could to make a deal for him, but Kanarek said he didn't want a deal. He just wanted to know what the FBI knew and what he was facing and then he would decide for himself what to do. He was getting ready to go underground."

"Have you talked to Harry?"

"I called him two days ago, right after I got back from talking to Kanarek. He didn't deny it. He didn't seem surprised I found out. He said he'd made some anonymous inquiries for Kanarek, but they were dead ends. The FBI wasn't interested in him. He had nothing to be afraid of."

Seeley said, "But that's not what Harry told him. Harry had his own plans."

"Harry told me he took complete responsibility for what

happened. But he also said it was Mayer Bermann who gave Kanarek's name to the investigators."

"Why would Bermann be involved?"

"The federal investigators were winding down their work in Hollywood. The state people had been hanging back while the committee took on the writers and directors, and now it was their turn to go after whoever was left. They put together a stack of files the federal investigators had started on but hadn't closed, and Mayer Bermann and United Pictures were way up on their list. Bermann had never paid for the stand he took on the blacklist. Although it wasn't something he could be investigated or prosecuted for, they still wanted to rub his face in what he'd done. For some reason, the feds had stayed clear of him. Harry thinks he made a deal with them. I don't. I think they were just afraid of him. But Bermann couldn't intimidate the state investigators. They decided to punish him by organizing a boycott of his films. Wall Street figured that if the boycott worked it would make United easy pickings for a takeover, so they gave the state people the go-ahead."

Just like when Bermann teamed up with local union officials to drive his fellow theater owners in Albany out of business. "So," Seeley said, "Bermann went to Harry Devlin for help, and Harry gave him Max Kanarek as his sacrificial offering. One real Communist in return for saving Mayer Bermann's studio from the predators."

Julia said, "Bermann gave Kanarek to the state investigators, and Harry negotiated the deal for Kanarek. They wouldn't prosecute if Kanarek left the country. Harry got it delayed for three months so he could finish *Spykiller*. But you're right. Harry used Kanarek to save Mayer Bermann's studio from Wall Street." Julia's tone was so dispassionate she could have been a court stenographer reading back testimony. But the drawn face and wrecked eyes told Seeley she was devastated, and he wondered why.

"And," Seeley said, "Max Kanarek got a steamship ticket to Mexico." He didn't see much difference between whether you thought Bermann turned Kanarek in or Devlin did. By letting Bermann do the informing, Devlin maintained the fiction that he had not handed his client over to the government. Legal fictions didn't bother Seeley; they were standard issue in the lawyer's kit of tools. But what Devlin did went miles beyond a lawyer's bending of the rules. Even if the deal he struck for Kanarek was the best the writer could have hoped for, Devlin had violated his trust. To Seeley, the thought of intentionally betraying a client was incomprehensible.

"When I talked with him on the phone, Harry said he was glad I found out. He said that after all this time it felt good to get it off his chest."

"I wonder how good his client felt."

Seeley saw Julia wince at the bitterness in his voice, and reminded himself that his anger wasn't at her. He had misjudged her badly, and regretted that. But why had she struggled so hard to hold this back from him? And why had that touched him so deeply?

Julia said, "I can't understand why Harry did this for Bermann. Until a couple of days ago, I didn't even know they talked to each other."

"Did you ask him?"

"He said it was complicated."

"Any friendship is complicated—if that's what you want to call their relationship."

Seeley told her about their union racket in Albany. "When they moved to Los Angeles, and Bermann started building his studio and Devlin began representing a better class of racketeers, my guess is they continued doing favors for each other. I doubt Bermann knew any big secret that he was holding over Devlin, just a lot of bad acts that neither of them would want to see splashed on the front page of the *Los Angeles Times*." He remembered Bermann in the library telling Devlin that Julia believed he walked on water; Max Kanarek was the secret Bermann had been holding over him. "They still blackmail each other, even today."

At the next table, two middle-aged couples, sunburned and with Qantas tour bags on the floor next to them, suddenly broke into uproarious laughter, shattering the quiet of the room.

"When are you leaving?"

Seeley said, "I still need to find Max Kanarek."

"Why? If Bert Cobb's dead, why do you need anything from Kanarek?"

"What I told you about how Cobb died was the newspaper story. I don't know whether it was intentional or an accident." Recalling the precision of the boxer's blows, Seeley thought it was more likely murder than negligence. "Either way, the man who killed Cobb was working for United."

"Film studios don't hire thugs to intimidate people."

"What were we just talking about? Mayer Bermann destroyed Max Kanarek's life to save his studio. What makes you think he wouldn't hire someone to beat up an old portrait photographer out in Pacoima?"

"But he had no reason to kill Cobb. He needed him to sign over the rights."

Seeley told her about the deed from Verna Cobb transferring ownership of *Spykiller* to United. "United knew it would get the rights either way: intimidate Cobb until he signed, or kill him after it bought the rights from his widow. Maybe that's why they got careless."

"But if Max Kanarek wrote the script, he owns it. How could Cobb's widow sell the studio something she doesn't have?"

"As long as the copyright office records show that Bert

Cobb is the author, no one's going to question that Verna got the rights when he died or that she transferred them to the studio. But if I can get Max Kanarek to sign a declaration that he wrote *Spykiller*, and get it recorded in the copyright office, that will be enough to put a cloud over the studio's rights. No bank will finance a sequel until that's resolved, and when that happens, Max Kanarek will own the rights."

"What makes you think that whoever killed Bert Cobb won't try the same with Max Kanarek? Or Carlotta? Or you?"

"Once Max Kanarek signs a declaration that he wrote *Spykiller*, he'll be safe, and so will Carlotta. No one would gain anything by killing them."

"Why is it any of your business if United gets to make another one of these ridiculous movies?"

"I'm being paid," Seeley said. "Enough to set up my own practice when I finish here."

"I think you'd go after Kanarek even if you weren't being paid."

Mayer Bermann had said that, too. It bothered Seeley that he was becoming so transparent.

"You think it's up to you to fix every injustice you find."

"No," Seeley said. "Just the big ones."

"I'm sorry about scaring Kanarek off." Julia glanced at her watch, but Seeley knew she wasn't going to leave. "I can help you find him."

"How can you do that?"

"I know what he looks like. You don't."

"So the two of us just wander around Germany looking for Max Kanarek. Or do you have an idea where we should start?"

"Something will turn up."

Seeley didn't hear her, for a thought had stopped him. Pacing the carpet in his suite, he had concluded that only a declaration of authorship from Max Kanarek could reverse the effect of

Verna Cobb's deed to the studio. Kanarek would own the rights and United would have nothing. But this was precisely what Mayer Bermann had asked him to obtain, with the promise of a million dollars if he succeeded. Why would Bermann want to undermine the transfer of rights the studio had already obtained from Verna Cobb? Either Bermann was wrong about the effect of a declaration from Max Kanarek or Seeley was. And Mayer Bermann didn't impress him as a man who was often—or ever—wrong when it came to the welfare of his studio.

SEVENTEEN

Seeley was finishing a room service breakfast when Carlotta telephoned. "A friend from Max's *Stammtisch* called."

Seeley hadn't heard that word since he'd left his parents' home. It was the best table in the tavern, the one reserved by pride and custom for his father and his drinking circle at Germania Hall.

"Two men were asking about Max. At the hotel, at the shops in town. One spoke German, the other said nothing. They wanted to know where we live. Why are they looking for Max?"

"This friend who called you. Does he know where Max is?"

"I can't tell you."

There was a slyness in Carlotta's voice that Seeley hadn't heard before. He remembered her fearless performance as a Russian spy.

Seeley said, "Max is in danger from the men who are looking for him. I want you to come to Munich as soon as you can."

"Is this something to do with the American girl?"

"No." A trace of Julia's perfume lingered in the back of his consciousness. He remembered Carlotta telling him that Kanarek and Bermann had grown up together in Poland. "Does Max have anything from when he was a boy—a diary, a journal?"

"No, nothing. Only a picture album."

"Please, bring it with you. But don't take the train from Starnberg. These men may be watching for you. What's the next closest train station?"

"Mühlthal. What if Max comes back?"

"Take the next train from Mühlthal. I'll wait for you here. Call Max's friend and tell him Max should stay where he is. Don't waste time. Do this now."

Carlotta let Seeley take her elbow as they crossed Neuturmstrasse, but fiercely clasped the leather album under her arm when he offered to carry it. Behind them, a line of tourists and locals jostled to get into the packed Hofbräuhaus, its three stories throbbing with the sodden beat of an oompah band. Across the street, the local Planet Hollywood outpost was all but abandoned, the awnings rolled and chairs tilted against the outside tables.

They took a table inside under a larger-than-life photograph of an action hero, his biceps bursting from a leather vest, an automatic rifle in his beefsteak hands, and a smudge of grease across his brow. It occurred to Seeley that Hollywood, not Silicon Valley, was California's nursery of invention: an Austrian bodybuilder becomes an American movie star, then reinvents himself again as the state's governor. Carlotta put the album she was carrying on the table. It was not as thick as the one she'd shown him at the cottage, and the well-worn binding was from an earlier age. Seeley ordered a glass of Riesling for her and coffee for himself.

"You and Max have to stay away from Starnberg. Just for a while."

"Here is the album." Carlotta already had it open. "A different place. A different time. Only God knows how, but with all that happened in that little town, this was saved."

She swiveled the book so that it faced Seeley and turned a page only after she was sure he had taken it in. There were two or three photographs on a page, each neatly mounted with gilt corners on black paper, like the photographs in the *Spykiller* album. A few were formal, sepia-toned portraits of individuals or family groups made indoors, the clothing and the furniture in the background dating the pictures somewhere between the two world wars. Most, though, were snapshots taken in rustic settings or enclosed courtyards. A single subject was common to them all. As Carlotta turned the pages, Seeley saw the figure he assumed was Max Kanarek evolve, as if in stop-motion, from an infant cradled by a stern and stiff woman to a tall, bushy-headed youth in a cloth jacket and knickers.

Carlotta reached over the album and placed a fingertip on a photograph of Kanarek leaning against a stone wall, one arm resting lazily along the top of it, the other thrown around his companion, a boy who, though much shorter, looked about the same age. Kanarek had on a rough farm shirt buttoned at the neck, the other boy a coat and vest with a neatly knotted necktie. Unlike his companion's set jaw, Kanarek's easygoing grin engaged the camera lens directly. The short boy had his hands jammed into his suit trousers and his eyes fixed on a point over the photographer's shoulder, somewhere in the middle distance.

"Do you know who that is?"

Seeley didn't have to guess. The aloof companion—was he staring at someone behind the photographer, or was it a thought that triggered the faraway look?—was the boy who, after shedding several names, became Mayer Bermann.

"Look at what friends they were! From what Max told me,

nothing could separate the two of them. You wouldn't know it to look at the picture, but of the two of them it was Bermann who was the troublemaker. No one in their little town was safe from his practical jokes. Later, when things turned bad—after the SS took Bermann's parents away—Bermann's adventures became more reckless. He would sneak around the countryside, taking food from the farmers' storage places. Later, Max told me, he got even more daring. Many times he broke into the local SS encampment to steal food, blankets, even fuel oil. Some of this he would share with Max and his parents. The rest he would barter.

"You can guess what Max's part was in this. He wrote little stories—boys' stories—about Bermann's adventures. Of course, he made Bermann's attacks grander and bolder than they really were. He made his opponents smarter and stronger, too. Max said Bermann would take his stories as a dare to do something even more reckless, as if he had to keep a step ahead of what Max wrote about him.

"So as bad as the times were, these two boys shared a bond that for Max is only a memory." Carlotta let her finger trace the outline of the two figures in the photograph. "In all the time I've known him, Max has never smiled like that. And do you know why?" She turned the next page. There were more snapshots of Bermann and Kanarek. "This"—she pointed to Bermann—"is why. As close as they were—*because* they were so close—Mayer Bermann destroyed whatever chance Max had for a happy life. Even so, I have forgiven him for what he did to Max."

Seeley closed the album and pushed it across the table. "The men who are looking for Max are killers."

She rested her hands on the album. "Why should killers be looking for Max?"

"Do you remember, before, we talked about Bert Cobb? The photographer?"

"Of course I do. He's the man whose name is on Max's script."

"He was murdered five days ago."

It took Carlotta a few seconds to take that in and, once she did, she rapidly crossed herself. "I'm sorry, of course, but what does this have to do with Max? Why should he be in any kind of danger?"

Seeley told her about Bert Cobb's refusal to sign over rights he didn't own, and the fraudulent transfer of rights from Cobb's wife to the studio. "I didn't realize how far the studio would go to save *Spykiller*. If they killed Bert Cobb to get the rights, they'll do the same to Max to keep them."

"And you think Max is going to get himself into trouble by telling the world he wrote the script?" She shook her head vigorously. "You don't know Max."

"It doesn't matter what I know. What matters is that whoever sent these men doesn't know Max. As long as he's alive, there's a risk he'll start talking about the script. They can't afford that." He hesitated, then decided she should know the truth. "You're also a problem for them."

"They wouldn't have come after Max if you and the girl hadn't stirred this all up. Nobody would have known about Max and that script." Carlotta immediately pressed her fingers to her lips like a chastised child and gave him a small, embarrassed smile. "I'm sorry. I didn't mean to be rude."

"It wasn't the girl's fault. It was mine. I'm the one they followed here."

"And now, we're supposed to leave our home? Just disappear?"

"As soon as Max signs the declaration that he wrote *Spykiller*, and I get the declaration recorded, they'll go away. His authorship will be part of the public record, and no one will bother you or him."

"You're telling me a piece of paper is going to do this."

"Once it's recorded in the copyright office, it will override the deed from Cobb's widow. Max just has to swear the declaration is true and sign it. He will be the owner of record of the script. If anything happens to him, you will own the rights. No one would gain anything by harming you."

Further steps would need to be taken. Also, Seeley had to find a local lawyer to initiate the recordation procedure in Germany. But recording the declaration was a start and would be enough to get the studio to call off its thugs. For now, this was all Carlotta needed to know.

"Max will never do anything to help Mayer Bermann's studio."

"Max's signing this paper isn't going to help the studio. He'll still own the script. He can sell the rights to anyone he wants. He doesn't even have to sell them. If he wants to, he can stop Bermann from making any more *Spykiller* movies."

"If you're Mayer Bermann's lawyer, why are you doing this?"

"I don't work for Mayer Bermann. He's not my client anymore." Seeley had made the decision while waiting for Carlotta.

Carlotta was shaking her head. "This is too complicated for me."

Seeley noticed that she hadn't touched her wine. "You're wondering, why should you trust me?"

"It doesn't matter whether I trust you. I don't want anything to upset Max. He won't trust you."

"If Max doesn't sign the declaration before these men find him, he's not going to have the chance to decide whether he trusts me or not."

"Max is a sick man, Mr. Seeley. For years, he can't hold down the little he eats for breakfast. The last few months all he spits up is blood. He doesn't know that I know. He tries to hide it from me, but Max was never a tidy man, and I see it when I clean up. But every day Max lives is precious to me, even when he goes off like this."

"Then let me see him. If you want him to live, you need to do this."

"This declaration—you give me your word it will get him the credit he deserves for writing the movie?"

When Seeley nodded, Carlotta pushed the wineglass aside and lifted her purse onto the table.

Seeley said, "Tell Max I want to see him in Munich, not Starnberg."

Carlotta continued searching for something in the purse, whispering to herself, then snapped it shut. "Do you have a pen?" She pushed a napkin toward Seeley. "Write this down." She gave him the name of a café and an address on a side street off Leopoldstrasse in Munich's Schwabing district. "Max will meet you there at 8:30 tonight," she said.

"When did you talk to him?"

"That doesn't matter. Just make sure you are there on time." Her voice slowed. "On the phone, he sounded so weak."

"Are you sure he'll be there?"

"If I tell you Max will be there, he will be there." Her voice softened. "Thank you for what you're doing, Mr. Seeley."

"Where will you go?"

"I have a friend, a dressage student of mine. She lives in Neuhausen, out by Nymphenburg. It's a short ride on the train."

Seeley tried, but could think of no words of comfort that wouldn't sound false. He signaled the waiter and asked him to call a taxi to take Carlotta to the station at Marienplatz.

Carlotta pulled the photo album onto her lap. "Do you remember what Natalia's last line was in *Spykiller*? Just before the American shoots her?"

Seeley remembered, but Carlotta said it before he did.

"I am completely in your hands."

EIGHTEEN

The offices of J. Hanauer and Partners were in Bogenhausen, a leafy district of large villas and broad avenues east of the Isar, an easy walk from the Königshof. The stuccoed villa at 24/26 Maria-Theresia-Strasse was set well back from the street behind an iron fence and a neatly trimmed lawn. A bronze plaque on the gatepost put the Hanauer firm on the first floor. Another law firm occupied the second floor and an architectural firm, the third. Seeley had found the firm in the listings under *Patentanwalt* in the Munich telephone book; he recognized Hanauer's name from the advisory board of an international law journal he occasionally read. For the small service he needed, Professor Dr. Joseph Hanauer would be substantially overqualified.

The receptionist's desk was in what had once been the foyer of the old villa. She told Seeley that Professor Dr. Hanauer was in Frankfurt on business and would not return until Friday.

"Can I see one of the other partners?"

"Dr. Reiman may have time to see you."

"Is he a partner?"

"You wish to speak to a lawyer, yes?" Before he could tell her that Dr. Reiman would be fine, she lifted the receiver and punched in a number.

The man who came into the reception area was too young to be a partner in a German law firm. He was slightly stooped and almost painfully thin, but when he grasped the hand Seeley offered, the grip was muscular and sure. The blue eyes behind the gold-rimmed glasses were lively, even shrewd, and when he read Seeley's business card they showed amusement.

"Avenue of the Americas. Sounds very cosmopolitan."

"That's why New Yorkers call it Sixth Avenue."

"How can we help you?"

Seeley nodded in the direction of the hallway Reiman had come from. "May we?"

"Of course," Reiman said, glancing briefly at the receptionist. "Come with me."

On the way, they passed three offices, all dark behind panes of frosted glass.

"Are you the only lawyer here?"

"How many do you need?" Reiman glanced over his shoulder, the same amusement playing in his eyes. "Not many German lawyers come to the office on Saturday. I'm sure we will be able to help you."

Reiman's office had evidently been the sun parlor when the villa was a private home. The windows looked out onto a small, sequestered garden, and early-autumn light flooded the neat, well-ordered room. The young lawyer was doing well; this was the equivalent of a senior partner's corner office. A single pile of documents was aligned perfectly with the edge of the desk. The only thing out of place was a well-worn University of Michigan sweatshirt hanging off an old-fashioned wooden coat stand.

Seeley said, "I need to have some copyright papers filed. It shouldn't be very complicated."

Reiman made himself comfortable in his chair before responding. "Tell me what this is about."

If the young lawyer's extraordinary self-confidence wasn't genuine, it was an accomplished pose. Seeley remembered how, in his own first years of practice, that mask of assurance had been his constant disguise.

"I have a client in California that would like to arrange for a German domiciliary to execute and record a declaration of authorship. He wrote a movie script many years ago."

How many lies had he just told?

The young lawyer looked up from the pad on which he was making notes. "Is that how they conduct business meetings on the Avenue of the Americas? Standing up? Leaning against a chair?"

Reiman didn't look like much. The attempt at a mustache was a wispy failure, his shirt collar was three sizes too large, his nails were bitten down and the fingers that held an old-fashioned fountain pen were stained with ink. But Seeley was now certain the self-confidence was genuine. He took the chair.

"Does this client have a name and address?"

"You can send the bill to me."

"It is a necessary procedure that we check for conflicts of interest. I'm sure you follow the same procedure in your own office. It will just take a few minutes on the computer. I need to know who our client will be."

Seeley gave him the studio's address in Burbank and told him to send the bill to the attention of the general counsel.

"What do you want us to do?"

Why was it Seeley had the feeling that this *we* and *us* were no more than Reiman and the receptionist in the foyer.

"I'd like you to prepare whatever form you use for a declaration of authorship to be filed in the German Patent Office. After it's signed, you can arrange for the filing."

"Do you also want us to prepare the form for filing in the United States?" When Reiman saw Seeley's surprise, he gestured in the direction of a wall with several framed certificates on it. "I am a member of the Michigan bar. I received my master of laws degree at the University of Michigan."

Reiman's fluent English had impressed Seeley. "How long were you there?"

"Two years. The master's program is one year, but I liked Ann Arbor, so I stayed for a second year as a teaching fellow."

"Why Michigan?"

Seeley would have figured Reiman to be a city dweller, more at home in New York or Boston than in a college town like Ann Arbor.

"The Wolverines," Reiman said. "No other American university with a graduate law program has a football team that comes close to matching the skill of the Wolverines. Wherever you go, the courses and faculty are the same. But the football team—that set Michigan apart. Did you play?"

"In college, sure."

"I thought you did. Quarterback?"

Seeley nodded.

"Big Ten?"

Seeley laughed. "I went to a small Jesuit college in Buffalo, New York. That's the only reason I got to play at all."

"But still, you played."

"Just not very well."

Seeley looked at his watch. The meeting with Kanarek was in four hours. "It will be fine if you prepared the form for the U.S. Copyright Office."

"What is the author's name and his address in Germany?"

"His name is Max Kanarek. Why do you need the address?" Too many people already knew where Kanarek lived.

"I believe it is required for the U.S. filing. But even if it is not, the German regulations require the address to be included in the filing."

"Leave it blank, for the time being," Seeley said. "We can fill it in after Mr. Kanarek signs."

"That will not be possible. The address must be part of the statement he is signing."

Seeley liked Reiman, but the officiousness was beginning to wear on him. "Is Dr. Hanauer still involved with this firm?"

"If you were speaking with Dr. Hanauer now, he would tell you exactly the same. We must have the address."

Seeley noticed that as Reiman became more insistent, the German accent grew more pronounced. He gave him Kanarek's address in Starnberg.

"Will you obtain Mr. Kanarek's signature, or would you like us to?"

Seeley thought, Will you get the signature or shall we? If only it were that simple! If Carlotta was right, there was only the most remote possibility that Kanarek would sign a document that Seeley put in front of him. "I'll take care of it."

"Do you also want us to prepare the form for transferring the rights?"

"That won't be necessary."

Time was running out. All Seeley needed was a declaration. He was thinking about how long it would take the lawyer to prepare the document.

Reiman crossed his arms over his thin chest and studied Seeley, judging him. "If someone requests a declaration of authorship, it is usually because he is arranging for the author to transfer his rights. Why else would you need a declaration?"

"Fine. Go ahead, prepare one."

"That's not what I was thinking about," Reiman said. "Something is not right here. There are facts you are not disclosing to me. Declarations of authorship are always followed by a copyright transfer, yet you don't seem to want a transfer—"

"I already said, prepare a transfer."

"That is not my point. It's *why* you didn't request a transfer that concerns me. Also, why you were so reluctant to give me the declarant's address. If I may be blunt, Mr. Seeley, I believe you are being less than open with me, and that presents a risk for this firm. Unless our clients place their complete confidence in us, we cannot advise them on the legality of their affairs. Without this knowledge, the firm would be exposed to legal sanctions for any possibly unlawful conduct we undertook on your behalf."

"There's nothing unlawful here. All I want is a form. This isn't the Magna Carta."

"I have the impression, Mr. Seeley, that you have never been a client before. It is not always easy being a client. I am sure it is difficult to trust a complete stranger with your confidences. But with us it is a necessity. You are certainly at liberty to ask some other firm to provide you with these forms."

Seeley had already considered and dismissed that alternative. He needed the form tonight and had no reason to think that another lawyer, if he could find one on a Saturday, would be any less intractable than Reiman. Paring down the facts, he told Reiman as little of the story as he thought the young lawyer would accept: that when Max Kanarek lived in California he had written a film script under someone else's name; the film had become the basis for the popular *Spykiller* series; Kanarek was now gravely ill, and it was necessary to see his name restored to the script before he died. Then, deciding this didn't sufficiently convey the declaration's urgency, Seeley said, "There are people here in Munich looking for Kanarek. They don't want him to sign a declaration."

Reiman listened calmly, chin resting on an open hand, not speaking. German lawyers take author's moral rights seriously, including the right to receive credit for their works, and Seeley expected that Reiman would find the story persuasive.

"From what you say, Mr. Kanarek is not the only one who is in danger. Does he have a wife? A family? They are also in danger. You are in some danger yourself."

"And now that I've given you the full disclosure you asked for, you also are at risk."

"I am your lawyer. We only get in trouble when we don't know enough about our clients."

Seeley let the smug reprimand pass. "When can you have the forms ready?"

"This time tomorrow." He gave an embarrassed shrug. "So, you see, I am in the office on Sundays, too. The work never stops."

"I'm meeting with Mr. Kanarek tonight. I need them by seven."

The address in Schwabing that Carlotta had given him was no more than a ten-minute taxi ride from the hotel but unless Reiman was different from every other lawyer Seeley knew, the papers would arrive later than promised.

"You are not our only client, Mr. Seeley."

"They're, what, one-page forms? How long can they take?"

Reiman gestured at the pile of papers on his desk. "These are all regular clients. You just dropped in from out of nowhere, a stranger. What would you do in my place?"

"In your place," Seeley said, "if a fellow lawyer—particularly one from the United States, with control over a substantial amount of foreign copyright and patent work that he can assign as he wishes—if such a lawyer came to me and said the matter was urgent, and that more than just money depended on its prompt resolution, I would drop everything to get the work done."

The amusement returned to Reiman's eyes. "Let us say, Mr. Seeley, the papers will be at your hotel—delivery to the hotel is agreeable, yes?—no later than seven this evening."

NINETEEN

Föhn, the warm dry wind that periodically rolls down the lee-ward slope of the Bavarian Alps, had settled in among Munich's avenues, alleys, parks, and plazas. Unlike its close cousin, the harsh Santa Anas of Southern California whose gales can turn a brush fire into an incinerating tornado, föhn works its havoc insidiously—an indiscernible speck in the eye; a hum felt, but unheard; a mental irritant. In times of föhn, office workers stay home; jewelers leave their shop windows barred; some doctors in Munich hospitals cancel elective surgery while others, over-worked, irritably dismiss the precaution as foolishness.

At the sight of Hersh Landau in the lobby bar of the Königshof, Michael Seeley's insides clenched. As he came closer, he saw that Hersh did not look well. His cheeks, closely shaved, were pale and drawn and had a bluish cast. His hair was slicked back as if he had just come from the shower. The deep-set eyes were uneasy. Seeley lifted Hersh's folded Burberry from the empty chair and handed it across the table. Hersh balanced the garment as if to weigh it before tossing it onto a neighboring table.

"Let me guess," Seeley said. "You and your fraternity brothers are here to raise hell at Oktoberfest."

"I just spent thirty hours in airplanes and Red Carpet Clubs eating stale pretzels. You screwed up and so did Bermann. I told him we shouldn't hire you, but no, he said, you were the right man. It's what I told you in my office: Bermann makes a mess and I get to clean it up. You wouldn't sign the E&O opinion. You scared Cobb off."

"But I didn't kill him."

Hersh gave him a mild stare. "An intruder killed him. You should believe what you read in the newspaper." He stubbed out the cigarette burning in the ashtray. "You watch too many movies. People die in accidents all the time. Burglaries. It's too bad about the old guy, but he was . . . an old guy. The police said he fought back. If he was smart, he wouldn't have done that."

Hersh's hand moved across the table. Reflexively, Seeley drew back from his touch—instinct, not reason, told him this man was responsible for Bert Cobb's death—but he had only been reaching for the crumpled cigarette package that lay on the table between them. He shook out a cigarette and took his time lighting it from a slender gold lighter, making a show of how calm he was.

Seeley said, "What are you doing in Munich?"

"I told you. Cleaning up the mess you made. Nobody knew anything about Max Kanarek until you started poking around. Everyone thought Bert Cobb wrote *Spykiller*. For all I know he *did* write it. But now we have to find this guy Kanarek. If you're smart, you'll help us."

We. Us. The men looking for Kanarek in Starnberg.

"Why would I want to help you?"

"You're still our lawyer."

Two well-dressed women laden with shopping bags settled at a table next to them, and Hersh lowered his voice. "We're paying for your time."

"I get to decide whether I'm working for you."

"Working for United? Or for Mayer Bermann?"

When Seeley didn't answer, Hersh said, "You know, you're really not as smart as everyone says you are. You don't have a clue why Bermann sent you here."

Mayer Bermann had humiliated Hersh in his office and Seeley, against his will, had witnessed it. For that, it was now Hersh's turn to humble him. Seeley shifted in his chair; he was having a hard time getting comfortable. Hersh was right. He had no idea why Mayer Bermann should want Max Kanarek to sign a declaration but not a transfer of ownership.

"Why don't you tell me?"

Hersh said, "I don't know what went on between the two of you. But I do know Bermann's not paying you to get Kanarek to sign over his rights to *Spykiller*."

"Why wouldn't Bermann want the rights?"

"If he wanted the studio to own *Spykiller*, don't you think he would have gone out and talked to Bert Cobb? If he wanted the rights from Max Kanarek, don't you think he'd have told me or Phil Mendelson where to find him? I had to track you down through the studio's travel office. It's real simple, Mr. Seeley, and you're the only one who hasn't figured it out. Mayer Bermann doesn't want the rights because he doesn't want *Spykiller* to get made. Not this sequel, not any in the future."

"That's crazy. Why would the chairman of a studio want to shut down its biggest franchise?"

Hersh's long fingers toyed with the tableware, pulled the

salt and pepper shakers across the cloth, arranging and rearranging them as if to make a point. Black against White. Yin against Yang. Us against Them.

"Mayer Bermann wants to gut the studio. He wants to shut down *Spykiller* so he can buy the studio back from Beau Callaway for next to nothing. Five cents on the dollar, just like when he was buying movie theaters in New York."

"That's what it would be worth. Nothing. He'd have to be crazy to do that."

"United Pictures is Mayer Bermann's whole life. If he had to throw his daughter in front of a train to get the studio back, he'd do it."

Bermann's daughter; Hersh's wife. The violence of the image told him something about Hersh that he had blindly ignored from the start. His mistake—how many others had he made?—was to assume that Hersh's complaints about Bermann were the resentments of an embittered underling, yet one who had no choice, ultimately, other than to be loyal to the man who had hired him. But Hersh had made his deal with Beau Callaway: get *Spykiller* made and the studio was his to run. The flight from Los Angeles took thirty hours because he had stopped in New York to meet with Callaway. It was Hersh, not Bermann, who wanted control of the studio.

A good way to entrap a witness into telling the truth, Seeley knew, was to play to his pride. "And you think you can turn this around, that you can stop the man who runs the studio."

"I already run the studio," Hersh said. "Bermann hasn't had any real power for years. Most of his time he spends with his foxhunts and his charities and his English girlfriend."

"Which one of you gets to green-light a project?"

"You don't know anything about the industry if you think that's where the power is. No project gets to Bermann without going through me. He doesn't get to approve anything unless I approve it first. It's that way for the theme parks, too. The merchandising deals. I'm the one who decides what he gets to look at."

Across the lobby at the concierge desk, Schreiner was writing in an oversize ledger. Outside, just visible through the gauze curtains, a single automobile rumbled along the cobblestone street. The very banality of the scene made Seeley wonder whether he was embarking on another of his grand mistakes.

"So you're a high-priced secretary. You handle his appointments. Who handles operations? Who actually runs the studio?"

Hersh pulled on his cigarette, the tired, undervalued executive.

"I'd have more time to run the studio if I didn't have to fly around the world putting out the fires he starts. No one is in charge of operations but me."

"When the Supreme Court took away half of your film library, who arranged for the writers to sign back their rights to the studio?"

"I did. Bermann didn't have a clue how to deal with it. The lawyers handled the details. Phil Mendelson's people. I made the executive decisions."

"But you were busy running the studio—you had all these distractions—so it took you some time."

"I had the lawyers out on the street getting assignments of rights the day after the Supreme Court decided the case. I figured that if we gave them any time to think about it, the writers would hire lawyers and it would get a lot more expensive for us."

"You did that with Bert Cobb? You went right after him?"

"You know that. You talked to him."

"And Mrs. Cobb?"

"Sure. Her, too. Husbands and wives, everybody got treated the same, give or take a week or two."

"And both of them signed?"

Color crept into Hersh's face in angry red splotches and his voice rose. "Of course Cobb didn't sign. You know that."

"I meant his wife."

"She signed."

"Right away?"

A frightened boy caught in a lie peered out from Hersh's eyes. "Why wouldn't she?"

"I'm asking because her assignment is dated just one week ago."

Hersh hadn't expected him to know when Verna Cobb signed over her rights.

Hersh said, "Maybe she was like her husband and held out. I don't know. Our people went out to see her the same time they saw all the others, right after the Court's decision came down."

"That's quite a coincidence, wouldn't you say? She signs over her rights and three days later, her husband is murdered."

"I told you in my office, that's Bermann's way of doing business, not mine."

"But you just told me that Bermann doesn't want the studio to get the rights to *Spykiller*. He'd push his daughter—your wife—in front of a train to stop that from happening. If you're right about that, I'd think Bermann would do everything he could to keep Bert Cobb alive, so his wife would have no rights to sign over. Do you think maybe you're wrong about Bermann wanting to destroy the studio?"

Hersh's hands, finally, went still. "You don't know what—"

Seeley ignored him. "No, I figure you're the only one at the studio with an interest in seeing Bert Cobb dead. When he wouldn't sign over the rights, and I wouldn't sign your opinion, getting his wife to sign and then murdering him was the only way you could get your E&O policy."

The color had left Hersh's face, and the hands were in motion again, the gold cigarette lighter sliding over and through his long fingers like a magician's coin trick.

"Why would that be in my interest?" The question was halfhearted. He knew that Seeley knew.

"Because you made your deal with Beau Callaway. Get *Spykiller* back on track and you're the studio's new chairman. That's why, when I saw you in your office, you told me to go home. It's why you said you didn't need the opinion letter or Bert Cobb's signature. You had just gotten the assignment from his wife and all that was left was for her husband to die."

As Seeley thought about it, the fact stunned him that he was sitting across from a murderer, talking about his crime as easily as the two women at the next table were chattering about the collected treasures of their shopping expedition. No sane man, if you gave him a moral calculus, would tell you it was possible to compare Hersh's crime with Mayer Bermann's Machiavellian scheming. Why was it, then, that as much as it revolted Seeley to look at Hersh, it was the machinations of Mayer Bermann, manipulating him from six thousand miles away, that pricked like a needle at his every nerve?

"You're overlooking the most obvious point, counselor."

Seeley waited.

"Why I'm here. If Max Kanarek really wrote the script, we need him to sign over the rights."

Seeley remembered the moment in Mayer Bermann's office when, choosing sides between Hersh and Bermann, he decided to go along with Bermann in keeping Max Kanarek's authorship from Hersh. If he had spoken then, Hersh would have called off the attack on Bert Cobb and would instead have come to Munich to get Kanarek to sign over the rights. Having made one self-assured but deadly error, was he now making another by not telling Hersh where he could find Kanarek? By such murderous increments, Seeley thought, does my own guilt grow.

"Those were your men who were looking for Kanarek."

"Looking where?"

"One of them smells like a spice chest. Swimming in aftershave."

"We can't get Kanarek to sign an assignment if we don't know where he is. You could help us with that."

"Where's the form you're going to use for the assignment?"

"Why—you mean, now?"

"You'd think someone who flew all this way to get an author to sign over his rights would bring a piece of paper for the man to sign."

"Mendelson's people are reviewing it. They'll fax it to me when they're finished."

Even for Hersh, that was weak. It took a simple two-page form to accomplish a transfer of rights. The studio stocked the forms by the ream. Seeley had taken one with him on his trip to Pacoima to see Bert Cobb. Jack Elm had brought one for Verna Cobb to sign. No lawyer needed to review the form.

"Do yourself a favor, Mr. Seeley, and stick to your side of the street."

"Am I supposed to interpret that as a threat?"

"I don't make threats. I issue orders."

"I'm wondering. When you practice that line, do you look at yourself in the mirror? Or do you do it blind?"

It was less than three hours until Seeley's meeting with Max Kanarek. For all Seeley knew, Hersh's men had already found him.

"You know," Hersh said, "you're a hard guy to get traction on. Your wife's kicked you out. From what your partners tell us, your law practice is falling apart. You're about to get disbarred."

Seeley rose. "I guess some of us are just born under a lucky star."

It was 5:45 p.m. in Munich, which meant it was 8:45 a.m. in California and 11:45 a.m. in New York. He had two calls to make.

When Hersh put a hand on his arm, Seeley shrugged him away. Maybe it was the föhn, but he'd had enough of Hersh Landau. He'd had enough of himself, too.

TWENTY

Girard answered the telephone on the first ring, before his secretary could pick it up. "I thought you would call. What's up?"

"What do you know about Beau Callaway?"

"Nothing," Girard said. "He's Daphne's client."

"That makes you the only lawyer at the firm who's not working for him."

"I'm doing the corporate work on an acquisition in San Diego. A television station. But I've never met the man."

"Who's arranging the FCC approvals?"

"The D.C. office."

"Doesn't the FCC do background checks on broadcast licensees?"

"I'm sure he came up clean. He's been buying stations for years. You don't really think he has something to hide? What are you doing in Germany?"

"Who told you I'm here?"

Seeley knew Nick Girard as well as he knew anyone, and through four thousand miles of telephone line he could hear the ticking of his friend's brain.

"Daphne doesn't seem pleased that you're there. What kind of trouble are you in?"

"Not as bad as the trouble the firm will be in if you don't drop Intermedia as a client."

"They do all their deals here. They can't drop us and stay in business."

Girard hadn't heard what he'd said. "Did Daphne tell you how United got a guy's wife to transfer her rights to them, and three days later the husband's dead?"

"I'm sure there's an explanation."

"I just got off the phone with the widow. According to her, United's president lied when he told me they talked to her about signing over the rights five months ago. The first time she saw anyone from the studio was three days before her husband died."

There was a long pause. Girard had become thoughtful over the past month.

"I'm still the best friend you have, Mike, so I can tell you this. When you go charging off on your white horse, you don't always pay attention to the consequences. You leave a lot of pain behind you. And it's not just me who thinks that. Maisie says so, too."

Girard's mention of his wife was to let Seeley know that the reproach encompassed his treatment of Clare.

"I wasn't looking for your approval," Seeley said. "I thought you would be interested in protecting the firm."

"Everyone's fine here. It sounds to me like you're the one who's in a fix. Stick with your friends, Mike. You know, this disbarment proceeding isn't going to go away unless the firm lines up behind you."

Evidently Mayer Bermann and Harry Devlin didn't have a monopoly on blackmail and extortion. The invisible barrier that had always separated him from Girard was acquiring depth and dimension.

"You know," Seeley said, "I never understood why you left Buffalo."

"I told you—"

"Sure, I know—the four generations of Girards, a dying city. But of all the law firms you could have gone to, why did you pick mine?"

There was another of Girard's new, thoughtful pauses.

"I admired you, Mike. Hell, I still do. You're someone who shakes things up. I'm not. I liked being where you were."

In the twenty years Seeley had known him, he had not once heard Girard talk like this.

"But this time you've gone way over the line. If you want the partners to support you, you've got to pull back."

"What kind of deal did you make with Daphne?" When Girard didn't answer, Seeley said, "You're going to be the next head of corporate, aren't you?"

"Bill Kellerman was just nominated for the SEC. It's a big win for the firm. I'm next in line."

Girard wasn't next in line. Daphne was promoting him over at least three other corporate partners with more seniority and higher billings.

"Well," Seeley said, "congratulations."

"You know, Mike, you don't leave people much room to be human." There was a brittleness Seeley hadn't heard in Girard's voice before. He had changed.

"Are you still cutting down on your drinks?"

"I quit."

"That's typical, isn't it? You always have to overdo it. Either you drink too much or you don't drink at all. Come back to New York, Mike. There's nothing for you in Germany."

"What's there for me in New York?"

This time the silence was shorter. "Take care of yourself, my friend."

The patronizing "my friend" confirmed what Seeley already knew: he had lost the one friend he thought he had.

Seeley knew how deceptive legal papers can be. Ponzi schemes, stock frauds, cooked-up escrows, wire transfers to countries without extradition treaties—every one of these scams has the look of biblical truth, yet every one of them is constructed out of nothing more than paper. In the past month he had been asked to sign a fraudulent legal opinion, had himself unwittingly tried to persuade Bert Cobb to sign over rights he didn't own, and was now waiting on yet another piece of paper, this one for a dying man to sign to save his wife's life and what was left of his own.

When Seeley came into the lobby, the night concierge told him no papers had arrived for him. By eight o'clock, he knew he had misjudged the self-assured young lawyer. Three telephone calls to Reiman's office got only an answering machine. As he went through the revolving doors, heading for the taxi stand, Seeley caught a reflection in the glass of the flying, outsized trench coat that hung in the center of the lobby. He had the feeling that it was mocking him.

The moment Seeley walked through the gates on Maria-Theresia-Strasse he knew something was wrong. The villa's grand double doors, closed and locked on his first visit, were flung open. When he entered, moonlight illuminated the vestibule. The receptionist's desk was bare, her chair pulled snugly up against it. There was no sign of life. Then, from the end of the dark hallway where Reiman's office was, came the sound of heavy objects crashing against a wall, followed by scuffling and a harsh, unfamiliar voice. "*Wo ister?*"

Seeley raced down the corridor to the brightly lit office. An acrid scent, rank and viscous like old engine grease, met him at the threshold. The office was a disaster. The coat stand with the Michigan sweatshirt was on the floor. Drawers hung from Reiman's desk like turned-out trouser pockets. Papers lay in pools on the floor. Reiman's framed admission to the Michigan bar, its glass shattered, lay next to an overturned wastebasket.

In the center of the room, his face creased with pain, Reiman was swinging above the floor, feet flailing. A tall, muscular man was holding him by his belt, and with his other hand had twisted Reiman's arm up behind him, so high that the lawyer's frantically grasping fingers rose above his shoulder. Reiman's eyes were resolute, his jaw clamped. "*Wo ister?*" the man barked at him, swinging Reiman back and forth, his lank hair brushing the lawyer's cheek. Where is he?

Across the room, the back of a familiar brown windbreaker hunched over a file cabinet, its drawers hanging off their runners. The boxer was pulling file folders out of the drawers, frantically searching their contents before throwing them aside.

Reiman's eyes found Seeley. Neither intruder, busy at his work, had yet seen him. Seeley put a finger to his lips. He knelt and lifted the coat rack, grasping the top of the heavy post with both hands so that he held it as he would a baseball bat. The length gave him heft and momentum, the four wooden feet still more heft. Seeley's eyes fixed on the base of the tall man's spine. He swung the cudgel back, then with all his strength propelled it forward, willing it to strike at its target. There was a grunt of surprise, then pain, followed by a release of body odor—the stench of old engine oil that hung over the room intensified—as the man collapsed to the floor, taking Reiman down with him.

The boxer turned from the file cabinet and quickly took in what had happened. There was no surprise in his reaction; he could have been waiting for Seeley.

"You should have gone home," he said. "Like I told you."

Seeley charged at the man, holding the stout post before him like a battering ram. Even as he did, he saw his mistake. The boxer deftly grabbed two of the wooden feet—he could have been a juggler catching ten pins—and twisted them until he had wrenched the post from Seeley's grip. Looking first at Reiman, who was still on the floor but had separated himself from his attacker, and then at Seeley, the boxer edged to the French doors, opened one, and tossed the post into the garden as easily as if it were a javelin.

Seeley searched the room for a weapon, or even a shield, but found none. The boxer came toward him, disgust mixing with the sweat that poured down his face. The sharp fragrance of his aftershave mixed with the other, sour odor in the room.

"Like in LA, you really want to hurt, don't you?"

The tall man was still on the floor, motionless. Reiman had raised himself to a crouch, and Seeley watched him move toward the boxer's back.

Seeley shook his head. The gesture was not for the boxer, but to warn off Reiman.

"I've always been a slow learner."

Reiman pounced, leaping onto the man's back, clawing at his throat, slippery with sweat. Triumph crossed the young lawyer's face. The boxer shrugged and, reaching behind him with one hand, lifted Reiman off. His eyes still fixed on Seeley, he hurled Reiman against the wall.

Seeley had backed himself against the desk. It was already past 8:30, and if Carlotta was right about her husband, he wouldn't wait. Seeley's only chance of meeting Kanarek lay somewhere between him and the man in the brown leather jacket. He could, if he moved quickly, make it to the French doors and out to the garden, but that would leave Reiman, who was in no condition to escape. Seeley realized that even if he left, he might succeed only in leading the boxer to Kanarek. Whatever happened next, he could waste no more time.

He felt behind him on the desk for a scissors or a letter opener, anything that would serve as a weapon, but the only solid object his fingers found was a squat, glass container. Reiman's ink bottle. The boxer's eyes remained fixed on Seeley's. From the groans close by and the stench wafting up to him, Seeley sensed that the other man had begun to move. Seeley palmed the ink bottle out of the man's sight.

"You have to wonder what's wrong with someone," Seeley said, "that he has to pour on so much aftershave." As Seeley spoke, he twisted the cap off the ink bottle, uttered a quick, silent, prayer—thank God for Reiman's fastidious habits, the bottle was large and filled to the top—and when the boxer took another step forward, Seeley hurled the black liquid directly at his eyes.

The boxer staggered. Seeley threw a fist, then another, into the man. A jagged bolt of pain shot up his arm as if he had punched a stone wall.

The tall man was on his feet, but bent over. Seeley wondered what damage the blow had done to his spine. Nick Girard was right. Michael Seeley inflicted pain wherever he went. His partners. His own wife. But sometimes, like now, it felt entirely right.

The boxer tripped over a file drawer, then quickly righted himself, rubbing his eyes with the balls of his hands. The tall man came up beside him, steadying him with a hand on the collar of his jacket. For an odd moment, they presented the picture of an old-time organ-grinder and his chimp on a leash. Reiman had the telephone in his hands; he was speaking into it, giving the office address.

The tall man saw what Reiman was doing, started to move toward him, then stopped and turned. He thrust his free hand, open-palmed, at Seeley, not to strike him, but to protect his exit. "*Raus!*" he shouted at the boxer, the man's collar still gripped in his hand. "Get out!"

Seeley started toward the men. The police would come and Seeley could leave and find Kanarek himself. "No," Reiman cried out. "Let them go." When Seeley continued toward them, he said, "For God's sake, let them go!"

In the next moment, the two men, the tall one still hunched, but guiding the other, were out the French doors into the garden.

Seeley's heart pounded. "I could have held them long enough for the police to come."

"There was no call." He showed Seeley that he had depressed the receiver hook. "You don't want the police here."

"But—"

"You know nothing about the police in Germany. They would demand to know about our business together. I would tell them nothing. But I would have to identify you as my client. You would be detained until you explained what this was about. This would take hours. You have an important meeting. Already you are late."

"What were they after?"

"They wanted to know what work I was doing for you." Reiman stopped to consider. "They knew I was working on something to do with this Max Kanarek. Was I in contact with Kanarek, they wanted to know. Was I preparing a legal instrument for him? They asked me where he lives."

Reiman's breathing had become more even, but his effort to speak without moving his injured mouth gave his voice a strangled quality, like a vaudevillian's imitation of a German accent.

Seeley could not have objected if Reiman had saved himself a beating by handing over Kanarek's address. "What did you tell them?"

"I told them nothing. It would not have been professional." Reiman rose carefully from the chair. "But we are wasting time. You have your meeting."

A breeze rushed into the room through the French doors. Seeley stepped over the threshold into the garden. The men were gone. The flowers exhaled a rich perfume, but Seeley recognized none of the mingling fragrances. It seemed a lifetime ago that he had stood in the perfumed air at the edge of Mayer Bermann's driveway, looking out at the lights below.

Seeley went back into the office. Reiman was entering commands at his keyboard. It was after 9:00, well past the time set for the meeting with Kanarek. Seeley lifted a Munich telephone directory from the floor—the rust-colored smudge on the cover might have been blood—and found the number for Julia's hotel. If Kanarek was no longer at the café in Schwabing where Carlotta said he would be, and Seeley had to search for him, he wasn't going to recognize him from photographs taken more than fifty years ago. He would need help. When Julia came on the line, he told her what had happened and asked her to meet him outside the café. Then he called a taxi for himself.

Reiman removed two sheets from the printer tray, evened them on the desktop, and handed them to Seeley. "The declaration. One for the German Patent Office and one for the U.S. Copyright Office."

Seeley said, "Are you all right?"

"Go," Reiman said. "You are already late. Go!"

TWENTY-ONE

Munich's Schwabing neighborhood was barely a ten-minute taxi ride from the dark, empty streets of Bogenhausen where Reiman's office was, but its noise, neon, and crowded sidewalk cafés could have placed it in a different city entirely. Only three close stops on the U-Bahn—Odeonsplatz, Universität, Gisela-strasse—separated Schwabing from the center of the old city where Seeley's hotel was. The tourist guidebooks called it the city's Bohemian, or arts, quarter, but in fact few artists had worked or lived in the district since its heyday in the 1920s, and the street vendors who tacked up their oils, pastels, and photographs on the weekends came from neighborhoods farther out from the city center, where the rents were lower.

Julia was waiting for Seeley outside the café. "Kanarek isn't here. The bartender said he and his friends left half an hour ago."

"Did he know where they went?"

"He said they usually don't go far. They might come back later."

"We can't wait. There are too many people looking for him, and I don't want to be the last one to find him."

Seeley wasn't a bar drinker—he did most of his drinking alone, at home, in the office, or in hotel rooms—and over the next hour he found himself in more bars than he'd been to in the last ten years. A few of the places were vast drinking halls with tables overflowing onto the sidewalk. Others were hardly more than a cramped corridor. The walls breathed alcohol: yeasty Pilsners, the decaying leafy fragrance of pale ale, spicy Rhine wines, oaty Weisbier just coming into season. Beneath the malty offerings *vom Fass*, and pulling like an undertow, were the spirits—Cognacs and Armagnacs that made Seeley's eyes water, peaty scotches, bracing dollops of gin. In his mind Seeley could taste every one of them.

They found Kanarek and his friends in a tavern at the edge of Schwabing, close to Universität. The front rooms were filled with students, smoking, drinking, and talking over the noise of the jukebox and coin-fed video games, but as Seeley and Julia moved farther into the place through a jumble of smoky alcoves, the din subsided and the patrons were mostly men in the dark clothes of office workers, unseasonable woolens, sodden browns and grays.

Julia put a hand on Seeley's arm. "That's him."

Although the light in the room was dim, Max Kanarek threw off an energy that seemed to illuminate him. His arm was draped over a companion's shoulder with the same easy grandeur as in the long-ago photograph of him and Mayer Bermann. Animatedly lecturing his tablemates, one foot planted on the floor, the other on a chair, Kanarek could have been poolside at the Beverly Hills Hotel. He had on a multicolored, carnival-striped shirt and wore his trousers low on the hips, cinched tight with a braided leather belt. The white loafers had gold buckles.

Julia said, "I'll wait for you at the bar."

"I thought you wanted to talk to him."

"No, it's your turn."

"Are you sure?"

She thought for a moment, then nodded, giving him the smile he hadn't seen since Los Angeles.

Kanarek turned at Seeley's approach. When Seeley offered his hand, it appeared for an instant that Kanarek was going to lose his balance, but he brushed aside his companion's effort to steady him and, in the same movement, gave Seeley a soft, spongy hand. He was over six feet, as tall as Seeley, but he held himself with a stoop, as if the ceiling were too low for him.

"Here's the great lawyer! He can't even get to a meeting on time!"

One or two of the men moved to make room for Seeley at the table, but Kanarek pulled him away. He was still shaky and used the arm he had thrown heavily across Seeley's shoulder as much to support himself as to guide them to an empty table in the corner. He kept his eyes on Seeley the whole way. This was a man, Seeley thought, who would stride toward a precipice, eyes fixed on the void, knowing that to look down would make him appear weak.

Kanarek took a seat at the table and immediately threw both hands into the air. "Schmidt!" Three times he hoarsely cried out the name, stopping only when the waiter arrived.

"Zwei Kirschwasser. Doppel."

Finally able to study Kanarek from across the table, Seeley saw that the man had chosen his costume to disguise a profound illness. In the low light of the tavern, Seeley's first impression had been that Kanarek's face, though cross-hatched and seamed, was deeply tanned. But there was no pinkness beneath the glow, only a sallow bronze, the waxy yellow of jaundice. The rosiness Seeley had mistaken for a healthy flush came from the red blotches that rose high on his cheeks and spiderwebbed across his nose. Beneath the man's long, shrunken chest, a huge

belly protruded, so obscenely out of proportion that it belonged on a different frame. But it was Kanarek's eyes that ar-
rested Seeley. Of an indeterminate color, they were stained by
the same yellowing pigment as his complexion. Though cun-
ning, the eyes offered an astonishingly unguarded admission
into the depth, the very bottom of his disease.

The waiter set two tumblers before them. Seeley had tasted
the clear cherry brandy once and, apart from the fact that it was
alcohol, hadn't cared for it.

"As I get older, I find myself enjoying these fruity drinks.
Do you care for sweet drinks, Mr. . . . ah . . ." Kanarek was trying to distract him from what was happening on the table. With
the knuckles of one hand, he was edging the glass into the waiting, half-open grip of the other. Still using his knuckles to hold
the glass steady in the trembling claw, he lifted the glass in Seeley's direction. "Prosit!"

Seeley hadn't anticipated the alcohol fumes coming off the
liquor in fat layers. "Prosit." He lifted his glass in reply and,
with an effort, returned it to the table.

Kanarek was momentarily disconcerted by Seeley's failure
to drink the brandy, but took his own down in two long gulps.

"How do you like Carlotta?"

Seeley wasn't certain what he meant. "She's fine."

"Just *fine*?" Kanarek shook his head. "You're lying. You saw
the movie, didn't you?"

"*Spykiller*? Sure."

"Any man who sees that movie falls in love with her."

"Maybe with the character, but not the actress."

"No," Kanarek said. "In this case it's the same. She's taken
a liking to you, you know. Carlotta." The voice was edgy, and
the smile was tentative, taunting in a way that Seeley suspected
could in an instant turn violent. "I bet a sport like you is a real
winner with the ladies."

Seeley said nothing and tried to keep the man's eyes fixed to his own.

"Well, let me tell you, you don't know the first—" The yellow face turned red, inflated like a child's balloon, looked like it would explode in the paroxysm of coughing that overcame the man. The large head went back and fists drummed the table. Kanarek's torso writhed as if some frantic creature inside was fighting to escape. Then, as quickly as it came on, the seizure ended and Kanarek lifted Seeley's glass, finishing it off in a swallow. Seeley had the odd sensation that the scorching liquid was pouring down his own throat, the quick thrill of it racing into his blood.

Seeley said, "Do you know why I'm here?"

"Carlotta told me. You want me to sign a piece of paper that says I wrote *Spykiller*. But I'll tell you right off, you're wasting your time. Mine, too."

"Do you remember Bert Cobb?"

"Why would I need to sign a piece of paper? *I* know I wrote the damn movie. Cobb? Sure. Strange little fellow. Black fingernails."

"He's dead."

"Carlotta said that. People die." Abruptly, his arms thrust upward. "Schmidt!"

"The police say he surprised a burglar."

"Hah!" Kanarek gave no content to the exclamation. He could have been agreeing with the police version or dismissing it.

The waiter came and took an order for two more tumblers of brandy.

"But you think he was murdered. A real California murder mystery. Carlotta told me everything you told her. But you're right about one thing. If this fellow—"

"Bert Cobb."

"If he's dead, Mayer Bermann's somewhere behind the curtains, pulling levers."

Seeley hadn't told Carlotta that Bermann was responsible, only that the studio was involved. The leap in logic was Kanarek's or hers. Kanarek's, he decided.

"Mayer Bermann's not why I'm here."

"Of course he is! You're his lawyer. You're here to cover up for him with some piece of paper you think you're going to get me to sign."

Kanarek lowered his head to just inches above the table and, with lips that puckered like a baby's eager to nurse, sipped at one of the two glasses the waiter had brought. When he finished, he leaned back and rested his arms along the chairs on either side.

"I can tell you things about your client that would make you piss your pants."

Seeley had met men like Kanarek before, starting with his own father. Like any mean and stupid drunk, Kanarek wanted Seeley to correct him; it was a setup so he could freely lash out at him.

"Carlotta said you grew up together in Poland. She showed me pictures."

"Carlotta talks too much. She's always looking at old pictures of me because she can't stand to look at me the way I am now. You don't want to know about Poland. You wouldn't believe it anyway."

"You let Mayer Bermann bring you to America."

"Do you know what people in those villages would do if they thought it would get them to America? Do you have any idea what you would have done, Mr. Lawyer?"

Mud, Seeley thought. *Mud and barbed wire*. Could this be why his father had left his small town—not to escape the Nazi hunters, but simply to try for a better life? That Lothar Seelig had been miserable in America didn't mean he was any less so in Germany.

"I had no parents, no family, except an uncle who was of no use to me. But once I got to America I had nothing to do with Mayer Bermann. I made my own way. I paid him back for everything, even if he tells you I didn't."

"He bought your script when no one else would."

Kanarek massaged one half-clenched hand with the other, as if he were washing them under a faucet. "That shows how much you know. It was Mayer Bermann who sold me out to the investigators. You didn't know that, did you? The girl didn't tell you. She's a cute little trick. She's your girlfriend, isn't she?"

Kanarek's smile was the wretched grimace of a man who had forgotten how to smile, lopsided teeth hanging out of a crocodile jaw, looking sadder, more vulnerable than he would ever want to know.

"That's the kind of favor Mayer Bermann does: first, he destroys you and takes everything you own, then he gives you a blanket and a plate of soup and demands your gratitude. That's how he got the script from me. He got me blacklisted, and then he does me a favor by making a movie from my work."

"But you let him make it."

"You lawyers can't understand that, can you? When you go back to your fancy house—where do you live, Bel Air? Brentwood?—you ask your taxi driver if he's got a screenplay folded up there under his window visor. They all do. You ask him what he would do to get that script made into a movie. Ask him if there's anything he *wouldn't* do to get it made. Listen to what he tells you. Murder is nothing to a writer." He stopped to sip at the glass. "But you're right about one thing. It was my mistake. I should never have let him take my script. What good did it do me to have that movie made?"

"You took his money."

"He took my art. The great Mayer Bermann. Did he tell you how he was the only one who stood up to the committee?"

"I heard the story."

"Well, you listen to me. He was under their thumb. Not just about the blacklist. The committee controlled the movie, too. Did you read my script?"

Seeley had looked at the studio's copy of the script, but solely to confirm that Bert Cobb's name was on it as the author.

"No."

"Then you don't know who the double-crosser really was. How I wrote the story. It wasn't Natalia, the Russian, who was going to betray the American. It was the Brit. The English spy. He was a treacherous bastard. But, no, the lawyers for the committee told Bermann, 'The British are our friends. The villain has to be the Russian.' So Bermann changed the ending. He turned my story upside down, completely changed its meaning. The single point of my script was that it is our friends who betray us, not our enemies."

That, Seeley now realized, was why the movie had seemed so off balance to him, truncated.

Kanarek threw back the remaining brandy in his glass. "Now you come here and tell me I'm supposed to forgive this man and sign this piece of paper for him. So, you tell me, why is it so important that my name be on my work?"

"It's the only way the public knows whether to trust a work: if the author puts his name on it." Seeley didn't believe that any more than Kanarek did.

"The public? So they can whisper behind my back, 'There goes the great writer, Max Kanarek?' Do you know how many novels I've written since I left California? Novels—not screenplays, not stories—finished novels, polished so they shone. Thick ones. Not *War and Peace*, but major works. This is hard work, not like writing arguments or contracts or whatever it is you lawyers do. I put in four, five hours a day on them and at the end of it I'm exhausted. Eight full-length novels. I'm working on number nine right now. That's an honorable life's work."

"But you don't publish them."

"Why should I? I already told you, I'm a writer. I'm not a publisher. I know what I wrote. Why should I care what the public thinks of my work?"

The old drunk's diatribe was getting them nowhere.

Seeley said, "The truth is, you're a coward. If you weren't a coward you would have claimed authorship of your script years ago. You would have published these books. You would have put your name on what you believed in. You're vain, you're selfish, and you're full of fear."

Kanarek brushed the table, as if chasing off a fly. "Carlotta said you were a prickly type."

"Have you even thought about Carlotta?"

"How's that?"

"What it would mean to her if you took credit for the movie."

Kanarek made a dismissive gesture with his hand.

"Did she tell you two men were looking for you in Starnberg? These are the people who killed Bert Cobb."

"And you're saying they want to kill me?"

"I don't care about you. You're going to die on your own, soon enough. It's Carlotta I'm worried about."

That stopped Kanarek. For the first time, Seeley thought he saw a shiver of human emotion behind the yellow eyes.

"You know, you're not all that bad." The crocodile grin transformed his face once again. "I could get to like sparring with you."

Seeley noticed that the men from Kanarek's table were watching them.

"If you sign a declaration stating that you wrote the script, and if I can get it recorded in time, that will be enough to keep Carlotta alive. Once you're on record as the author, there won't be any profit for these people to get rid of you. You'll own the rights. Carlotta will own them when you die. She'll get to decide if she wants to sell them and who she sells them to."

The hideous smile folded back into Kanarek's face and the dark expression returned. It made Seeley aware of the gray, heavy figures moving about in the room.

"Why should I trust you? You work for Bermann."

Bert Cobb had said the same thing. "I don't work for Bermann. Or the studio. I don't have a client anymore."

"And you're doing this out of the goodness of your heart."

"I'm not asking you to trust me."

From inside his jacket, Seeley removed the documents Reiman had given him. "Show this to your own lawyer. Tell him to call me if he wants."

Kanarek looked at the piece of paper. "You're not having your . . ." Embarrassment flooded the man's face, and he looked down and then at Seeley.

Seeley waited while Kanarek fumbled for the word, until he saw there was no chance he was going to retrieve it. This was what Julia had told him about, the man's inability to remember the simplest words.

"Drink?"

Kanarek said, "I don't drink alone."

Seeley studied the full tumbler in front of him and thought how his life might change if he took just this one drink. Hadn't Harry Devlin told him that this is what the trip to Munich would come to? Don't go chasing after Max Kanarek, Devlin said. If you find him, or if you don't; if you get him to sign your piece of paper or if you don't; one way or another, you're going to end up drinking, and this time you may not be lucky enough to stop. You'll end up dead like the lawyer who thought he had escaped from living under the bridge.

"No, thanks."

Kanarek continued staring at him. The jaundiced eyes that had for the briefest moment revealed his love for Carlotta, now reflected nothing at all. This was a jackal waiting for its prey to move.

"A sport like you, all dressed up in a coat and tie. I bet you can't hold your liquor. Before I talk about signing your papers, you have to have a drink with me."

"I don't drink." Seeley had never said that to anyone before.

"Everyone drinks!"

One sip, Seeley thought. I can handle it. This is just dumb pride, my perfect pride at not taking a drink.

"In my whole life, I never drank alone," Kanarek said. "Only drunks drink alone, and I'm too old to go down that road now."

Observing the insanity of Kanarek's behavior, Seeley couldn't help but think of his own. Why wasn't it the tragedies, like Bert Cobb's death, that he drank over, but instead the petty insults, like Clare's sad words or Max Kanarek's pathetic taunts? Max Kanarek wasn't going to goad him into taking a drink. The man's signature on a declaration wasn't worth it. Nothing was.

"A big fellow like you. I bet you're afraid of what a little glass of alcohol will do to you."

"Afraid?" Seeley said. "I'm terrified! If I drink that, I'm not going to stop drinking until I'm dead."

A glint of emotion—triumph? fear? yearning?—passed behind Kanarek's clotted eyes. His upper body shuddered violently, giving a moment's impression that it was, on its own, lifting the rest of him. As he rose, he pressed down on the table as if to jackhammer it through the floorboards.

"I never drank alone, and I'll be damned if I'm going to waste my time with a man who won't drink with me."

Kanarek turned and, staggering, drifted back toward the table where his friends sat. Midway, he wheeled and, grasping a chair, threw back his head as if to roar at Seeley. The crocodile's jaw dropped wide, but no sound came other than a harsh sputtering from deep in his throat. He was searching frantically for a word, just one word, but it was beyond his reach, and this time Seeley could not think of one to give to him.

TWENTY-TWO

Seeley telephoned the home number Bermann's secretary had given him. The secretary, Hobday, answered, told Seeley that Bermann was out by the pool, and put him on hold. Recorded music came on—a frantic bombast of strings, woodwinds, brass, and chorus that Seeley guessed was Mahler's Second, the *Resurrection* Symphony—and then abruptly cut short.

"Mr. Seeley, it is good of you to call. You are well, I hope. Do you find the Königshof agreeable? It is not too ancien régime for your tastes? No? Good. Have you obtained Max Kanarek's signature?"

"That's not why I'm calling."

"But you have seen him?"

"I saw Hersh."

"Ah, my son-in-law," Bermann said.

Was it possible, Seeley thought, for Mayer Bermann to refer to Hersh without sighing?

"And that is why you are calling."

"I don't like it when clients lie to me. I expect it, but I don't like it. You should have told me why you wanted Max Kanarek to sign a declaration."

"Why, to document his authorship, of course. What did Mr. Landau tell you? I hope you remember it was he who treated you to that fantastic tale about Herman Göring and my paintings."

Seeley remembered and, for all he knew, Hersh was right about the paintings.

"He said you want to use Kanarek's declaration to destroy any claim the studio has to *Spykiller*. You want Callaway to sell the studio back to you."

"I see that this time desperation has truly inspired Mr. Landau. It is no secret that I have arranged financing against the event that Mr. Callaway should put the studio up for sale. Any prudent businessman in my position would do that. Indeed, my bankers have fully informed Mr. Callaway of this."

Seeley imagined Bermann poolside in bathing trunks and silk robe, as serene and cool as any eighty-four-year-old would be who possessed a good measure of health and an estate worth a few hundred million dollars. What was it like to be Mayer Bermann, to live with the memories he must possess? What does it do to a man to lose everything—parents, home, village—only to invent a life a million miles away that no one, not even he, could have imagined? The paintings, the Hermann Göring collection, were the link for Bermann between past and present, his chord of solace or revenge. But it was his control of the studio—the studio, not its film library—that connected Bermann to the present. It told the world that the qualities of shrewdness and will that it required for a young immigrant to carve this institution into American life had not diminished.

"You are of course free to question my motives. But what

can you find in my conduct that is wrong? Surely there is nothing about Max Kanarek signing a declaration of authorship that is illegal or unethical. I am restoring his name to his work."

"You're aren't doing this for Max Kanarek. You just want your studio back."

"If I remember correctly, it was you who said there is no morality to the ownership of art, only to its creation. It is Max Kanarek's creativity that I am seeking to honor. If I should happen to have some other motive, too, well . . ." Bermann's voice faded, then returned. "I understand you represent starving artists pro bono publico. Out of a commitment to public service, you devote yourself to these clients who cannot afford to pay for your services—am I right?"

"What's your point?"

"But you also take credit for the work you do on their behalf. You puff yourself up, you think what a terrific fellow you are, donating your valuable time to these struggling artists."

"I don't advertise my pro bono work."

"Of course," Bermann said. "I am sure that even your law partners have no idea how much good you have done. On the other hand, you do congratulate yourself, do you not, for performing this work, even though self-congratulation does nothing to help either your client or the public. What I am saying, Mr. Seeley, is search behind any fine gesture, even your own, and you are certain to find at least two motives, one of which is far less noble than the other. You get to pat yourself on the back for your work on behalf of artists. For obtaining acknowledgment of Max Kanarek's authorship I, perhaps, get my studio back."

Bermann's grandiose speculations held no interest for Seeley.

"When you wreck the studio and Beau Callaway puts it up for sale, who's going to finance you?"

"You know, Michael—may I call you that?—I have grown to admire you greatly. I now regret that I have not sought your personal counsel on my studio's affairs. Should I reacquire the studio, I will be looking for a new general counsel. Phil Mendelson is not at all suitable. I hope you would consider taking the position. As to the purchase, there will be some of my own money, of course. But most of the funds will be Chinese. An industrial company in Shanghai. Heavy machinery, construction equipment. They have no connection to the arts."

"What makes you think you'll get along with the Chinese any better than with Beau Callaway?"

"Humility, Michael. Humility is the difference. Mr. Callaway has none of it. He believes he is capable of complete success in any endeavor he puts his hand to. If you listen to him, you would think he knows more about creating motion pictures than someone who has been running a studio for over sixty years. The day I met him, I knew he was going to meddle in our production decisions. My Chinese colleagues are humble men. They have no illusion that they know anything about motion pictures and they have no interest in interfering in my running of the studio. All they desire is a return on investment."

"What kind of return can they expect? Without *Spykiller* the studio is nothing more than a shell."

"Did Mr. Landau say that? That sounds like him." This time the sigh of resignation was inside Bermann's voice. "Can you believe, after all his time in the industry, he understands this business no better than the most uninformed outsider. A motion picture studio has only one asset, and for all of Mr. Callaway's financial genius, it is not an asset that is created in the marketplace. The asset is the insight and judgment of the man who runs the studio. All the rest are commodities—contracts with talent, with writers, directors, producers, lenders, distributors—these are things you can buy on any street corner in Los Angeles. But the studio itself is just one man. Mr. Callaway has tried to turn it into something different, a business-school exercise with management committees, strategic planning, and all this other nonsense. I am sure you understand. You have litigated cases for my studio for, how many years?"

Seeley stopped to think about how to phrase the next question. "What did you know about Bert Cobb's death?"

"A terrible occurrence. In his own home, and for what? Nothing, now that Mr. Kanarek's authorship is about to become a matter of public record. I know you had a particular affection for Mr. Cobb. That is why I sent you the news clipping."

"You didn't answer my question."

"I could say that I had no knowledge, because that is what you expect me to say. But that would not be entirely true. I did not know they would kill him, of course. But I do know that these are absolutely ruthless people. Mr. Landau is a man with no morals at all, but you have figured that out for yourself by now. I would imagine he is Mr. Callaway's lieutenant on this project."

"You are as responsible for Cobb's death as he is."

"That is an absurd statement. Even if I had known it was going to happen, what could I have done to stop it? It is no concern of mine whether you believe this or not, but I had nothing to do with your friend's death, either directly or indirectly. I admit that in building my studio I occasionally engaged in dealings that even some of these MBA graduates might characterize as sharp practice. This was the ethic of the time and I have no apologies to make to anyone. But my parents died in a concentration camp in Poland, so you will understand that where human life is involved I place a higher value on it than does your generation."

Bermann's allusion to the death of his parents struck Seeley as grossly self-serving; it was heartening to see that the man was capable of a misstep.

"You're the one who put Bert Cobb's name on Max Kanarek's script."

"That was many years ago, under entirely different—and exigent—circumstances."

"You never told Hersh about Kanarek."

"I assure you, that would have made no difference."

"When I saw Cobb," Seeley said, "he as much as begged me to get you to see him. If you had gone out to Pacoima, he would have signed the papers, and none of this would have happened. The bank would have financed your next *Spykiller* movie and all the ones after that."

"As I already told you, my going to see Mr. Cobb would also have made no difference." Bermann's voice had turned to dry ice. "Have you considered, Mr. Seeley"—he was Mr. Seeley again—"that perhaps this is your guilt speaking for you? That had you not been so inflexible about refusing to sign the opinion letter, Mr. Cobb would be alive today?"

For how many minutes—seconds—had Seeley *not* considered this? If he had written the letter the studio wanted, Bert Cobb would be alive. But if that were so, why couldn't he convince himself that, had he known what was going to happen, he would have signed the letter? It was no consolation that Cobb himself would have told him not to sign it.

"If you think about it," Bermann said, "you have also put Max Kanarek's life in danger. Mr. Landau's hired men will kill him if they can find him. But I have placed it in your hands for you to redeem yourself. As soon as Mr. Kanarek signs the declaration, he will be safe. There will no longer be any advantage to be gained by harming him. That is why you must obtain his signature on the declaration."

Once again, Bermann was playing him like a piece on a chessboard. Seeley said, "I'm terminating our engagement. I've decided not to work for you anymore."

After a silence, Bermann said, "It is not possible for you to resign. There are professional responsibilities."

"You're not my client. United Pictures is. The studio you're trying to destroy. If I have a duty to any client, it's to United Pictures and Intermedia."

"You understand that if you fail to obtain Mr. Kanarek's signature on a declaration you will be placing not only his life at risk. There is also his wife to think of." Reiman had said the same thing, but from Bermann it felt like a challenge. "This is to say nothing of the danger to Professor Walsh, who Harry Devlin tells me is in Munich, too. Do you feel morally comfortable making this decision for all these people? There is also a danger to yourself, but that, I am sure, is of no moment to you. You realize that if you choose this path you will be rewarding Mr. Callaway, giving him exactly what he wants—uncontested ownership of Max Kanarek's script."

"And Hersh will be the studio's new chairman. That's his payoff. You'll be out of a job."

"On the other hand," Bermann said, "if you were willing to persuade Mr. Kanarek to sign the declaration, you could secure retribution against Mr. Callaway for having your friend murdered, and you could save all these other lives as well. It will be the end of any value the studio may have for Mr. Callaway. He will sell the studio and I will buy it. But, of course, for you to take this path would reward me, which you seem disinclined to do, even though my connection to your friend's death exists only in your mind and, even there, you will agree, the connection is attenuated at best. You seem intent on denying it, Mr. Seeley, but there is a mutuality between our interests, yours and mine. As a lawyer, I am sure you understand that a decision not to act can be as consequential—perhaps even more so—as a decision to take action. It is true, is it not, that in law errors of omission are as indictable as errors of commission? Whatever you decide, you must make your decision quickly. We both know why Mr. Landau is in Munich and, for all his faults, he is not one to procrastinate. As I said, Mr. Seeley, you have a choice to make. I do not envy you. But, if I may—"

"I'm not looking for advice."

"Please indulge an old man for just a moment more." The earlier cordial tone had returned. "Whatever decision you make, Michael, I believe it would be a tragic mistake for you to make it on the basis of injured pride. You feel that I have manipulated you. Perhaps I have, but that is the way I do business. You are doubtless justified in these feelings. But you will never forgive yourself if you let this pride of yours influence the choice you make. Too many people will be injured."

"What is Harry Devlin's connection to this?"

"Did he tell you not to go to Munich?"

"He said it would be harmful to my health."

"Perhaps to his health, too," Bermann said.

"You think he was afraid I would find out that he informed on Max Kanarek."

"Possibly." Bermann's voice indicated no surprise that Seeley should know about Devlin's connection to Kanarek. "It is possible that, like me, Mr. Devlin had more than one motive concerning your presence in Munich. This means that you have indeed met with Mr. Kanarek."

It was Julia, not Kanarek, who told Seeley about Harry Devlin, but he did not want to bring her into this. Nor did he feel like reporting to Bermann on his encounter with Kanarek in the café.

"I know that it was you who turned Max Kanarek in to the state investigators."

"So now you understand why it is so important that I repair my relationship with him before he dies."

"Devlin was supposed to give me Kanarek's address, wasn't he? You gave it to me only because he didn't."

"For all of your legal experience, Michael, there is still much you do not know. In time you will learn that, in spite of all the relationships we busy ourselves with from day to day, at the end of our lives each of us is completely alone."

For the first time, Seeley heard something like emotion in Bermann's voice. Disappointment, even sadness, if he was right.

The line went silent, and Seeley was about to hang up when Bermann spoke again. "Tell me, does that grotesque overcoat still hang in the lobby of the Königshof?"

"What do you know about it?"

"Believe it or not, it is a work of art, a sculpture. It is by a German sculptor. Very fashionable, people tell me. I have forgotten what it is called, but ask the concierge. He will be able to tell you the history of it."

Then Bermann hung up.

TWENTY-THREE

The heavy double doors to the offices of J. Hanauer and Partners were closed and, when Seeley tried them, locked. It was Sunday. Reiman had been beaten badly, and Seeley had little hope that he would be in the office. Although he had no reason to think Max Kanarek would sign the declaration Reiman had prepared, Seeley also had no reason to stop trying. But if Kanarek did sign, the documents would have to be notarized—and if not by Reiman, Seeley would need to find someone else.

After several stabs at the buzzer, one of the doors opened an inch, exposing an eye and part of the angry frown of the receptionist from the day before.

"*Was möchten Sie?*"

"I would like to see Dr. Reiman."

The slice of face hardened. "Dr. Reiman is not available."

That was a mistake. She should have said Reiman was out of the office.

"We have an appointment," Seeley said.

"All appointments are canceled."

Seeley quickly moved his foot into the opening to keep her from closing the door.

"You know, if Dr. Hanauer learns you are canceling appointments for his associates, he will dismiss you at once."

The pressure against his foot eased, and Seeley followed the receptionist through the doorway into the anteroom. Avoiding Seeley's eyes, she pointed to the corridor leading to Reiman's office. The rooms along the hallway were still unlit behind their windowed transoms. Sunlight streamed into Reiman's office, illuminating the wreckage from the night before; in a corner someone had begun stacking the papers into a neat pile. Reiman's back was to the open door, his thin shoulders hunched over the computer screen.

Seeley tapped lightly at the door. "Dr. Reiman?"

The lawyer turned slowly, painfully. Behind the gold-rimmed glasses, one eye was swollen shut, the purple-black crescent beneath it livid against his white cheek. He blotted his lip with a blood-splotched handkerchief and focused on Seeley with his good eye. "I didn't want to call your hotel until I was certain you were up. I need to give you the envelopes for your documents."

"How are you?"

Reiman started to smile, but winced instead. "You should see the other guy."

Seeley thought about the force with which he had swung the coat stand at Reiman's attacker. More than was needed to separate the two men. He had hit him hard enough to crack his spine. The anger behind the blow—not only at the man, but at Bermann, at Hersh—had been growing in him since he'd learned of Cobb's death. Longer. As he thought about it now, it seemed as if he had been living with that anger forever.

There was a knock at the open door, and the receptionist came in. Ignoring Seeley, she handed Reiman what looked like a hand towel folded into a plastic bag. Ice cubes jostled inside the package. "*Für die Schwellung*," she said to Reiman. For the swelling. She surveyed the mess in the room and sighed dramatically.

"Later," Reiman said, putting the towel on the desktop. "You can clean up later."

He returned to Seeley. "You have no reason for concern. They didn't get the address for Mr. Kanarek."

"I'm sure of that," Seeley said. "I came to see how you were."

Reiman surveyed the papers scattered around the room. "The address is in the computer, nowhere else."

"You should have given it to them. There's a limit on how far you have to go to maintain a confidence."

"I instructed them that any information I had was privileged, that it was a lawyer-client communication."

This lack of imagination in someone so very smart startled Seeley. He asked himself what he would have done in Reiman's place.

"You could have said I didn't tell you where Kanarek lives."

"Whether my client told me anything or nothing is no one's business. Our ethical rules are no different than yours."

"I'm sorry I led them to you. I'm sorry for getting you into this."

Reiman said, "You warned me there was danger. I should have been more careful, taken precautions." He was clearly uncomfortable talking about himself. "Has Mr. Kanarek signed the declaration?"

"Not yet," Seeley said. "When he does, will you be able to notarize it?"

"Of course. Perhaps, if Mr. Kanarek needs to be convinced,

I can help you with that as well. My clients tell me I have a talent for coming up with solutions other lawyers don't see."

Seeley didn't want to get the lawyer any more deeply involved. "If I run into a problem, I'll call you."

"No, you won't," Reiman said. "You're someone who likes to do things by himself. You are an *Einzelgänger*. You know some German?"

"A lone wolf."

"Close enough. A loner."

"Not so much anymore," Seeley heard himself say. "I'm learning that some things are too big to take on by myself."

"Is there anything that is *not* too big to take on oneself?" Reiman looked around the office. "If you hadn't come by, who knows what damage they would have done."

"But you still wouldn't have given them the address."

Reiman dabbed tentatively at his lip to see if the bleeding had stopped, then put the handkerchief on the desk next to the computer keyboard. "Last night, with all the confusion, I forgot to give you the envelopes. After the documents are signed, how do you want them delivered?"

"Hand delivery to your patent office. Fax and overnight express to Washington. Whatever service you use here."

Reiman typed a command and inserted mailing labels from a folder resting against the printer. When they were printed, he handed them to Seeley.

"Thank you," Seeley said. He knew this was inadequate, but he also knew Reiman would take anything more as an insult to his professionalism.

"I know where to send the bill," Reiman said. "Is there anything else I can do for you?"

Seeley said no.

The lawyer gestured around the room. "Well, as you can see, this little adventure has set me behind in my work."

The reception area was empty. When Seeley opened the double door, there was a movement on the landing. Standing off to the side, holding her purse in front of her like a school-girl's satchel, was Julia Walsh.

Shouts of children at play rose from the park across Maria-Theresia-Strasse. The shadow of a flock of birds passed over the villa.

Julia said, "I have a message for you."

"I was surprised when you called me last night to help you find Kanarek. You don't seem like someone who asks for help."

They were jaywalking across Maria-Theresia-Strasse where it borders Isar Park.

Two times in one hour, Seeley thought. Was he really that closed off? "You mean I'm an *Einzelgänger*?"

Julia laughed. "What's that?"

"It's what Reiman—the lawyer—said I was. A lone wolf. A loner. I looked for you after I finished with Kanarek."

"It didn't seem important to stick around, so I left. How did it go?"

Seeley said, "It wasn't much of a conversation. He ranted and I listened."

"But he wouldn't sign the declaration."

"I haven't given up on him. How did you find me?"

"I asked at your hotel. The man who dresses up like the Kaiser told me."

Schreiner. Seeley had given him Reiman's address in the event Carlotta tried to reach him, but had instructed the concierge not to give it to anyone else.

Julia said, "How is he—the lawyer?"

"Reiman? Fearless."

"You don't hear too many lawyers described that way."

"Maybe," Seeley said, "because the ones like him don't get as far as middle age."

They came to a bench on a knoll overlooking a grassy playing field. On the field, several children kicked at a soccer ball while their parents lounged on blankets nearby, talking, drinking, smoking. Seeley remembered Julia's greeting in the doorway.

"You said you had a message for me."

Julia slouched against the back of the bench and crossed her legs. In her short, summery skirt and white T-shirt, she could have been a shopgirl on lunch break. A very smart, well-dressed shopgirl.

"I talked to Harry last night," she said. "After I left you at the café. He told me to warn you against trying to see Kanarek again. Harry's not usually melodramatic, but he said trying to get Kanarek to sign your piece of paper would be the same—these are his words—as putting a gun to your head."

The absorbed concern in her voice touched Seeley.

"He wouldn't tell me why, but he said you'd understand."

Was this why Devlin had tried to discourage him from going to Munich—that he cared about Seeley's well-being? Or had he feared that Seeley would discover his betrayal of Max Kanarek? Or was Bermann right, that more than one motive drives even our finest acts?

"I can't get Max Kanarek to sign the declaration if I don't see him."

"What happens if you don't get the declaration?"

"I already told you. The people who murdered Bert Cobb—Hersh, Beau Callaway—get the rights to *Spykiller*."

"And if you do get it?"

"Kanarek and Carlotta will own the rights, and Mayer Bermann gets to buy his studio back for very little money."

Julia tensed. "Mayer Bermann. The man who manipulated

Harry into betraying his client. The man who's been manipulating you since before you even met him."

"And you believe there's a moral equivalence between what Hersh and Callaway did and what Bermann's doing?"

"No, I'm thinking those can't be your only choices."

"If you come up with another, let me know."

Julia's arm brushed his, and for a moment Seeley felt the beat of her heart as intensely as if it were his own. He said, "Harry didn't call you just to give me a message."

"He wanted to tell me how glad he was that I finally let him down from the pedestal I'd put him on. I told him I hadn't let him off, not completely, and he said he thought I should. I told him I didn't care what he thought. That seemed to please him. I'm still going to work with him on the class action. He's juggling a dozen different projects and needs the help."

Seeley remembered the flashing lights on Devlin's office telephone. "How well do you know him?"

"Harry? Nine years. Maybe ten. Why?"

Seeley hadn't asked her how long she'd known Devlin, but how well.

"When I saw him in his office, it must have been close to midnight, but he had two or three phone calls holding all the time I was there. He was talking to someone in French."

Julia smiled. "Harry calls them his guys. The drunks he tries to keep sober. They come from everywhere. I don't know how he finds them. He's always got a couple of them staying at his place out in the valley. Lawyers, doctors, auto mechanics, even some of his clients."

Perhaps Devlin had in fact been trying to save him. "Are you one?"

Julia shook her head, but didn't meet his eyes. "Are you?"

"I don't know. He thinks so."

Seeley had successfully resisted Kanarek's demand to drink

with him, just as he had skirted the bars and restaurants in Santa Monica. But, as before, his new sobriety was fragile, and he didn't want to lose it by talking about it.

Seeley said, "Why do I get the feeling there's something more than a professional relationship between you and Harry?" The words were harder to get out than he thought they'd be.

Julia colored. "Harry and I had a relationship for a while. It was one of those things that happened without either of us expecting it to. The romantic part's been over for a long time." Julia's voice raced and braked; it was as hard for her to answer Seeley's question as it had been for him to ask it. "Do you have any idea what it's like to be researching your dissertation, and every couple of pages your boyfriend's name comes up?"

To Seeley, "boyfriend" seemed hardly the word to fit Harry Devlin.

"You're thinking Harry's old enough to be my father. Older. If my father's still alive, he'd be sixty-four."

"You don't know?"

"He left when I was eight. It was one of those things you read about in the paper. A man goes out for a pack of cigarettes, and his family never sees him again. But you don't think it's going to happen to you. He didn't say he was going for cigarettes. He just went to work one morning and didn't come back. I think my mother suspected he was going to leave, but she wouldn't talk about it."

"Why didn't you tell me? I had a picture of a spoiled little girl whose father carved dolls for her out of quarter-inch plywood."

"It's not a time I like to think about. I spent the whole summer in my bedroom watching for him. There was a big magnolia tree in the front yard that blocked most of my view, but I sat at that bedroom window, staring through it, waiting for his car to pull into the driveway. I was sure that if I concentrated hard enough, he would come. After that, I started doing really well in school. Straight As right through college. I thought if I could just be perfect, he'd come back."

Seeley considered which is harder on a child—having a parent who abandons you or having one who is at you all the time, a source of constant torment.

Julia said, "You think it's strange, to have a romantic relationship with someone older than your father."

Seeley ran through a rapid inventory of the feelings he might have about Julia and Harry Devlin—envy, anger, amusement, resentment—and finished empty. "It's none of my business."

"But, still, you're picturing an old man romancing a nubile young woman."

"I—"

"Don't say anything," Julia said, "unless you're prepared to make me a better offer."

Seeley didn't know if she was serious. He waited, but she gave no clue.

"In case you haven't tried it, it's not easy being a fearless, independent woman."

"You look like you pull it off pretty well."

"*Look*, sure. But inside . . . Anyway, thanks for saying that."

"You mean you're not an *Einzelgänger*?"

Julia said, "No one is, outside of the movies. At least no one wants to be."

"Do you want to go?"

"Sure," she said.

They walked back toward Maximilianstrasse and their hotels, Seeley struggling to remember the forgotten rhythms of courtship, the games of flirtation he had never really mastered. At some point Julia's hand slipped into his and stayed there. They took the several flights of wide marble stairs down to

Widenmayerstrasse, crossed, and started up Maximilianstrasse, the pink columns of the Maximilianeum floating above and behind them. Julia's hotel was a block away, Seeley's three.

Julia said, "What are you going to do now?"

"Wait to hear from Carlotta. Unless Kanarek calls me himself."

"Would you like company?"

"That would be nice," he said. "Sure."

TWENTY-FOUR

Hersh was in an easy chair in the Königshof lobby, directly under the giant trench coat flying off the column. He was pretending to read the *Suddeutsche Zeitung*. At the sight of Seeley coming through the revolving door, he folded the newspaper and started to rise, but stopped when he saw Julia following a step behind. In the moment before the newspaper went up again, Seeley glimpsed the desperation in Hersh's pale face.

Stepping into the elevator with Julia, Seeley had to remind himself that, as comical as Hersh appeared—the president of an important film studio slinking around a hotel lobby like a private eye in an old B movie—he was a dangerous man.

Julia went ahead of Seeley into the suite while he knelt to pick up a hotel envelope. The message was from Carlotta and the handwriting was loose, almost crazed, as if she had been rushed. "Dear Mr. Seeley," the note read, "Max is dying. You must come at once to St. Joseph Klinik on Schönfeldstrasse. A taxi driver will know where it is. Come soon. Please. (Mrs.) Carlotta Kanarek."

Seeley had not before thought of Carlotta's name in conjunction with Kanarek's. It was always Carlotta Reyes, or just Carlotta. The proximity of the two names, and the danger it implied for Carlotta as well as her husband, sent a shiver through him. He handed the message to Julia.

"I'm going with you," she said.

Seeley didn't bother to list the reasons she shouldn't come. Julia would have an answer for each and would follow anyway. He dialed the number for the concierge. Seeley didn't know if he could trust the man—against his instructions Schreiner had told Julia she could find him at Reiman's office—but he had no choice. Now, when Seeley asked if the new American guest was still in the lobby, Schreiner's tone was cross.

"Yes, Mr. Landau is here, reading a newspaper. You must understand, Mr. Seeley, he is a guest of the hotel, just like you. I cannot be spying on him."

"I'm sure you want to take good care of all your guests, Herr Schreiner, particularly those who have taken good care of you. If you would like to meet me on the roof by the service elevator in five minutes, I can introduce you to a president of the United States."

"Which President would that be?"

"Ulysses S. Grant."

"Ach! As I remember, General Grant was not one of your country's more distinguished leaders."

Was the concierge an American history buff, or did his blundering manner hide a finely honed mercenary instinct?

Seeley said, "If you can get me away from the hotel without Mr. Landau knowing, perhaps I can arrange for you to meet another great American instead. Say, Benjamin Franklin."

"Benjamin Franklin? Indeed, a very great American! 'There

are three faithful friends'—did you know Franklin said this?—'an old wife, an old dog, and ready money.' "

"I'll see you on the roof in five minutes."

Schreiner, incandescent in cream flannels and gold braid, was waiting for them by the open door of the service car. He nodded to Julia. "So, you found your man."

Seeley said, "Where is the service entrance?"

"It is in the cellar," Schreiner said. "I will take you there." He inserted a key into the button marked U.

"I appreciate this. You will understand when I tell you this is a business matter. Mr. Landau is a commercial rival."

"Have you been yet to Oktoberfest? The young lady?" He nodded at Julia, again, as if she were a stranger. "No, you are too busy, both of you. Too much business. Americans take no time to enjoy life. Tomorrow, everything closes down." Schreiner pressed his palms together, then opened them swiftly upward, as if releasing a small bird. "Pfft! Gone!"

The elevator doors opened onto a dark passageway stacked with empty produce crates; daylight shone at the far end where the service entrance led into an alley. Across the alley was the beer garden of the Hofbräuhaus, half filled at 3:30 with tourists and shoppers lounging at umbrella-shaded tables. Seeley thanked Schreiner and handed him a hotel envelope with a hundred-dollar bill inside. With Julia, he went past the iron gate into the beer garden, walked through a banquet hall, out onto Neuturmstrasse and from there up a cobblestoned incline to Maximilianstrasse, regularly checking to see if they were being followed.

Using a map from the hotel, Julia had located Schönfeldstrasse, six blocks up Ludwigstrasse not far from Universität in Maxvorstadt, the district next to Schwabing; the hospital was two blocks off the wide boulevard. As they walked, Seeley glanced into the side-view mirrors of the BMWs and Mercedes-Benzes that were parked half on, half off the broad sidewalk. Hersh might still be in the lobby, but he had at least two men working for him. In the moving, fractured reflections of the mirrors, one figure emerged—a tall man with lank hair that brushed the turned-up collar of a rumpled sport coat. He was leaning into a cell phone at his ear. It was the man who had attacked Reiman in his office. There was a gangly, simian looseness to his gait—he appeared to have recovered from Seeley's blow—and that and the hair made Seeley think of an orangutan gliding from perch to perch.

Julia said, "Someone's following us." She had seen him, too.

"He's one of the men who beat up Reiman." The unsteady image of the man—gaunt, hunched, unwashed—conjured the mixed odors of engine grease and sweat in Reiman's office.

Seeley said, "How far is it to the hospital?"

"Four blocks, maybe five. We're leading him right to Kanarek."

Marienplatz was fifteen or twenty minutes away, a crowded, jostling place filled at all hours with tourists. Beneath it lay an intricate network of U-Bahn entrances and exits through which Seeley calculated they could elude the man and then turn back toward Schönfeldstrasse. At the next intersection, he took Julia's elbow and, when the light turned, they crossed Ludwigstrasse. Even with the layers of exhaust fumes, he was aware of Julia's gentle fragrance, and for a moment let himself imagine what might have happened if the note from Carlotta had not been waiting for him in the suite. What hold did Harry Devlin still have on her? What hold did Clare still have on him?

The sight of Marienplatz brought him back to reality.

Six or seven people milled around the foot of St. Mary's Column and a short line waited at an automatic teller across the plaza. Three teenage boys on motorbikes looped in and out of the monuments. The lank-haired man was half a block away, in the shadows of the city hall, still talking into his cell phone. But, other than that, the square was empty. The tourists and locals were making their last visit to Oktoberfest.

Seeley surveyed the four corners of the square. He took Julia's hand and walked quickly to the nearest corner and onto a pedestrian mall lined with department stores and a jumble of food stands. Down the middle of the street, a succession of new-model automobiles glistened like trophies on canopied platforms. The mall ended after two blocks and automobile traffic resumed. The buildings became shoddy and graceless, many of them surrounded by scaffolds and industrial netting. The harsh pounding of pneumatic jackhammers drowned out all other sound and there was a pervading stench of boiling asphalt. The self-confident, well-ordered Munich Seeley had become familiar with was far behind them.

A sign for the Karlsplatz U-Bahn station jutted out over the street. The escalator to the station wasn't operating, so they took the steps down into a brightly lit shopping area almost half the size of Marienplatz. A few customers loitered at a deserted snack bar while wave after wave of bodies funneled onto an escalator to the next level down. Seeley checked an enameled wall map to confirm that they had been walking in the direction of the Theresienwiese, where he knew they would be able to lose the man following them. He felt the rumble of arriving and departing trains on the lower level. The escalator up to the street was operating, but when they got to it, the lank-haired man was waiting for them at the top of the moving steel steps. They went back to the stalled escalator. Above them, hands on hips so that his body filled the passage, was the boxer in leather jacket and tie. The two men could easily have caught up with them. This meant Hersh wasn't planning an encounter on the streets or subways of Munich. He just wanted them followed.

Julia said, "If we split up, one of them is going to have to follow me. It will be easier getting to the hospital if you only have to lose one of them."

"No. It's too dangerous."

Julia smiled. "For me or for you?"

"You don't know the city."

"How well do you have to know a place to get lost in it?"

Seeley accepted that he could no more persuade Julia to stay with him now than, half an hour earlier, he could have persuaded her to stay at the hotel. "Which one do you want?"

"The guy who walks like an ape is sort of cute."

"Walk a couple of blocks and find a taxi. Go back to your hotel. I'll call you."

Julia's grip tightened, and she leaned into him. "There's something I wanted to give you in your hotel room." Her cool fingers went to the back of his neck, bringing Seeley for a moment into the circle of her fragrance, and her lips touched his.

Before he could recover, Julia was gone, moving up the escalator where the lank-haired man was waiting. She didn't look at him when she reached street level, but strode directly onto the sidewalk. With a last look down into the station, the man turned and followed.

Seeley waited for the tremor that would indicate a train arriving beneath him. All he needed was to reach the Theresienwiese and Oktoberfest.

The boxer started down the stalled escalator just as a train rumbled into the level below. Seeley pressed himself into the crowd on the down escalator and, forcing himself past heavy bodies, muttering excuses—"*Entschuldigen Sie, bitte!*"—he let the movement of the human mass propel him forward. Carried by the crowd, he experienced no transition from escalator to platform to the interior of the fluorescent-lit train. In the encompassing crush of hips and elbows, he smiled at the thought that no ticket inspector could make his way through this dense mass. No one got on or off at the next stop, but at the Theresienwiese station, the bodies pushed out from the opening doors, swarming onto the platform, again carrying Seeley with them.

Seeley's first awareness of Oktoberfest was the clamor, an undifferentiated roar that rose and spread from the fairground less than a block away. The mass of people surged in the direction of the din. As he got closer, Seeley smelled roasting meats and, beneath that, the intense, malty fragrance of what must have been coursing rivers of beer. The promenade running through the center of the fair was twice the width of a city street, flanked on either side by massive beer halls the size of circus tents. The muffled rhythms of brass bands inside the tents and the mechanical tinkle of a Ferris wheel syncopated the buzz of the crowd. Each tent bore the banner of the brewery that operated it. Some—Löwenbräu, Paulaner, Spatenbräu—were familiar to Seeley from his Friday evening excursions into the bars of Buffalo with the other young lawyers in his firm. Others—Hackenbräu, Augustiner—he didn't recognize. In the distance, at the far end of the fairground, a broad marble stairway rose past a massive statue of a woman holding a wreath aloft, a lion crouched beside her. Behind the statue was a columned palisade and behind this, Seeley guessed, would be streets and taxi stands and his escape back to Schönfeldstrasse.

A step ahead of Seeley on the promenade, a mother held a boy by one hand and a leashed dachshund by the other. The threesome stirred the memory of an autumn when Seeley was still a boy and his father had taken him to the Erie County Fair. It was a special event—he had been on only two or three outings alone with his father. As much as he exulted in the adventure—the exclusive company of his father, the promising sounds of the amusement rides, the smells, the jostle of fairgoers—he was never unaware of the danger of separation. When his father refused to accept his hand—Be a man! he'd said—Michael pressed into him with cheek and shoulder and arm, his father's body reciprocating with an exhalation that, to the small boy, was the man's very essence: the cool smoky wool of his rough jacket, the aroma of tobacco, the deep oaky fragrances of beer and whiskey. The sensations enveloped him in an unaccustomed promise of safety.

The leashed dog on the Oktoberfest promenade was as overstuffed as a pork loaf, its belly barely an inch above the pavement. The grinning boy, his hand still in his mother's, bent forward, forcing his small tummy out of his waistband, so that he, too, became a grotesque—legs, hips, and arms rocking and pumping in studious imitation of the low dog's waddle.

Fingers hard as bullets drummed Seeley's shoulder and a steel trap gripped his elbow. "I'm getting tired of chasing after you." It was Hersh. "Take me to Kanarek."

"I knew you couldn't stay away. Where are the fraternity brothers?"

Seeley continued moving with the crowd, Hersh grasping his elbow. Seeley was confident he could break away. Hersh looked to be in reasonably good condition, but so was he. It was the thought of the other two men that concerned him. Hersh hadn't found him on his own; one or both of the men had directed Hersh to the Theresienwiese, and if they were here now, watching, Seeley's escape would only lead them to Max Kanarek. He would have to wait. He hoped that Kanarek could wait, too.

They came to the last tent on the mall. As they passed under the canopied entry into the Löwenbräu Festhaus, the vast roar from within the tent struck Seeley with the force of a physical blow. At row after row of long, planked tables, thousands of patrons drank, talked, sang, bellowed, swayed to the rhythm of the brass band high on a center stage, a tangled weave of arms and shoulders moving like waves in a crosscurrent. Above this sprawling organism, a dense cloud of tobacco smoke rose through the yellow light to the tent's upper reaches, three or four stories above. Suspended from the beamed canvas ceiling, tracing the circumference of the place, thousands of electric candles studded a wreath of glittering metal.

Seeley found a table with two free places and motioned Hersh to take the bench across from him. At the other end of the table, seven or eight ancient men smoked and argued, the quart-size schooners in front of them half drained.

Seeley stopped a sturdy waitress rushing past and ordered half a roast chicken for himself.

"*Fur Sie?*" she said to Hersh.

Hersh shot Seeley an uncomprehending look, spreading his long fingers on the table as if to rise.

"*Ein Mass für meinen Freund,*" Seeley said, and the woman went away. Seeley noticed a black, dime-size hematoma under Hersh's thumbnail and, imagining the trauma that had produced it—a slammed car door, the misplaced swing of a hammer—experienced a moment's pulse of sympathy for the man. Then he thought of Bert Cobb.

"Eat your food, and then your time's up. You can take us to Kanarek or tell us where he is. Those are your only choices."

Seeley said, "Tell *us*?"

"Beau Callaway wants this wrapped up by tomorrow morning."

"It must be wonderful being Beau Callaway, to be able to order people around like that. Professionals, like you. What's it like being Callaway's gofer? His lackey? I bet it really burns you that no one takes you seriously. Not Callaway, not Bermann. To them you're a guy who married the boss's daughter. You complain about being overworked, but what you really miss is the respect. That's what tears you up inside, isn't it? No one treats you like the big-time movie executive you think you are. I'll bet even your own kids treat you like crap."

The waitress arrived with Seeley's roast chicken, a steak knife buried in its breast, and separated two pitcher-size schooners from the five she held in her fist, sliding them across the table to them. Reflexively, Seeley pushed his over to Hersh.

"Go ahead," Hersh said, "dig your grave. For someone who's a failure, you've got a real attitude problem."

"You want to know the truth? I'm not usually like this. There's something about you that brings out the worst in me."

With the knife, Seeley cut into the mahogany-skinned chicken, the serrated blade slicing cleanly through crisp skin and moist, fragrant meat. The first mouthful reminded him that he hadn't eaten since an early breakfast, and after that he ate quickly but precisely. The last time he enjoyed a meal this much was the lunch with Elm in the studio commissary. While Seeley ate, Hersh sipped awkwardly at one of the schooners, looking more like a small boy tasting his first beer than the president of an American motion picture studio. Again Seeley felt an irrational pang of sympathy for him.

"Mayer Bermann never let you in on his dirty tricks with Harry Devlin, did he? His deal with the Chinese? You're Bermann's Ivy Leaguer, his operations man, but has he ever asked you for advice? Brought you into his confidence? How long did it take you to figure out that he wouldn't let Callaway keep the studio?"

Hersh glared at him.

"I have no illusions about Mayer Bermann," Seeley said. "He's done things as bad as anything you've ever done. If it weren't for him, Bert Cobb would still be alive. But he isn't the one who crushed Cobb's skull. You are. Or the thug in the leather jacket who works for you."

"I already told you, that's ridiculous—"

"After I saw you, I called Mrs. Cobb. She seems like a nice woman. She's not a gold digger. She said she didn't mind that I called her before 9:00 in the morning to talk about what she thought was her late husband's script and how you got her to sign the rights away. I think she feels responsible. She's beginning to understand that there's a connection between her signing over the rights to the studio and her husband dying like that. You lied to me about her. You said the studio talked to her five months ago. She told me nobody spoke to her until three days before her husband died. I got the feeling she really cared for the guy."

More than cared, Seeley remembered. She told him she had moved away because she couldn't bear to watch Cobb suffer the way he did for what he thought was art.

"I'm sure somebody from the studio approached her—"

"You're a liar, Hersh. And you're stupid, too. You don't even get it that Beau Callaway has set you up. Bert Cobb. The attack on the German lawyer. Whatever you've got in the works now to stop Max Kanarek from signing the declaration. Your fingerprints are everywhere. You won't even get to choose if you're prosecuted in Germany or in the United States. Do you have any idea what it's like to be a foreigner in a German jail, a man who doesn't speak the language?"

Keeping his eyes on Seeley, Hersh reached into the inside pocket of his jacket and lifted out a cell phone. He pressed an automatic dial button, spoke his name, listened for a few seconds before returning the phone to his jacket.

"All we want is for Kanarek to sign over the rights."

"And if he won't?"

"We go home." Hersh looked directly at him to give conviction to the lie, and Seeley made sure the eyes stayed locked on his.

Beneath the table, working with one hand, Seeley slid the wooden-handled knife up the sleeve of his shirt and then let it slip down a half-inch so the point lodged in the wristband of his watch. He pushed back from the table and rose.

"Where are you going? I didn't say you could go."

"Bavarians aren't all that fastidious when they're drinking, but they draw the line at peeing under the table."

"Hold on." Hersh put a hand over Seeley's and speed dialed the phone again, giving an order to the person on the other end. Seeley pulled his hand away but otherwise didn't move.

"Do what you have to do, and then we leave. You're going to take me to Kanarek."

"And if I don't? Are you going to have your hired men out there beat me up? You're not going to do anything in front of five thousand people."

"Nobody will notice."

It occurred to Seeley that he was right. Outside on the mall it was different, but the people in the poorly lit tent were so absorbed in their drinking and the noisy celebration that a bomb could explode and the geezers at the other end of the table wouldn't even look up from their argument.

The boxer arrived at the table. It may have been the shadows, but he looked heavier than he had in Reiman's office, the thick, porridgy cheeks folding into a rim beneath his eyes. When he turned into the light, Seeley saw that his forehead was glossy with perspiration; the ink Seeley had thrown at him in Reiman's office had left a stain like a raccoon mask around his eyes; it gave him the look of a cartoon burglar or an anonymous movie hero.

"I don't think the Lone Ranger here enjoys being a chaperone," Seeley said. "He's more a man of action. He likes working with his fists."

"Make it fast," Hersh said, and to the boxer, "Watch this guy. If he acts out, do anything you want to him. Just as long as he can still talk."

The boxer's fingers pressed into Seeley's back as they moved away from the table. Over his shoulder Seeley said to him, "I bet Hersh flew you coach. What did he fly? Business class? First? Upstairs where the seats fold out like beds? It must have been a rough trip for a big fellow like you, cramped in one of those sardine-can seats."

The patter wasn't particularly subtle, but as with Hersh, he wanted to keep the man angry and off balance.

"Tell me if I'm wrong: Hersh booked you into an Econo Hotel didn't he, one of those places with linoleum floors? You smell like you've been living on *Schweinerei*, that garbage they sell at the wurst stands. No wonder you look so crummy, all that greasy crap sitting in your gut."

The man came close to his ear, and Seeley could smell the aftershave. "Hersh told me you have a death wish."

"You don't think he's going to take the fall for this, do you? Beating up the lawyer. Killing the old guy in Pacoima. That was you, wasn't it? You do the dirty work and Hersh walks away. Farting through silk. Who is it gets to take me to the little boy's room? You or Hersh? That's how executives do it. They make the dumb guys do the dirty work."

The WC, when they got to it, was a makeshift affair, a thirty- or forty-foot cavern formed on one side by the wall of the tent and, on the other, by a canvas partition dropped from low inside the tent's ceiling. A steady procession of men streamed through the flap door, and a steamy mist of beer, urine, and smoke wafted out from it in waves. Seeley had been counting on the boxer's pride, but the stench was an ally, too.

"Do you want to come in and hold my hand?"

"To hell with you and this whole goddamned job. Just make it quick. If you weren't such a smart guy, you would've taken my advice back in LA. You could be in New York, right now."

Seeley pulled the canvas flap aside and stepped in. In the gloomy, umber light, men lined up in rows four and five deep waiting their turn at the long galvanized trough. As in pissoirs everywhere, the men looked straight ahead; no one looked at anyone else. Seeley shouldered his way through the lines until he reached the far end of the WC, lifted the flap and started out. The lank-haired man was no more than an arm's length away, lounging against a tent post, waiting for him. Seeley's heart skipped. What had happened to Julia? Seeley gave the man a small, tight grin and went back inside the WC.

From outside on the fairground, silhouettes moved past the canvas wall like a dumb show. Edging along the wall, Seeley moved back toward the other exit. Even if one of these damp, shuffling men should think to turn and watch him, it would make no difference. He knelt on the packed earth next to the wall as if to tie his shoe, letting the steak knife slip down his sleeve into his hand. He ran his index finger lightly over the rough serration. Using his other hand to tauten the coarse, waxed canvas just above the ground, he pressed the knife point into the fabric and rapidly worked a hole in it. He pushed the knife through, angled it, and, rising from his knees, with a single upward slash of the blade opened a slit in the canvas tall enough for a man to walk through. Next he made a quick horizontal cut at the top to form a flap. Then he stepped through the opening and was gone.

TWENTY-FIVE

St. Joseph Klinik occupied half a block of Schönfeldstrasse, with drawn curtains at every window. In the taxi from the Theresienwiese, Seeley succeeded in interrupting the driver's monologue on Oktoberfest long enough to borrow his cell phone. He called Reiman, and then Julia at her hotel, but there was no answer in her room. He thought of the boxer and the tall man searching for him among the bodies packed into the fetid WC. By now they would have found the cut in the canvas wall. They had probably already left the fairgrounds with Hersh. The hotel map showed at least seven hospitals or infirmaries spread over the blocks surrounding St. Joseph's. It was only a matter of time before the three men put together that this was where Seeley had been heading with Julia and that their object had been to see Kanarek. Once they figured that out, it would take no more than an hour or two, going from hospital to hospital, for them to find Kanarek themselves.

In the hospital lobby, two Sisters in the pale gray uniforms of nurses sat at an oval counter awash in fluorescent light, their backs to each other. Another, no older than a girl but in the same uniform, stood at attention beside the counter. Seeley gave Kanarek's name to the older of the nurses, a heavy-boned woman with coarse features. After consulting a card file, she whispered something to the girl, who signaled Seeley to follow her. As he walked through the broad corridor, the only sounds were the background hum of hospital machinery and the squeak of the girl's rubber soles on the polished linoleum floor. Dusk was falling, and the light coming through the narrow sky-lights was gray. When they reached Kanarek's room, the girl gestured for Seeley to enter, and left.

In the far corner of the room, the hospital bed was cranked up and Kanarek's head lay on a stack of pillows, his eyes shut. A flannel blanket covered him almost to the chin, and two clawlike hands rested on the blanket's satin binding. Kanarek's skin was yellow, as it was when Seeley last saw him, but features that previously seemed robust—jaw, cheeks, chin—were now hollow, sucked inward as if the plastic bags hanging from metal racks on either side of the bed were drawing out his essence. This, Seeley thought, is how I could die.

Kanarek opened his eyes and gave Seeley a tired, watery look. He hadn't been sleeping; he had been watching his visitor.

"So, it's the big-shot lawyer. Big man—won't take a drink!"

Seeley looked from the bed to the metal racks and back to the bed. "I don't think either of us has much of a chance of get-ting served in this place."

Kanarek's eyes moved in the direction of the racked bags. "These are my organs now." The voice was a raspy murmur. "The doctor says my insides are falling apart, they're useless." He looked past Seeley. "Isn't that what he said?"

Seeley turned. Carlotta, hands neatly crossed on her lap,

was on a chair in the opposite corner. A television, bolted to the wall precariously high above her, had its volume turned down to a low, barely audible drone. The evening news was on. Carlotta looked exhausted. Across her shoulders, the same dark shawl she wore on Seeley's visit to Starnberg now seemed to embody her weariness in its folds. But the dark eyes were bright.

Kanarek said, "Can you believe, I've been thinking about my life fifty, sixty years ago. I can't remember what this thing is called"—he tugged at the blanket to indicate it was what he meant—"I can't remember your name. But I can remember every detail, every taste and texture, of my life half a century ago."

The voice, though weak and lacking the vitality of the previous night in the tavern, was filled with bravado.

A "wasting disease" was what Bermann had politely called Kanarek's ravages and, although Bermann hadn't seen his childhood friend for more than fifty years, the diagnosis was uncannily accurate. Not the physical wasting—that was as much old age as anything. No, what startled Seeley was the moral depletion of the man, the layers of despair that rolled off him in waves, like exhalations.

Still, Kanarek chattered on. "You have no idea what it was like to be in the movement then. All of us were poor, no one ever slept, but we were heroes, at least to ourselves. We were intellectuals, we were going to change the world. This wasn't a bunch of show-off screenwriters. Not"—his mouth twisted to inflect sarcasm into the words—"not your Hollywood Ten. No, these were honest-to-God workers, committed Socialists. No one's like that anymore. They're all buffoons." His voice grew stronger, and dots of spittle danced on his lips. "And the girls! Dark beauties, all of them, with those serious, shining eyes. We ate nothing. We lived on cigarettes and coffee. Red wine from a jug. Can you believe it? I can taste that wine now! And her, over there, the most beautiful of them all, with kisses so sweet you could get drunk on them."

How much of this, Seeley wondered, was memory, how much fantasy? Kanarek wasn't describing the lone operator he had read about in the spare report of the state investigators. But there was nothing false about the ardor. Seeley looked over at Carlotta. Her hands were clasped tightly, and though her head was down, he could see her lips move silently.

"She does that to drive me nuts," Kanarek said. "She always has. Her prayers. That down-on-your-knees, Hail Mary, Mother of God business. The rosary beads, the reek of the chapel, the mystery of the sacrament. It was a lot more stylish when she was young. Those eyes could melt a bishop's will."

Where was Reiman? The lawyer's office was no more than twenty minutes from the hospital, and it was more than half an hour since Seeley had called him from the taxi. The German and American documents had to be notarized, and Seeley knew no one in Munich other than Reiman to perform the small formality.

A flash and then a muffled explosion came from the television screen and Seeley followed Kanarek's eyes to grainy footage from a war zone that could have been in Eastern Europe or the Middle East. Over Carlotta's head, figures ran frantically for cover against a staccato background of automatic-weapon fire. When the three newscasters came back on the screen, Seeley turned to Kanarek.

"I brought the papers with me. Are you ready to sign? We talked about it yesterday in the tavern."

He held his breath, hoping Kanarek remembered.

"You mean, moral rights? That bourgeois garbage? The slop the studio bosses give the workers while they're stealing the bread from their mouths?"

Carlotta said, "Behave yourself, Max. This man didn't come here to listen to your Marxist nonsense. Sign his papers so he can go home."

Kanarek scowled at Seeley from behind the breathing tubes. "Ever since you and the girl showed up here, all she can talk about is how I should forgive Mayer Bermann. Forgive, she says. Forgive."

Seeley said, "Whatever Bermann did when you were blacklisted, he made your movie. He's been supporting you ever since." He caught himself, not remembering whether Kanarek knew about the money Bermann sent to Carlotta.

"I know where she gets the money. Do you think she fools me with those riding lessons? It's Bermann's money. He never lets me forget that I'm in his grip. You're a smart fellow. Tell me how you forgive a man who has intentionally disfigured you, who has deformed every molecule of your being."

The man's monumental self-pity seemed as much a part of his disease as the jaundice. Seeley remembered Mayer Bermann's curious warning about Kanarek: Don't fall in love with this man. Seeley wasn't falling in love, but in the extravagance of Kanarek's complaint he was finding reflected images of himself—his anger at Clare for not taking him back, his resentments against incompetent judges who ruled against him and ungrateful clients who second-guessed him.

"Don't you think you have some responsibility for the way your life turned out?"

A furious, unhealthy color poured into Kanarek's face. From across the room, Carlotta put out her hand to calm him.

Kanarek moved his jaw with his fingers as if to test it. "You don't know anything," he said to Seeley.

"I know that you're a selfish old man."

Kanarek's head flew off the pillow. "You want to see selfish, Mr. Lawyer? Look in the mirror. You push yourself into the life of a sick, dying man. No excuses. No 'How are you feeling, Mr. Kanarek, I need your help.' You make no effort to understand his misery. You demand—*demand*—that I sign your piece of paper. And why should I do this? For no better reason than this will please you."

"I'm sorry. You're right." He meant it; this, he realized, was how Michael Seeley operated. "I get started on one of my causes, and before I know it, nothing else matters."

"I'll bet you do that a lot."

"More than is good for me."

"Tell him what happened, Max." Carlotta had moved to the side of the bed and adjusted the pillows so Kanarek could sit up. "Tell him the story and get the poison out of you." She grasped a withered hand and squeezed it gently before going back to her chair.

Seeley remembered the family picture album and Carlotta's remark that the split between Bermann and Kanarek went back to when they were boys together in Poland, the boy who went on adventures and his best friend who wrote stories about them.

"Go ahead," Carlotta said.

"You think this is about the blacklist? It's not. The blacklist was just Mayer Bermann's final twist." Kanarek hawked to clear his throat. "No, this is a story from childhood. Two friends. Inseparable friends. Remember, I'm a writer. I make things up— I create tales—except this one is true. I'll tell it to you, Mr. Lawyer, and you explain to me how I'm supposed to forgive Mayer Bermann."

Carlotta leaned forward in the chair. "And then you'll sign the papers?"

He ignored her. "Just listen."

With long pauses as Kanarek struggled for a word, and as Seeley or sometimes Carlotta supplied it, Kanarek told the story.

"This was more than sixty years ago, long before he became

Mayer Bermann. Who knows when or how we became friends; it seemed as if we had been friends forever. Bermann was three years older than me—at the time of his betrayal, he was eighteen and I was fifteen—so maybe he was the older brother I had secretly wanted. Of course, I worshipped him as a younger brother might. There were no secrets between us, or at least I had no secrets from him."

Kanarek looked across at Carlotta. "Did you tell him about the stories?"

She nodded.

"That was my start as a writer, you could say—writing up our adventures together or, as it turned out, Bermann's adventures. I often thought he did some of the things he did—the pranks, the thievery—only so he could later see what they would look like in a story. This is why he couldn't live without me. He called me his bright canary. Did you know that is what Kanarek means? It is the Polish word for canary.

"We—my family—lived in a small town, nine or ten kilometers from Lublin. In truth, Bermann and his family lived in the town and we lived outside on a small farm—not even a farm, just a cow, some chickens and geese, a garden for vegetables. My parents were both committed Communists, not a good thing to be in those days with the SS and the Wehrmacht on every corner. They weren't intellectuals like the Communists at the university. They were real Communists, working people who scratched out a living on their small piece of land and belonged to the party. My mother took in handwork and my father did some carpentry and machine repairs around the town. There was a roughness to them that comes from that hard kind of life, but they were good people. They were my parents, and they did nothing to harm me. It was unusual in those days to have only one child, so maybe I was a little spoiled.

"Bermann's parents—his father was a butcher—had been taken away in the first roundup. They got all the Jews except Bermann and a couple of the other boys who were out in the woods that day. I was with them—I told you, he and I were inseparable—and, when we found out what was happening, we knew enough to run as far from town as we could. After that, Bermann mostly stayed in the woods, joining up with the partisans who came through from time to time, going on raids with them. He survived on handouts or what he could steal from farmyards—there wasn't much difference in those days between charity and theft.

"Two or three times a week, always at night, he would come by our cottage and throw a pebble at my window. It wasn't necessary, of course, for I was always half awake, waiting for him. We would go off to the woods and from the cloth sack he carried with him he would empty out his loot—for my parents, sugar, preserves, sausage he had stolen from the mess at the SS encampment, and for me, always, the paper and pencils he stole from the secretariat there. In return, I had for him my latest chapter of his adventures. When winter came and it got bitter cold, we would return to my parents' cottage and he would hide for a day or two in the potato cellar before he went off again.

"My parents knew and didn't know what was going on. They welcomed Bermann's gifts, of course, and they liked him and wanted to help him. But they were also concerned for themselves and for me. If it was discovered that they were harboring a Jew, or even that I was associating with one, it would mean immediate transportation to one of the camps. What was a boyhood adventure for Bermann and me was a matter of life and death for them. So, finally, they forbade me to see Bermann. When I told him this, he was angry—much angrier, I thought, than he had any reason to be, but I was flattered by my importance to him. I later came to believe that he was more upset about the loss of my tales than of me. He demanded that I leave my parents and go off with him. But, as much as I knew I would miss him, in the end I obeyed my parents. That meeting was the last I saw of Bermann until I went to the United States.

"A week after this last encounter, I returned home from one of my solitary forays in the woods to find our house empty. A neighbor told me that my parents had been taken away; that a letter left in the offices of the SS by some anonymous informant had denounced them as Communists. I knew at once it was Bermann. Who else knew they were Communists and also had such free, undetected access to SS offices? It was his revenge against my parents for separating us, and his revenge against me for rejecting him, for choosing my parents over him."

Carlotta was staring at Kanarek and through him. How many times had she heard this story?

"My parents were transported to the camp at Neuengamme, where they died. Do you know what this did to me, the knowledge that, but for my decision, my parents would have lived? At the beach, a child chases a ball into a tide pool that empties into a raging current. His father leaps in to save him, but is swept out to sea and drowns. The small boy survives. What can this boy's life be like as he grows into a man? Guilt for being the cause of a parent's death holds you in its grip forever. No amount of knowledge or experience or time can dislodge it. This is why I cannot forgive Mayer Bermann."

It was a sad, even appalling story, but Seeley could not shake the conviction that it was Kanarek who was responsible for turning his life into the dark stew it had become.

"He paid your way to California. He gave you writing jobs. He tried to make it up to you."

"Only so he could betray me once again. Surely you can

appreciate the irony that, having denounced my parents to the SS as Communists, Bermann should then hand me over to the California investigators for being a Communist, too."

There was a knock at the door, but Kanarek's eyes didn't leave Seeley.

"That was the fate for which I saved my miserable life. The irony, of course, was intentional. Nothing with Mayer Bermann is by accident. His cruelty is unremitting. After that final humiliation I never spoke to him again."

"I have no doubt about Mayer Bermann's capacity for evil. But everyone bears some responsibility for how they live."

"Then you have understood nothing of my story—" Kanarek looked up sharply. "Who is this?"

Reiman was at the door in an overcoat that looked as if it had been borrowed from someone taller and broader. The eye was still bruised, but the swollen lip had returned almost to normal. A worn leather portfolio was under his arm. "I have only a few minutes," he said to Seeley. "Where are the papers?"

Seeley introduced Reiman, but the young lawyer remained in the doorway, giving Kanarek no more than a nod of acknowledgment.

"More lawyers," Kanarek said with disgust. "What does this one want?"

Carlotta pulled at Seeley's sleeve. "May I see the papers?"

As Seeley handed the documents to her, Reiman spoke into his ear that he was already late for a dinner meeting.

Seeley held on to the thin arm and leaned to his ear. "Just a few minutes and we'll be finished. He'll sign, and you can notarize the papers."

Carlotta put the papers down. "You must sign these, Max. If you forgive Bermann, God will forgive you."

Kanarek turned to Seeley, a mock frown on his lips, eyes pleading. "Do you see how she tortures me with these platitudes?" He was visibly pleased at remembering the word, but all Seeley saw was a vain and spiteful old man, a burlesque performer who believed in nothing but his performance.

The ancient head resting on the pillows, shrunken like an archaeologist's trophy, turned back to Carlotta. "You never got it, did you? This is what my books are about. All of them. Lives painted in every color of betrayal. My hatred for Mayer Bermann is the one fact that has given meaning to my life."

"Meaning? What meaning?" Carlotta said. "Look at who's dying and who's living. You drink poison and expect Mayer Bermann to die."

Seeley envied Carlotta's conviction; not the churchgoing slogans but the moral clarity that underlay them.

"Carlotta's right. You should do what she says."

"A big fellow like you. A lawyer. You don't believe in this God business."

"I believe she's fortunate to have faith."

"Ach!" Kanarek glared at the ceiling.

"If you sign, you're the one whose name gets saved."

"If I wanted to save my name, don't you think I would have done this already?"

Seeley said, "I'm not doing this for myself."

"Of course you're not. You're doing it for Mayer Bermann. You don't have the spine to say no to him."

"Think about Carlotta. You owe it to her. As soon as you sign, you'll own the rights to *Spykiller*. When you die, Carlotta will own them. She won't have to depend on Mayer Bermann's charity."

"Don't worry about Carlotta. She's strong. A lot stronger than you are. Smarter, too."

Carlotta said, "It would be nice for people to know what a fine writer you are. To know that I'm the wife of such a fine writer."

"See," Kanarek said, "strong as a bear. Smart." The hideous

grin relaxed, softening into a show almost of affection and delight.

"Show me these papers." With an effort, Kanarek raised himself, leaning unsteadily over the bed rail. He searched in the nightstand, indifferent to the intravenous tubes stretching so taut that Seeley thought they would snap or pull free. Finally he extracted a pair of half-frame glasses from the drawer. He slipped on the glasses and fell back onto the pillows, his eyes going back and forth between Seeley and Reiman.

As Seeley placed the two documents—the German version beneath the English one—on the blanket in front of him, Kanarek said, "I know that I'm dying, but don't kid yourself. You're not going to see any deathbed conversion." He shuffled the two sheets of paper. "What is this one?" He lifted the page and showed it to Reiman.

"It is a declaration," Reiman said. "In English. The other one is in German. You state, under oath, that you are the author of this film, *Spykiller*. Are you the author?"

"Of course I am! If I sign, what happens next?"

Seeley said, "Mr. Reiman records the declaration here in Germany and in the United States. You will own the rights to *Spykiller.*"

Kanarek looked at him blankly. "What would I do with these rights?"

Even in out-of-the-way Starnberg, Kanarek had to know that the *Spykiller* franchise was worth hundreds of millions of dollars to United, and would be worth the same to any of its competitors.

"The studios will be climbing over each other to buy the rights from you."

Kanarek said, "What about United?"

Seeley pictured Hersh poring over a map of downtown Munich, checking off the hospitals in the district one by one.

"If you don't sign the declaration, United will own *Spykiller.*

That's why they murdered Bert Cobb, the photographer. It's why they beat up Mr. Reiman here."

"That's not the way Mayer Bermann works. It's too crude."

"But it's not too crude for Bermann's son-in-law and the people who own United now."

"What's in this for Mayer Bermann?"

Seeley had anticipated Kanarek's question, but could think of nothing to tell him but the truth. "Mayer Bermann wants you to sign it. The reasons are complicated, but if you sign the declaration, it will help him get his studio back from these people."

Kanarek ran his fingers over the two documents as a blind man might, reading braille. "So, if I don't sign this declaration, I will be rewarding murderers. But if I do sign, I will be granting the wish of Mayer Bermann, a man who, I have told you, is worse than a murderer."

"Bermann's son-in-law is in Munich. That's how Mr. Reiman got beat up. If you don't sign the declaration, your life expectancy will be even shorter than it is now."

Kanarek beckoned Seeley to come closer. "What about Carlotta?" His voice was a whisper. "What happens to her if I don't sign?"

Perhaps Kanarek did know something about love. "As soon as you sign the declaration, Carlotta will be safe. They would gain nothing by harming her."

"Death doesn't frighten me," Kanarek said. He threw an arm, light as a twig, over Seeley's neck, drawing him in closer. "I will tell you a secret: for years now, I have been praying for death to come. Yes, Mr. Atheist, praying." It wasn't a smile, but a shadow of one that began to form on the wasted face, a parting of the lips, a crease at the corners of the eyes. A bitter, dying man's odor rose from Kanarek. "But for a decision like this"—with his other hand he tapped the papers—"I have no strength."

The arm slipped from Seeley's shoulder, as insubstantial as a shadow, and Kanarek's head fell back onto the pillows, mouth open, eyes clamped shut.

Carlotta gasped.

So close. How, Seeley asked, could Kanarek have come so close to resolution and then die? He couldn't. "You can't do this!"

"Let it be." Carlotta's voice was scarcely a whisper. She crossed herself and Reiman started to, as well, but then dropped his hand.

For a long time, the room was completely still, with only a background hum of hospital machinery coming from down the corridor.

Kanarek opened one eye, then the other. "So," he said, "you see I lack the strength for this. I leave the decision to you. Do I sign the declaration or not?"

"I can't decide that for you."

"I'm giving you no choice. You must decide."

Malice switched on in Kanarek's wretched eyes. He had a victim's instinct, honed over a lifetime, for locating a fellow victim's vulnerability. He held up the paper. "If I sign this, Mayer Bermann wins. If I don't sign, the murderers win. You tell me: Which should I do?"

Seeley said, "I could walk away right now. It's not my decision to make."

"But you know you can't walk away. Mayer Bermann made that impossible for you. He knew you would never let me turn the studio over to murderers. He's already made your decision for you." The withered crocodile jaw slid back and forth. "Now you know what it's like to be inside the grip of this man. He leaves his victims—and you are his victim as much as I am—only one choice: to do as he wishes. But that is not the worst part. No, the worst part is the humiliation. He sees to it that, in doing his will, we understand that we have surrendered to him. Or are you going to fight back and tell me not to sign these papers?"

Seeley thought about Mayer Bermann—not the Bermann he knew, but the eighteen-year-old in Carlotta's picture album. Robbed first of his parents and then of his closest friend, he instinctively struck back at his enemies—raiding the SS for supplies, informing on Kanarek's parents, making an orphan of the boy who lacked the courage to go with him. But if Seeley could understand Bermann's first betrayal of Kanarek, he could make no sense of the second. Had the threat from the state investigators and their Wall Street collaborators—these white-shoe anti-Semites, as Bermann called them—so imperiled his young studio that he saw no choice but to sacrifice Kanarek once again? Or had the loss he suffered in Poland lacerated him so deeply that he was still pursuing his revenge?

How little we know about the motives of those we would let control us. Not just Mayer Bermann, Seeley thought, but Randall Rappaport, Daphne Hancock . . . the long line of his oppressors, real and imagined. Our ignorance gives them a power over our lives that none of them would even dream of; our attempts to undermine their authority work only to enhance it. And Lothar Seelig. What in fact did Seeley know of his father's demons? That he shared a common history with Mayer Bermann's SS? Or that his unhappy life had set its own twisted course? His father was a brutal, sad man, and that was all it was necessary for Seeley to know.

We are victims of victims.

"Well, should I sign or not?"

What harm had Mayer Bermann done to him, as compared to what he had done to Max Kanarek? If Seeley was honest about it, Bermann had no more than bruised his pride. And, although it may have suited Bermann for Seeley to come to Germany, he would have come on his own anyway, without the man's support. Michael Seeley's presence in this hospital room was far more his own doing than it was Mayer Bermann's.

Seeley said, "Sign the papers."

Kanarek nodded, giving him a strained smile that came nowhere close to his eyes.

Seeley lifted the English and German documents from the blanket and placed a magazine from the night table under them for support. Kanarek lurched forward, the empty hand, yellow and waxy like a rooster's claw, clutching at the pen Seeley held out for him. Carlotta, at the foot of the bed, crossed herself again. Seeley showed Kanarek where to place his signature on the English version and, when he finished, did the same with the German document. After signing as a witness, Seeley handed the papers to Carlotta. Her eyes were filled with tears but, as businesslike as a clerk, she took them, signed beneath Seeley's name on both documents, and handed them back to him. Reiman was next, affixing a notary seal with a shiny metal device he retrieved from the worn leather portfolio. He, too, signed the two documents.

"Do you still wish me to arrange for the recording?"

"Please," Seeley said, as Reiman prepared to leave.

A tear rolled down Carlotta's cheek. Seeley started to put an arm around her shoulder, but she moved away, aware that Kanarek was watching. When Seeley turned, Kanarek's eyes were closed, his head averted as if he had seen something horrible. Nothing was left to be said or to be done, so Seeley walked out of the room into the corridor where the sound of Reiman's leather soles on the polished linoleum still echoed against the empty walls.

TWENTY-SIX

Seeley had finished with breakfast, but he felt no desire to move from his table in the light-filled lobby with its quiet, bustling rhythms. He'd had a pleasant chat with the usually overbearing concierge, in the course of which Schreiner, his hands busily twisting a brass paper clip, informed him that the giant trench coat hanging in the lobby was an "important example" of German postmodernism. Schreiner quickly added that the sculpture represented the taste of the general manager, and that his own preference ran to rustic scenes from the Bavarian Alps.

Earlier in the morning, Seeley had for appetite walked briskly up Maximilianstrasse, from there along the Isar, then down Prinzregentenstrasse, past the Nazi showpiece, the Haus der Kunst, and back to the hotel through the Hofgarten, its formal, hedged-in spaces still empty at that hour.

The night before, after returning from the Klinik, he had twice telephoned Julia at the Vier Jahreszeiten, without success, and then fell into as deep and untroubled a sleep as any he could remember; a telephone call from Carlotta woke him at six.

Max Kanarek was dead. Carlotta was not in Kanarek's room when he died. In the late evening, a nurse had led her from the chair in which she had fallen asleep to a room down the hall where there was an empty bed, promising her she could see her husband in the morning. When Carlotta returned to the room at dawn, Max was spread-eagled over the collapsed bed rail, his feet twisted in the bedcovers and his head resting on a tangle of tubes and plastic bags filled with fluid. The doctor on duty told Carlotta her husband had apparently suffered a seizure, but it occurred to Seeley that it wouldn't have taken much effort for Hersh's men to find an unattended entrance to the hospital, locate Kanarek's room, and then suffocate him by holding a pillow over his head. They could have thrown him across the bed rail to make the death look natural. Seeley would never know. For a patient that ill, no doctor would think to order an autopsy. Even if Seeley could persuade Reiman to initiate one, how could anyone prove that Hersh was responsible?

"Are you brooding, or would you like company?" Julia had come into the lobby without his seeing her.

"Where were you? I called you last night. Twice. When I called this morning the operator said you didn't want calls."

"I was exhausted. Our friend followed me back to Marienplatz."

Julia's hand went to her watch as if she was planning to leave in a moment, and Seeley wondered what it was that, in her own fearless way, she was afraid of.

"I took the train to Starnberg to divert him. When I got there I walked around for a while, but I don't know if he followed me. Then I came back to Munich."

"He didn't follow you." Seeley was struck by how readily

Julia had put herself at risk; whatever she feared, it wasn't physical harm. "Hersh or the other one called him off."

"When I got to the hospital, Kanarek said you'd already been there."

"I have bad news," Seeley said. "Carlotta called. Max is dead. He died sometime in the night."

Julia glanced at her watch. How often had she done that, waiting for her father to return?

"When I saw him, he didn't look good, but he didn't look like he was getting ready to die." She saw Seeley studying at the watch and drew her hand away. "How is Carlotta?"

"She sounded okay. She's been preparing herself for a long time."

The morning crowd in the lobby had thinned. With a swooping, balletic flourish, the single waiter still on duty brought a coffee service to Julia's place along with a fresh basket of pastries. Seeley hadn't eaten sweets for years, but since coming to Munich he discovered that he craved them.

"Did he tell you that he signed the declaration?"

"He just said you were there, not what you did."

"What did you talk about?"

"Nothing at first. I got the feeling he didn't want to be alone. I didn't know where Carlotta was or when she was coming back, so I stayed. After a long time, he motioned me to bring my chair over to the bed, and he just started talking about his novels. He said the books were so sorrowful—'wretched' was his word—that even if he could find a publisher, who would possibly want to read such a work? After the first one, he tried to introduce some lightness into his writing, some aspect of hope or redemption. He tried different genres—romance, mystery, science fiction, even a satire of contemporary German politics. But in the end, he said, the same themes— loss, guilt, betrayal—consumed every book he wrote, no matter how hard he worked to escape them. So they went on the shelf.

"The joke, Kanarek said—he called it that, a joke—was now that he was dying, the words of hope he had looked for so desperately were springing up around him as if they were mushrooms in a forest. If only he had time left, he could write the book he always wanted to write. He told me that when everything was quiet in the hospital room, he could hear his mother and father talking. Not to him, but to each other. He hadn't heard these voices since he was a teenager, and he didn't know whether it was ghosts he was hearing or just the power of memory. But it was their words he wanted to write down. I'm sure he was hallucinating. Anyway, after that, he became quiet and fell asleep, so I left."

It pleased Seeley that Kanarek had evidently achieved some measure of peace before dying.

Julia said, "What happens with *Spykiller*?"

"It's up to Carlotta to decide if any more movies get made."

"What if Hersh challenges her ownership?"

"He'll get a long fight in federal court. Even if he wins the suit, he loses. Carlotta's lawyers can stretch the case out for at least three or four years. No bank or insurance company will touch *Spykiller* if there's litigation over the rights. Don't underestimate Carlotta." He remembered Kanarek's words: She's strong. Smart. "If Hersh and Callaway are foolish enough to litigate, she'll fight back. Lawyers would line up to take the case."

"You?"

"I worked on this for United. The disciplinary committee frowns on conflicts of interest." Almost as much, Seeley thought, as it frowns on a lawyer being drunk in judge's chambers.

"The studio won't sue. Hersh knows that once a case gets started he won't be able to control where it goes. Facts come out in litigation that you don't expect, and there are facts here that can put him in jail."

"Like how Bert Cobb died?"

"So far there's nothing to tie Hersh or anyone at United to Cobb's death. The police are calling it a botched burglary and unless Hersh gets careless, that's how it's going to stay. Reiman's not going to file charges against the men who beat him up. Hersh and his hired man are out of the country by now. The police won't find the other one. I'll write a letter to the DA in Los Angeles describing everything that happened. He may assign an investigator to look into it for a day or two, but in the end they'll shove it in the back of a file drawer. There's nothing I can do to change that."

"So Mayer Bermann gets his studio back. But not *Spykiller*."

"That's for Carlotta to decide. Every studio's going to bid for the rights. The independents, too. Any one of them would pay a fortune to steal the franchise from United. She'll have a good lawyer representing her."

"But not you."

"Reiman."

Seeley knew he might not be representing any clients for a long time. The choice he made in Max Kanarek's hospital room eliminated any possibility that Daphne or the firm would help him fight the disbarment proceedings. What saddened Seeley when he thought about that morning in Judge Randall Rappaport's chambers was not the incident itself, or its consequences, but what it revealed about how he had led his life—desperate, disengaged, too numbed by alcohol and work, his all-consuming cases, to understand how wrong everything had gone.

He had told the story of that day to no one—not Clare, not Girard. But now there was Julia. Either they were going to become close, in which case he wanted her to know what happened, or he would never see her again, in which case it wouldn't matter.

"Do you have some time?"

"Did I look at my watch again?"

"No."

Seeley told her everything, starting with the two tumblers of gin in the University Club bathroom that morning in New York. Julia didn't interrupt or take her eyes from him. The rest of the story—what had brought him to that day—he could tell her some other time, if she was interested. He said, "This is where you get to run screaming from the room."

"I'm glad you told me. It makes you less of a stranger. You must have had a lot of demons."

"At the end, even the demons wanted nothing to do with me."

All Seeley had ever wanted was to be a lawyer. He would fight the disbarment—a lawyer was still what he wanted to be—but practicing law and winning cases no longer seemed to be the only thing in life that mattered.

Julia said, "What are you going to do next?"

"I've got a flight out at seven tomorrow morning."

"Los Angeles? Or New York?"

"Buffalo."

"*Buffalo?*"

"It's where I grew up. I thought I told you."

"You told me about the museum, not where it was."

"I was a trial lawyer there before I moved to New York. I'm thinking I'll go back and see what solo practice is like."

Buffalo had been present in the shadows almost from the moment Seeley arrived in Munich. He hadn't realized it at first, but the cosmopolitan glow of the locals strolling on Maximilianstrasse, the heavy silks, sleek cars, and abundant jewelry were no more than a disguise. Up close, the natives were in fact as familiar as the tired, worn-down shoppers in babushkas and heavy woolens pushing through the crowds at the Broadway Market on Buffalo's far east side.

"You could have a solo practice in Los Angeles. Harry does."

"Do you know what his office rent costs?" Seeley had money saved, but a divorce, if there was one, would take half, and fighting the disbarment could run into six figures. There was always plenty of cheap office space in downtown Buffalo, and the county law library had all the books he needed. Without thinking about it, he had over the past few days been planning out every detail of his move.

"What about the money Bermann promised to pay you?"

"I fired Bermann. No client, no fee."

"You *fired* him?" The astonishment was that of a small girl.

Seeley smiled. "Lawyers fire clients every day."

"What I meant was, you went to all that trouble, you may have risked your life to get Kanarek's signature, and you knew you weren't going to be paid?"

"The problem with academics is they think they have a monopoly on doing foolish things for noble reasons."

"What about the artists you represent?"

"Artists have problems everywhere. If they need me, they'll find me. I'm just going to practice law. It may not look like it, but starting out, all I wanted was to help people who had been crushed by the system."

The need to trim expenses was one reason for returning to Buffalo, but it wasn't the only one. Seeley had left Buffalo for Cambridge when a college adviser told him Harvard was the best place in the country to study law, and left again for Manhattan because New York had the most sophisticated clients and the most complex litigation. For now, at least, riding the top of the wave had lost some of its appeal. Buffalo seemed as good a place as any to practice law—if he could manage to hold on to his license.

"You don't think you're running away?"

"From what? New York? I was running away when I went there."

"Is your wife going with you?" The catch in Julia's voice was unmistakable.

"Why would that matter to you?"

"It's the kind of question women ask."

"I only made the decision this morning."

Julia waited for him to answer.

"She doesn't have any reason to come."

Seeley had no idea what would happen when he saw Clare again, but at this distance his heartache at losing her had become an abstraction; he could examine his marriage without the accustomed despair of the past. His relationship with Clare, if he was honest about it, consisted of a yearlong courtship discovering interests in common, another year or two playing at being a young married couple in Manhattan, and then seven or eight years revisiting, with increasing indifference, the memories they had accumulated. Working and drinking had left him little time for a wife, or for anyone. He wondered what it had been like for Clare. That he didn't have a clue told him all he needed to know about the marriage.

Seeley said, "Some people aren't hardwired for relationships."

"Do you think I came on to you too strong? Chasing after you to Europe?"

"You got here first," Seeley said. "I had to track you down."

"Still, I was chasing you."

Julia Walsh was no abstraction.

Seeley said, "I liked you from the first time I saw you."

"What's Buffalo like?"

"It's a generous city. Wide avenues, grand old houses, parks."

"And an art museum." Julia didn't seem convinced. "It sounds like the Paris of the Rust Belt."

"It's better than its press."

"Do they have telephone service?"

"Intermittently."

"Will you call me if you feel like talking?"

"You can do the same. I'd like that."

Seeley hadn't expected this. It gave him hope. "When are you leaving?"

"I have a flight to Los Angeles tomorrow afternoon."

"What are you doing today?"

"I've never been to Oktoberfest. Your concierge said it's the last day."

"Picture thousands of people, most of them drunk, singing and shouting, but mostly crashing into each other. Carousels. A Ferris wheel. Oompah bands."

Julia made a face.

"Have you been to the English Garden?"

"Near Reiman's office?"

"Not far. What about a picnic?"

"That sounds good."

For some time, neither of them spoke. There was no traffic in the lobby and the waiter was now literally dancing among the empty tables, removing crockery with grand, lunging gestures.

"What do you think his name is? The dancing waiter? Guess."

"Herr Ober," Seeley said, not thinking.

"I was in Prague for a film conference last year, and we had a waiter who danced around the tables like that. He had a plastic name tag that said Paczek. For some reason we thought it was hilarious. *You pay check, please?*"

Seeley was going to miss her. He thought of an eight-year-old girl waiting at her bedroom window for a car that would never come. This was what Max Kanarek had failed to understand. It is not the bad memories that destroy us but the good ones, those fragments of deceit that, pretending to console, inflate our dreams with calamitous expectations. How real they seem, how utterly they promise the one object that we seek! The memory of a father carving dolls from a sheet of plywood. The boozy camaraderie of young lawyers sharing a pitcher of beer in a parkside tavern on a Friday evening in spring. A father's rough tweed coat, fragrant with whiskey and tobacco. These murderous shards that promise intimacy, but never deliver.

"I talked to Harry," Julia said. "He said the alliance wants you to handle the lawsuit."

A month ago, Seeley believed that law should protect a work's integrity, and he had been ready to fire his client Gary Minietello for wanting to cash in on that principle. But knowing that Minietello was wrong did not make the principle right. If a work of art truly has integrity, no one can destroy it.

When Seeley didn't answer, Julia said, "Harry thinks you're an idealist."

"I know. Tell him he's wrong. Right now, all I want is to take the world as it is. If he thinks he can get something more than that for his clients, good for him."

Julia was looking at the trench coat hanging off the column.

Seeley said, "That's a sculpture, if you can believe it."

"Do you know who made it?"

"He's anonymous. The concierge said he was inspired by a German artist who made gigantic overcoats out of felt and animal fat."

"Joseph Beuys," Julia said. "He died fifteen, twenty years ago. He was a political activist more than he was an artist."

"Sounds like someone you'd like."

"He spent too much time preaching. He talked about art more than he made it. There was a slogan he was famous for."

She made her voice deep and solemn. "To make people free is the aim of art, therefore art for me is the science of freedom."

"*Die Kunst tröstet uns, selbst wenn sie uns befreit.*"

The corners of Julia's mouth turned down.

Seeley nodded in the direction of the trench coat. "It's the title of the piece: *Art Consoles Us, Even as It Sets Us Free.*"

"Oh. I thought maybe it was about the emptiness of materialism. Or"—Julia gave him the smile from the alliance lunch—"the triumph of British rainwear."

For the first time in God knows how many years, Seeley laughed.

ACKNOWLEDGMENTS

For their good help with this book, I am grateful to Meg Gardiner, Daniel Goldstein, Lizzy Goldstein, Joel Levis, Bill Petig, Frank Ratliff, Jan Thompson, and Bob Weisberg.

Victor Navasky's *Naming Names* (1980) provided valuable background on the blacklist, as did *I'd Hate Myself in the Morning* (2000) by Ring Lardner Jr. and *Goldwyn: A Biography* (1989) by A. Scott Berg. Julia Walsh's thoughts on the connections between Wall Street, the blacklist, and the transformation of the American film industry draw on Jon Lewis, " 'We Do Not Ask You to Condone This': How the Blacklist Saved Hollywood," 39 *Cinema Journal* 3 (winter 2000). Richard Lukas, *The Forgotten Holocaust: The Poles Under German Occupation 1939–1944* (2001), supplied pertinent details on events in Poland.

Lynne Anderson not only typed the manuscript but offered insightful editorial suggestions along the way. She has my lasting gratitude, as do Wendy Strothman at the Strothman Agency and Gerry Howard at Doubleday. No writer could hope for a finer agent or a finer editor.